Confed

4⁰⁰
argos

base 101

20. Rao RR p. 61

Secty. G. dis Nov 1861 p. 79
cipher p. 104, 146, 170
arrested p. 123
tip off· p. 131
Mayor of Wash 155·
s. Lucretia p. 156
to Old Capitol p. 190
out of " " 230
fee paid p. 237
to Europe 246
book 255
returns to Oorah 266

REBEL ROSE

*

Books by Ishbel Ross

✳

REBEL ROSE

PROUD KATE

CHILD OF DESTINY

ISLE OF ESCAPE

FIFTY YEARS A WOMAN

LADIES OF THE PRESS

HIGHLAND TWILIGHT

MARRIAGE IN GOTHAM

PROMENADE DECK

REBEL ROSE

Life of Rose O'Neal Greenhow,

Confederate Spy

By ISHBEL ROSS

Illustrated

Harper & Brothers   Publishers   New York

Library of Congress catalog card number: 54-8986

To
A. A.

CONTENTS

ILLUSTRATIONS

ix

ACKNOWLEDGMENTS

I have drawn material for this biography from numerous sources on both sides of the Atlantic, and am indebted to a number of librarians, curators and historians for generous aid in assembling facts on Mrs. Rose O'Neal Greenhow.

Among direct descendants and others by marriage who have supplied me with information are Mrs. Greenhow's great-grandson, Colonel L. E. Marié, Jr., and his wife, of Edgewater, Md., Mrs. Mary Greenhow Johnston of Richmond, Va., and Miss Cora B. Powell of Baltimore, Md. I am also indebted to Margaret Leech, author of *Reveille in Washington*; Harriet H. Shoen, author and historian; Colonel Louis A. Sigaud, author of *Belle Boyd, Confederate Spy*, and David Rankin Barbee, all of whom have special knowledge of Mrs. Greenhow's history.

In the manuscript division of the Library of Congress I had access to the papers of Henry Wilson, James M. Mason, Joseph Holt, Angela Singleton and Harriet Lane; to letters given by Mr. Barbee bearing on Mrs. Greenhow; and to the diaries of Mary Greenhow Lee and Martha Wright Morris. I wish to express my appreciation for the courtesy extended to me there by Dr. C. P. Powell, Miss E. G. McPherson, Frank White and Wilfred Langone.

I received most generous aid and co-operation also at the National Archives, where I was able to study Mrs. Greenhow's seized correspondence; many of her personal letters; the Dix-Pierrepont report; the Prisoners of War Correspondence 1861-62; the Confederate States of America Despatch Book, and sundry documents bearing on Mrs. Greenhow and other Confederate agents. I should like to express my thanks to Richard G. Wood, chief of the War Records

Section of the National Archives; to Dr. Carl L. Lokke, chief of the Foreign Affairs Section; and to his assistants, Mrs. Julia Bland Carroll and R. O. Wells, who greatly facilitated my task.

In the preparation of this manuscript I have made extensive use of the U.S. War Department Official Records of the Union and Confederate Armies and the U.S. Navy Department Official Records of the Union and Confederate Navies.

My warmest appreciation goes to the custodians of the American History Room of the New York Public Library who have given me the most tireless, intelligent and constant co-operation in rounding up material, and I hereby convey my thanks to Gerald D. McDonald, James J. Heslin, F. Ivor D. Avellino and Mrs. Maud Cole.

I am particularly indebted to Mr. Avellino in New York, and to Miss Margaret I. Foley, of the San Francisco Public Library, for help in hunting up obscure aspects of Mrs. Greenhow's history. Mrs. Carma R. Zimmerman, State Librarian, and Allan R. Ottley, of the California State Library, Sacramento, Calif., were also most helpful in this respect.

Generous co-operation was given me by Milton C. Russell, of the Virginia State Library, Richmond; Miss Eleanor Brockenbrough and Miss India W. Thomas, of the Confederate Memorial Literary Society, Richmond Confederate Museum; and Mrs. Ralph Catterall, Curator of Prints and Manuscripts, Valentine Museum, Richmond.

Further afield, I am much indebted to the Earl of Buckinghamshire, to Simon Nowell-Smith, Arthur E. Davies and Oliver Stallybrass of The London Library and to M. Amédée Outrey, Chef du Service des Archives, Ministère des Affaires Étrangères, Paris.

Herbert L. Ganter, Curator of Rare Books and Manuscripts at the College of William and Mary, was kind enough to let me have excerpts from Robert Greenhow's diary of 1837, and I had access to Lamar William Smith's thesis on Mrs. Greenhow, now in the possession of the University of Alabama.

The United Daughters of the Confederacy have been both inter-

([Acknowledgments

ested and helpful in the preparation of this work, and I am deeply grateful to Mrs. Gertrude J. Howell, of the Cape Fear Chapter, Wilmington, N.C., for the documentation she so generously shared with me, including letters from members of the Greenhow family, her own articles on Mrs. Greenhow, and a wealth of material bearing on the subject. I am similarly indebted to Louis T. Moore, chairman of the New Hanover Historical Commission, Wilmington, for much useful data on Mrs. Greenhow, including Harry Hayden's account of her death. I also wish to acknowledge with gratitude the assistance given me by John Sikes, Julien Dwight Martin and Harold Ludwig, of the Star-News Newspapers, Wilmington, N.C.

Among the many individuals who have helped me to trace Mrs. Greenhow's ancestry and childhood circumstances are: Roger Thomas, Senior Archivist, Hall of Records, Annapolis; Miss Ella R. Plummer, Land Office, Rockville, Md.; Roger Brooke Farquhar, Silver Spring, Md.; Zelda Branch (Mrs. William Walton Brown), Port Tobacco, Md.; Miss Elizabeth C. Litsinger, Enoch Pratt Free Library, Baltimore; Miss I. Hardin, Division of Institutional Education, Department of Welfare, Frankfort, Ky.; and Foster Edwards, of New Hanover County, N.C.

I. R.

Part One

CHAPTER I

Prologue to Politics

Rose o'neale was little more than an infant when her father, John O'Neale, was killed by his Negro body servant in 1817. He was a planter with extensive lands at Port Tobacco, a small Maryland town brisk with shipping and commerce in the days before the Civil War but today a rural community. When his estate was broken up his family moved to Poolesville, and from there his daughters in time found their way to the capital.

In later life Rose boasted of having revolutionary blood in her veins and traced back her ancestry to one of the Roman Catholic colonists who landed on the Western Shore in 1634. The family name was spelled O'Neale at the time of Rose's birth, but the final "e" was dropped in her early years.

She may well have inherited her wit, her zest for life, her eloqence, dashing good looks and romantic inclinations from her father. Although he was more of a legend than an actual memory to Rose, she was to learn from different sources as she grew older that he was known as a "great fascinator of women." It was no family secret that he had indulged himself to the full in the lusty pleasures of his day —fox hunting, horse racing, cockfighting and the lavish hospitality of the manorial region.

He left large sums to charities and his church, and dowered his daughters with land as well as money. All married in the tradition he

3

had wished for them, and two became well known in the social life of Washington. In 1833 Ellen Elizabeth married James Madison Cutts, Dolly Madison's nephew. Two years later Rose became the bride of Robert Greenhow, Virginian lawyer and linguist.

She was to know nine Presidents and to flourish as the intimate friend and adviser of one—James Buchanan. But she stood out chiefly among the women of her era for the espionage she did on behalf of the Confederacy. In the 1860's Mrs. Greenhow was known as a traitor in the North, a patriot in the South.

Her early years were free and happy, passed largely in the country, where she galloped on horseback across the rolling acres of Montgomery County at the same fast clip as her father. The landscape she knew was laced with white pine, hickory, locust, ash, beech and persimmon trees. Mountain laurel, wild roses and black-eyed Susans abounded. The fields were tilled with oats, rye and barley.

Although little more than thirty miles away, Washington seemed distant in these early days—the capital where Rose was first to flourish; then in another, grimmer phase, to find melancholy satisfaction from behind prison bars in comparing herself to Mary Queen of Scots and Marie Antoinette. She took the first step toward this life in her early teens, when she and her sisters went to live with their aunt, Mrs. H. V. Hill, who ran the fashionable Capitol Hill boardinghouse.

By this time Rose was developing into a tall dark beauty, supple in her movements and full of grace. Her finely chiseled features and flashing eyes were remembered by all who knew her. Their luster betrayed the shifting moods of a tempestuous nature. Her olive skin was delicately flushed with color, causing the guests at Mrs. Hill's to call her the Wild Rose. She was dynamic to men from her sixteenth year to the hour of her death.

From her first appearance in Washington Rose's fresh looks, her knack for repartee, the swing of her agile body, the sparkle of her vivid face between the slats of her bonnet, tended to ruffle the emo-

4

tions of political warriors who found cold comfort in the boarding-house atmosphere of the capital while Congress was in session.

Mrs. Hill kept her nieces busy but on display. They attended classes. They were schooled in the social graces. They went to parties carefully chaperoned. She steered them adroitly through all the mud and excitement of the Jackson era. Rose's true education came not from her schooling, which suffered from all the inadequacies of the period where girls were concerned, but from the accomplished man she married. Beyond this, her political preceptor was John C. Calhoun.

In later years, when Rose worked heart and soul for the Confederacy, she always credited the South Carolinian statesman with having shaped her political philosophy and influenced her life. After months of imprisonment in 1861-62 she summed up the role he played in the development of her character:

I am a Southern woman, born with revolutionary blood in my veins, and my first crude ideas on state and federal matters received consistency and shape from the best and wisest man of this century, John C. Calhoun.

These ideas have been strengthened and matured by reading and observation. Freedom of speech and of thought were my birthrights, guaranteed by our charter of liberty, the Constitution of the United States, and signed and sealed by the blood of our fathers.

Mrs. Hill's became a house of enduring significance for Rose. She tended Calhoun in his dying hours under her aunt's roof. There, too, she passed the months of her imprisonment in the surroundings of her girlhood, where she had met with wit and gaiety the compliments of urgent lawmakers, and decked herself in flounced ball gowns to go forth with them to dances, soirées and levees.

Externally the building had a bleak unfinished air, like much else in Washington during the Jackson era. It was three stories high, broad in effect, with clumsy chimneys and a lower extension to the rear. Tall arched windows matched a handsome doorway. Trees

5

straggled at irregular intervals around the front and sides of the building. Congress had assembled within its walls after the burning of Washington, so that it was already baptized with words of historic implication.

Mrs. Hill's long dining table reflected the hearty interests of the period. Politicians from various parts of the country foregathered to discuss the day's excitement on Capitol Hill. The place had the seething vigor of a frontier boardinghouse, linked by the worldly Mrs. Hill to the damask and silver touches of a more settled civilization. Breakfast was served at seven-thirty o'clock, dinner at two, supper at seven. A gong boomed between courses. Ruffed grouse, wild turkey, wild pigeon, terrapin and black bass from the Potomac, along with Indian cakes, berries, pies, sweetmeats, jellies, tea and coffee, made up the supper fare.

Many of the men who gathered for meals at Mrs. Hill's were lonely for the wives and families left behind in distant states. They were harassed, hard-worked, ambitious, eloquent, and snatched at vicarious pleasures. The O'Neal sisters, with their good looks and vivacious manners, were a refreshing spectacle for the guests, who talked politics freely with them.

Rose often climbed the windy hill to the Senate chamber, where hickory logs smoked in two rusty stoves, streams of tobacco juice trickled across the floor, and Senators huddled in hats and blankets trying to keep warm, or came strolling in from the Hole-in-the-Wall, the Capitol pub that sustained them in their labors. She acquired her first knowledge of law—always a strong interest in her life—from listening to Chief Justice John Marshall in the plain chamber in the Capitol basement that housed the Supreme Court. It was fashionable in Jackson's time for women to cluster on the cushioned sofas that flanked either side of this room.

The social graces did not flourish greatly in Washington during this era, although Dolly Madison and the Monroes had swung the pendulum toward elegance and lavish entertaining. With Andrew

6

Jackson in the White House, the frontier spirit spurted like naphtha in the ribald, spitting, cursing, gambling atmosphere created by the shrewd and vigorous men who dominated the political scene.

Figures of power and consequence from earlier administrations towered among them—orators like Calhoun, Henry Clay, Daniel Webster and Thomas Hart Benton. These were the spokesmen of the evolving civilization, who stoked or banked the fires of current American history. Their passions were strong; their speech often intemperate; their rhetoric a blaze of abuse or inspiration.

All this was heady fare for the girl in sashed muslin who held spermaceti candles for men who chewed tobacco, roughed up the English language, swore, drank and ate with gusto; wore the fringed buckskins of the West, or the lace ruffles and embroidered waistcoats of Charleston. Rose responded with equal attention to the plain accents of New England and the soft gallantry of the South.

Life at Mrs. Hill's was specialized preparation for a role of political influence, and it helped to shape her character. She was always to work as potently with rough-hewn men as with the gallants and diplomats who later paid tribute to her powers of seduction. She learned to be tolerant of their manners if their wits were bright, their passions strong, or they warmed her with the intangible force she possessed in full measure herself—personality.

She and her sisters had the grim example of a namesake held up to them—the much discussed Peggy O'Neale, whose marriage to Senator John Henry Eaton of Tennessee started the uproar that split Andrew Jackson's Cabinet apart. In a boycott led by Mrs. Calhoun, she had received the most thorough snubbing ever accorded a Cabinet member's wife in Washington.

Rose was still in her early teens when the crisis over Mrs. Eaton developed, but the mere mention of her for years thereafter started a flurry of gossip. She often heard Peggy defended at Mrs. Hill's, for some of the men who came down from the Capitol deplored the ring of fire that had scorched the tavernkeeper's daughter. The courteous Martin Van Buren, when Secretary of State, took a stand and publicly escorted her on his arm. Rose heard much about Mrs. Eaton, too, from her own first serious beau, Cave Johnson, who also came from Tennessee.

He was already a mature lawyer when Rose met him, and a silent figure in Congress. He was familiar with frontier life, had awkward manners, and was good-looking in a solemn, long-jawed fashion. He had weathered a hard childhood in Tennessee and had fought the Indians in Mississippi. Speculation in land had made him comparatively wealthy. He came to Washington moping over a girl from his own state who had rejected him, but who was to recant and marry him years later, when she had become a widow with three children. In the meantime Rose caught his eye, glowing as the flower for which she was named, and with plenty of spirit. She was a rare exhibit to squire around the capital and Johnson took pride in her.

Although dour in nature, he entered freely into the social life of the period. The waltz had come into favor. Mrs. John Quincy Adams had introduced dancing at the White House and it was now in high favor with Washington hostesses. As many as twenty-four fiddlers lined up for some of the soirées. At the age of sixteen Rose found Johnson an attractive partner. He had not yet become the sober figure whose gloom was to oppress her when she encountered him in later years as Postmaster-General in President James K. Polk's Cabinet. By that time Rose had grown in worldliness. Cave had narrowed in outlook and was known as the Cerberus of government circles.

But every facet of Washington life in Johnson's courting days was absorbing to the young girl who was equally happy riding in a carriage or jumping ditches and getting over stiles with true country dexterity, as she promenaded with him through the sprawling town. The White House and the Capitol had dignity, even then. A few imposing buildings stood near by. Beyond that, the capital was scattered, dirty and disorderly.

8

Pennsylvania Avenue had the gimcrack look of broken china. It was full of gaps and cracks, and was bare of paving until Jackson finally had this corrected. Dusty shops, cheap boardinghouses, hencoops, shabby homes that rented for anything from fifty to three hundred dollars a year, stood huddled together in clusters, interspersed with trees, gardens or untidy areas of grass or mud.

Washington in perspective suggested a series of country hamlets, except that its composition lacked both unity and beauty. It was no novelty to brush past cows browsing in the roads. Spring flowers burst like exploding stars along the swampy paths. And a Senator's wife setting out from Gadsby's or the Indian Queen to pay calls took nearly all day to make the round of four or five homes in a jolting carriage.

When out promenading with Johnson, Rose was sometimes brought to a halt in the street by the sight of Jackson striding along with tasseled cane and tall white beaver hat. None could fail to notice the gaunt figure, the crested hair, the deep-set eyes fiercely blue in their scrutiny. He had brought the White House to life with the vigor of his ways. It was being embellished after the spare but dignified regime of John Quincy Adams. Building was under way. The North Portico was headed for completion. The East Room was refurbished with blue damask satin. Silver, china and cut glass were replenished. Twenty spittoons were ordered for the state parlors, a much needed addition. Magnolia trees were planted in memory of Jackson's wife, Rachel, and racing stables were established. Slaves abounded. Political excitement ran high.

Rose knew that Jackson lounged in a dangling coat in his private quarters, slouched in a big rocking chair by a wood fire, smoking his long reed pipe with red clay bowl. She did not penetrate this inner sanctum but attended levees with Johnson, where wax candles spread a soft glow over the assembled company, and the horseshoe table in the state dining room was laden with fine fare, flanked at either end by enormous salmons in aspic.

All these impressions were part of Rose's worldly education as she ranged from suppers at Mrs. Hill's to White House levees and diplomatic receptions at Georgetown. Quite early in life she acquired a taste for the gold braid and insignia of the diplomatic corps, a set that was to loom large in her later political maneuverings. Even at this early age most of the talk to which she listened was of politics. The slavery issue came sharply to her attention as early as 1830 when Daniel Webster made his "Liberty and Union, now and forever, one and indivisible" speech, and predicted that civil war would be the inevitable result of sectional interests.

She was only a schoolgirl at the time, but the excitement at Mrs. Hill's was intense. Two years later she watched Vice-President Calhoun break with Jackson over the nullification issue. It was a period of reckless living and extravagant oratory, of the division of spoils and hot fights in Congress. Not until the days of the Compromise of 1850 was Rose to live again through such political tension. But she thrived on it as she moved close to its center in the company of Cave Johnson.

She was escorted everywhere, either by him or by her sister Ellen, who had swung her into Dolly Madison's orbit when she married Cutts in 1833. The young pair honeymooned at Montpelier and Ellen was always "my pet" to the genial Mrs. Madison. Rose was treated with equal warmth and was to go through life with many intimate memories of Dolly, and the levees she held in her home on H Street after her husband's death.

Mrs. Madison adored Ellen's small son James and often kept him beside her at these receptions, introducing him as her little Madison. Later, when Rose's daughters were born, they were to share in some of this attention. It was Dolly's traditional custom to tell the children that the statue of Jefferson in front of the White House invariably went to dinner when the bell rang.

Her encompassing warmth blanketed everyone who touched her circle, and Rose was devoted to her. As the years went on she fre-

10

quently spiced her dinner table conversation with tales of Dolly, and she visited the grand old lady of Washington to the end. She knew her best in her declining years when Mrs. Madison lived as a private citizen, but a rich store of legends about her White House days spread through the family.

In recalling them for her friends Rose usually dwelt on Dolly's good nature and kindness of heart; on the "dove parties" she gave for the Cabinet wives; on her pearly complexion and large, limpid eyes; on her feathered turbans and elaborate gowns; on the white bays that drove her through Washington; and on her great affection for James Madison.

Dolly was a pacemaker at a time when lace and ribbons, false hair sprinkled with gold leaves, and thick make-up, were affected by some of the older women. She did not spurn these frivolous touches, and her family often speculated on what she would wear next. When Rose knew her she appeared most often in black velvet, with the stiff quilled net that always rose around her neck like a ruff.

But she had intimate knowledge of Dolly's White House costumes, and the turbans so far removed from the Quaker bonnet of her girlhood days. She had often heard of the rose-colored satin gown with white velvet train, lined with lavender satin and edged with lace, that Dolly had worn against her new yellow damask upholstery. To this were added a gold girdle, gold necklace and bracelets, and a white velvet turban with ostrich tips. Rose did not doubt that it all looked queenly on Dolly.

She had watched her being dignified with diplomats in full regalia, but encouraging Henry Clay—Cousin Henry, she called him—to dip into her snuffbox at every opportunity. Washington Irving's description of her as a "fine, portly, buxom dame who has a smile and a pleasant word for everybody" was true enough, but although Madison was "Oh! poor Jemmy! a withered apple-john" to the new Ambassador to Spain, Rose noted that he was always "my darling little husband" to Dolly, and she was "my beloved" to him.

11

When the time came for Rose to marry none who knew her was more interested than Mrs. Madison. She met young Robert Greenhow in the 1830's through her Cutts connections. At that time he maintained his own home in Washington, engaged in studious pursuits, and was well known on the social front. There was little need for Rose—in the phrase of the day—"to set her plaits" at him. He showed interest in her at once and escorted her to parties.

Johnson soon saw how the wind was blowing and bowed out of the picture to a younger and handsomer rival. Ellen Cutts encouraged Greenhow's courtship. Everyone considered them well suited to each other. They were married in 1835, with the blessing of Dolly Madison, whose own husband was to die within the year. It was a love match, but Rose had the added luck, like Dolly, of finding a mate with chivalrous instincts and fine mind. He was handsome, erudite and much beloved by all who knew him. Dr. Greenhow was to cherish Rose as long as he lived and to find her a working helpmeet as well as a seductive wife.

He was born in 1800, the grandson of John Greenhow, an English settler who became mayor of Williamsburg in 1805, and of Richmond eight years later. Young Robert was graduated from William and Mary College in 1816 and took a medical degree at Columbia University. Then he went abroad, studied medicine at Edinburgh University, walked the hospital wards of London and Paris, and finally switched to a law course at the Sorbonne.

Uncertain in his aims, Robert tried belles lettres, studied languages, became one of Lord Byron's friends, and enjoyed the salons of Paris. On his return to America in 1825 he hung out his medical shingle in New York but soon turned to writing, and to lecturing on chemistry before scientific societies.

He had many substantial Knickerbocker friends, but his shifting interests caused one of his Richmond cronies, Moncure Robinson, to write smugly of Robert to his father, John Robinson: "Poor fellow! I am afraid he will not succeed anywhere; he has committed one

12

great error, that of attending to everything except his profession. I will endeavor to make his example a warning and to act in some degree on the opposite system."

But when Moncure landed in New York from Paris in 1827, Greenhow entertained him at the Athenaeum and Lyceum clubs, and took him to dine with Daniel Webster, a craggy figure in bright blue coat with gilt buttons and various dandified touches. From the respect with which Webster treated Robert, Moncure decided that he must be making headway. All doors seemed to be open to him. He was so much the favorite of the powerful Edward Livingston, later Jackson's Secretary of State, that in 1828 he was offered the post of translator, librarian and interpreter in the State Department. This was to be Robert's work for the next twenty years. He had become an expert linguist during his travels and spoke French, German, Italian and Spanish.

When James Buchanan was appointed Minister to Russia in 1832 Livingston besought him to make Greenhow secretary of the legation. He was reluctant to lose his services, the Secretary of State wrote, but he felt that the youth would be a great asset in the post, both in social and diplomatic terms. He commended him as a fine linguist who had made good use of his time abroad and was "well calculated by his manners, deportment and usage of the world" to aid Buchanan in Russia. "Dowdies—dowdies won't do for European courts," John Randolph had told Mrs. Livingston.

The appointment did not go through, and Robert had to content himself with reading the dispatches Buchanan sent back to Livingston on a country where there was "no freedom of the Press, no public opinion, and but little political conversation." The Emperor, in Buchanan's opinion, was a despot. The court was the most formal in Europe, the people were ignorant and barbarous, but the peasants were "jolly, good-natured rogues with long beards and tanned sheepskins."

Buchanan reported that the American "system of attending to our own affairs, and leaving other nations to do the same, has had the happiest influence upon our foreign relations." The Monroe Doctrine was taking effect, or so it seemed at the moment.

All these interests loomed large with Robert in 1835 when he settled down with Rose in a house on F Street. It was he who first swung her thoughts toward foreign policies. She was already well indoctrinated in domestic issues, and was alert to the agitation over slavery that flashed up strongly in the 1830's, led by William Lloyd Garrison.

Three decades later, and across the chasm of the Civil War, Robert's half-sister, Mrs. Hugh Lee of Winchester, was to recall in her diary how sweet the Wild Rose was at the time of her marriage. As Mary Greenhow, Mrs. Lee lived with them for some months. She remembered the quiet intimate evenings they all had together, with Rose reading William H. Ainsworth's "Crichton" in a "mellifluous voice," and Robert adding to her enjoyment with his "perfect knowledge" of Paris and of the history and manners of the time of Henry II. "I do not believe there ever was a person blessed with such a memory," she said of her brother. "I wish such things were hereditary."

The Greenhows were a striking pair as they set up housekeeping. Robert was darkly handsome, with a sensitive face, always faintly touched with melancholy—a reflection of the tragedy of his youth. His mother, Mary Ann Wills Greenhow, was burned to death in the Richmond Theater fire when he was twelve years old, and his father, Robert Greenhow, barely succeeded in dragging him to fresh air and safety. He rarely talked to Rose about this but he never forgot it.

Flashes of Robert's early devotion to his wife show in the diary he kept as he traveled to Mexico by way of Pensacola and Vera Cruz in 1837. He watched eagerly at various points for letters from his "dear Rose," and kept looking for ways and means to get others back to her. He traveled by rail, stage, carriage and steamer. Stopping at

14

Brazos, in Texas, he sent a letter to his "dear Rose" by a ship captain who promised to post it from New Orleans. Sailing off Vera Cruz on July 6 he scribbled an entry: "I wrote to my Rose." He went ashore at Pensacola on August 12 and was blissfully happy to find "three letters from my dear Rose." In later life his wife was to be noted for the extent, variety and diffuseness of her correspondence.

This habit was built up as she worked with Robert, who wrote continually when not out on one of his exploratory missions. He was a pamphleteer as well as a translator, and his writings were always of interest to Rose. They involved journeys of a pathfinding nature, at a time when the country was still undeveloped. He studied the journals of explorers in their original languages. He traveled to remote spots to check on disputed claims and assemble fresh material. It was his habit to dig deep into root sources, and Rose helped him in his research. When she could break away from the duties of child-bearing, she accompanied him on some of his earlier trips. She was a spartan traveler, an intelligent observer, and Robert enjoyed her company.

At the time of their marriage he was writing about Tripoli. Some of his titles suggest the scope of his later inquiries: *Kendrick's Passage Through Fuca's Strait; Seizure of the Argonaut Voyage of La Pérouse; Results of Cook's Discoveries; Bering's Voyage to the Arctic Sea; Spanish Colonies in New California; Expulsion of the Jesuits; Voyage of Drake* and *Improvements in the Navigation of the Pacific.*

But Robert's most practical contribution to the State Department was the intensive study he made of the natural features of North America—the coastlines, mountains, geology, climate and rivers. To this he added his own symposium on the early inhabitants, and comment on the "settlements of the claims of civilized nations," a burning issue during the years that he was with the department, and one that was tied closely to the slavery issue.

Rose helped him in all these matters during their long and happy evenings together when they were not out at social gatherings. She

15

read what Robert wrote. She contributed ideas and suggestions. He came to value her judgment. She, in turn, acquired some scholarly values lacking in her superficial education. Both talked well, and Rose had a remarkable memory. Robert found her an apt pupil and took pleasure in widening her horizons.

No discordant note from their marriage emerges in any of the Greenhow papers, although there is plenty of evidence that men of power and magnetism shared in Rose's counsels, heeded her advice and openly admired her. Even before her husband's death there was gossip about her influence with James Buchanan. But the breath of scandal did not settle heavily on Rose until after Robert's accidental death at the age of fifty-four.

Their home was a center for travelers from abroad, for Robert had friends in many quarters, and he spread ease by addressing a foreigner in his own tongue. Rose added to this her vivid charm and deep understanding of the needs and interests of men. She was a good housekeeper, too, setting a bountiful table in the fashion of her day. Her invitations were prized.

Although Robert engaged in the outer forms of social life, he was essentially a studious type and preferred his library. He was also frequently away on long expeditions in connection with his work. But Rose had genuine zest for worldly pleasures and made the most of them. One of her earliest political encounters after her marriage was with Conte Federico Confalonieri, the Italian nationalist arrested by the Austrians after the outbreak of the Piedmontese revolt. He was sentenced to life imprisonment but later was pardoned and exiled, coming to America in 1836. Rose wept as she listened to Confalonieri talk of his imprisonment, never suspecting that a similar fate awaited her.

"I thanked God that my destiny had been cast in a land where crimes like this could never be committed," she wrote in her wartime memoirs. "I did not then foresee that the scourge of Black Republican rule was to come upon us, and sweep from the New

16

World every vestige of civil rights and freedom, as had been often done in the Old."

In time Rose was to bear four daughters—Florence, Gertrude, Leila and Rose. During this significant decade of her life, instead of withdrawing from the social round as her contemporaries did, she continued to move more deeply into the political developments of the capital. She roamed freely about Washington. She haunted the Senate gallery, attended the outstanding functions, was admired by men of affairs, and flourished in the official circle in which the Cutts family and Robert moved.

Before long Rose had become adept at intrigue. She had a gift for conversation and her good memory was an asset. As she went around she gathered information for Robert, who by this time was deeply enmeshed in policy-making counsels. She added her own political prescience to the detailed knowledge of geographical boundaries, historical background and contemporary European politics, which made him valuable to the Secretaries of State through six administrations.

Livingston died soon after Rose's marriage, and she had little contact with him. But she was close to John Forsyth and his wife, two well-known Virginians; to Abel P. Upshur, also from her husband's state, and to John Middleton Clayton, who opposed Jackson on his United States Bank policy but supported him during the nullification crisis. None of the Secretaries of State except Calhoun and Buchanan interested her more than Daniel Webster, who was her husband's chief between 1841 and 1843. Rose and he had many spirited arguments over the soft shell crabs, terrapin, fried oysters and canvasbacked duck cleverly prepared by Webster's Negro cook. They never agreed on political issues, but loved to spar, and Webster was much attached to Robert.

Her husband's associates found her a fascinating, clever and sometimes scheming belle. In spite of his natural gifts Dr. Greenhow was not ambitious, but Rose was, and pulled strings in all directions

17

to further his interests. Colonel William E. Doster, who became Provost-Marshal of Washington in 1862 and for a time was Rose's official jailer, gave a skeptical appraisal of these years of her life when he came to write his memoirs:

> Surrounded by such advantages the vain girl did not fail to promote her ambitions and in the circle where she was at first only tolerated, soon became a leader, famous for her beauty, the brilliance of her conversation, her aptitude for intrigue, the royal dignity of her manners and the unselfish perseverance with which she accomplished whatever she set her heart upon.

CHAPTER II

Calhoun the Preceptor

ONE of the great disappointments of Rose's life was Calhoun's repeated failure in his strivings for the Presidency. From the time of the nullification crisis in 1832 she and Robert followed his leadership and championed him in all the bitter fights that followed. Because of this close association they were automatically swept into the engulfing tide of controversy that roared over the barriers in 1861.

The link between the Greenhows and the Calhouns was strong and constant. Floride Calhoun, like Rose, was a woman of substance, charm and character. She was the mother of nine, was devoted to John, and ran her home with spartan authority. She had deserted Washington society for the quiet beauties of Fort Hill, their home in South Carolina, before Rose had become a really potent figure in the capital. But Floride was glad to have the young Greenhows entertain her husband during the months he passed in Washington. Sometimes he stayed for weeks at a time on F Street while the Senate was in session.

Rose encouraged him when he grew weary in his struggles with Jackson over nullification and the United States Bank, two of the chief issues of the period. "The very existence of our constitution is at stake," he exclaimed as he arrived at the Greenhow house, hot and tired, on a June day in 1841. The immediate problem was Jackson's bank policy.

The heat and "incessant occupation" were wearing Calhoun down, for he drove himself hard and every fight was life or death to him. But Rose refreshed him with cool drinks, and listened by the hour to his stern exposition of his views. He ate and drank temperately and tried to keep fit by walking two or three miles a day through the streets of Washington.

That year he was again angling for the Presidency and he persuaded Robert to abandon the State Department temporarily to work with Robert Barnwell Rhett, another strong protagonist of states' rights from South Carolina, on a group of campaign newspapers designed to whip up support for his aspirations. Rhett planned to invade the New York field, but he did not get far beyond the Petersburg *Republican*, which Robert edited. From there Greenhow moved to Richmond, to sound out this familiar field, where he was liked for his own, as well as for his grandfather's, sake. Sipping Madeira and eating iced fruitcake, Rose took this occasion to beguile her husband's family and friends with her spirited tales of life in Washington and the recent visit of Charles Dickens and his wife.

Rose had met both Washington Irving and Dickens at the levee held by President John Tyler, which gave the visiting English novelist ammunition for some of his sharpest observations on American life. She shared Calhoun's impressions of Mr. and Mrs. Dickens. When he called on them he found that "Mr. Dickens' lady was quite homely and somewhat countrified in her manners" but amiable and sensible.

She continued to sew during Calhoun's visit, and never took her eyes off her needle except when she joined in the conversation, which was infrequently. Dickens struck Calhoun as having a "pleasant countenance, with easy simple manners." He thought that he was received civilly and politely in Washington, with "none of the ridiculous parade of Boston and New York."

Calhoun little knew that Dickens would return to England and

write in *American Notes* that in Congress he saw "the wheels that
move the meanest perversion of virtuous Political Machinery that the
worst tools ever wrought." Or that he would blast Washington as
unhealthy and ugly, the faces of its politicians swollen with tobacco,
their spitting habits disgusting, their costumes grotesque, their pushing and shoving at levees objectionable, their tactics and their manners unspeakable. He wrote of the new-born capital:

It is sometimes called the City of Magnificent Distances, but it might
with greater propriety be termed the City of Magnificent Intentions; for
it is only on taking a bird's eye view of it from the top of the Capitol, that
one can at all comprehend the vast designs of its projector, an aspiring
Frenchman. . . . To the admirers of cities it is a Barmecide Feast; a pleasant
field for the imagination to rove in; a monument raised to a deceased
object, with not even a legible inscription to record its departed greatness.

Calhoun corresponded with Rose when he was away from the
capital and she and Robert often visited Fort Hill, his pillared white
house fringed with cedar trees and surrounded by a park of poplars.
White birches gleamed in the distance. Wild orange trees scented
the flower garden. Floride had made it a home of sophisticated charm
to which the warrior of many battles could return for restoration.

She filled the family dining room with heirlooms from his country
home—austere pieces of pine, spinning wheels, ladder-backed chairs
and the old sleigh which had been their nuptial couch. The state
dining room, on the other hand, had all the formal touches that
were characteristic of Floride's French inheritance. There she held
banquets for thirty, and afterward played on the spinet with the
firmness that was part of her nature.

She welcomed Rose as a guest long before Calhoun became Secretary of State, but Rose needed little official shepherding through
the thickets of social life. She seemed to be born with the grace to
make her way. From the start of her married life she mixed freely
in all diplomatic exchanges and concentrated on visiting Britons and

21

Frenchmen at a time when both nations watched the expansion of America with close attention and edged in when they could. To talk to Rose was to get a vivid impression of any issue, since she knew no halfway measures.

She was at once involved when Oregon became a controversial issue between Britain and the United States, for Robert was deep in policy counsels behind the scenes. He had already exerted quiet pressure aimed at Great Britain through his book *The History of Oregon and California*. This had its beginnings during the Van Buren administration when he was commissioned by the congressional committee on American claims to the Oregon territory to write a pamphlet on the geography and history of the Northwest coast of America. This developed into the larger work, designed, in Greenhow's own words, to clear up the "mistaken and distorted view of North America common to all popular histories used in other countries."

This was Robert's major work and Rose helped him to compile, edit and correct his material. When the crisis developed between Britain and America it served as a tract for American interests, done on a broad and scholarly base. Robert played the role of diplomat, with the aid of Rose, who made it her business to get his book published in Britain, where it promptly came under attack.

Buchanan pushed the book hard and soon after it came out revealed in the Senate that Robert was making only $1,600 a year at the time and "must sell 2,500 copies of his work in order to make himself whole." The Senator from Pennsylvania cannily added that he had no disposition to do anything for Dr. Greenhow except what was just.

Soon after this, Buchanan followed Calhoun into office as Secretary of State, and Rose had another powerful friend in court. On August 30, 1845, Calhoun wrote to his successor:

It is beyond the power of man to trace the consequences of a war between us and England on the subject of Oregon. All that is certain is,

22

that she can take it and hold it against us, as long as she has the supremacy of the ocean, and retains her Eastern dominions. The rest is left in mystery.

Buchanan consulted Dr. Greenhow on matters of policy, as Calhoun had done before him. Because of his particular experience his opinions were valued where boundary disputes and the temper of regional groups were concerned. Thus, when the Mexican War broke out during President Polk's administration, on top of the Oregon dispute, the Greenhows were again at hand with strong opinions on all the issues involved.

While the war was in progress Buchanan maintained that the United States should give the European powers some assurance that it would not acquire California or any other part of the Mexican territory. Otherwise he thought it "almost certain that both England and France would join with Mexico in the war." President Polk replied that neither as citizen nor as President would he tolerate "any intermeddling of any European Powers on this continent" and that sooner than give the pledge proposed he would "meet the war which either England or France or all the powers of Christendom might wage."

Polk did not altogether trust his Secretary of State, who was known to have Presidential ambitions, and during this crisis he leaned heavily on Benton. While all this jockeying was going on in the background Rose became so deeply involved that Jessie Benton, who by this time had become Mrs. John C. Frémont, insisted she was pulling strings behind the scenes and was feeding confidential information to the British.

Rather than give Dr. Greenhow important documents coming in from agents in Mexico, Buchanan took them to Senator Benton for translation, according to Jessie. Her father and Senator John Adams Dix, both of whom spoke Spanish, then read the translations to Buchanan, and Jessie and her sister made written transcriptions.

Senator Dix lived on the same street as the Bentons. The two

23

families were intimate friends, and Dix often strolled in for an evening of music and talk in the large drawing room where the Benton family sat with workbaskets, books and portfolios, reading and writing by the light shed by tall candles in silver holders.

Taking note of the fact that Dr. Greenhow was official translator for the department, Jessie charged that Buchanan decided to cut Rose out of the picture, for she was "in the pay of the English Legation as a spy and our private information reached them through her." The only way to silence her, in Jessie's opinion, was to keep the reports from Mexico out of Robert's hands. But if these charges had any foundation, and Buchanan thought Rose a traitor at the time of the Mexican War, why did he trust her implicitly and move so close to her in later years? Or was his own stand equivocal in the negotiations?

In any event, this interchange led to a lifelong feud between Rose and Jessie. Both were clever, witty and had considerable influence with the politicians of their period. When they applied venom, it stung. There was no specific substantiation for Jessie's theory but when Rose was arrested for espionage in 1861 the story blazed into the open that she had long been in the pay of the British. This dated back to the Frémont charge at the time of the Mexican War.

In these early years Rose may well have been more indiscreet than deliberate in her operations, chattily giving away secret information through her intimate knowledge of her husband's affairs. She was always a free talker and was passionate in her political convictions. Not only was she in Robert's confidence but she had choice opportunities for gathering information on her own account. She dined, danced and promenaded with the leading statesmen and diplomats. As a State Department hostess with unofficial status, she was a lively social link between nations warily boxing behind the scenes. Moreover, by this time Rose's love of power was extremely well developed.

She carefully cultivated Richard Pakenham, who was British Minister at the time, and she and Robert enjoyed his bachelor hospitality,

24

which often included music and tableaux. He was an expert on border affairs, having been stationed in Mexico during the war between that country and France. He had gone to Vera Cruz in 1839 to help effect conciliation.

Rose was equally friendly with the popular Sir Henry Bulwer, who followed Pakenham into the Legation, and with Lady Bulwer, niece of the Duke of Wellington. She was also close to Sir John F. Crampton, chargé d'affaires at the time of the Mexican War, who later became Minister but was never genuinely popular with American statesmen.

Rose was a sharp observer of shifting currents, and maintained amiable relations with Presidential wives as well as with their husbands. She was friendly both with Mrs. Tyler and Mrs. Polk, for she cultivated *noblesse oblige*. When young Julia Tyler came on the scene, and set up a miniature court, Rose observed with interest her maids of honor, her white horses, her purple velvet train and the raised dais on which she received. She was young, beautiful and inoffensive, and when she gave a ball for two thousand persons in 1845 Mrs. Greenhow was among the dancers.

Rose liked Mrs. Polk for many reasons, one being the honor she always paid Dolly Madison, who had fallen on hard times through the extravagance of her son, Payne Todd. Like everyone else in the inner circle, Rose in the 1840's went to Mrs. Madison's straight from her New Year's Day call at the White House. Dolly still held court, although none could fail to observe that her home and her attire had grown shabby. When James Buchanan pushed through congressional support for her at the end, she blossomed again in décolleté white satin at the age of eighty-one. Rose watched her being escorted by President Polk across the room at her last White House reception in 1849.

Sarah Polk was a close friend of Buchanan's, and although she was not in sympathy with her stand on dancing, wine, horse racing and cards, Rose paid tribute to her good sense and all-round intelligence.

There is no record of President Polk's view of Rose, but if Jessie Frémont was right, she must have caused him some disquiet during the Mexican War.

President Zachary Taylor, beyond doubt, knew her to be up to her ears in intrigue in 1849, when she gave open and active support to General Narciso López in his attempt to overthrow the Spanish Government in Cuba. In this she was again the echo of Calhoun, who led a Southern movement to back up the Venezuelan-born filibuster in fomenting revolution. When López was exiled from Cuba and landed in the United States, Rose gave a large reception in his honor. She shared in the secret councils which promoted an army of American volunteers to back him up.

"The men of the South ought to flock down there in open boats the moment they hear the tocsin," said Calhoun, and Rose applauded. But neither Jefferson Davis nor Robert E. Lee would head the López army, and Colonel G. E. White, who had fought in the Mexican War, took command. An invading fleet was scheduled to sail in secret.

Spurred by protests from Spain, President Taylor issued a proclamation describing the expedition as a "criminal enterprise," and warning Americans not to join it. But Rose considered this a mere face-saving gesture on the part of the President. She professed to have inside knowledge that he did not mean it. She gave López refuge at her home and on August 29, 1849, after breakfasting with him and seeing him off, she wrote to Calhoun that the expedition was ready to set forth in a steamer from New York bearing a thousand picked and armed men, and another from New Orleans, with twelve or fifteen hundred more, "ready for the perils and honors of the venture." She added:

We think that all the elements of success are with them, as every chance has been calculated and everything which prudence and forethought could suggest done to ensure full success. The Government here are in the secret

26

and have done no more in the matter of the Proclamation than regard for appearances demanded.

The first fifteen days is the time of trial, and they invite the moral aid of all true hearts, who desire the incorporation of that ocean gem, in our sisterhood of States—and of all who sympathize with a people groaning under the yoke of tyranny, determined to achieve freedom or die in the struggle.

But Rose's hopes were dashed. The coup failed. The ocean gem retained its political status, and López returned to the United States, where he was received again with some acclaim. In the following year he tried once more and failed. There is no evidence that Rose was further involved. Calhoun was close to death and her interest may have faded. In the end López was put to death in Havana. He was one of many picturesque characters who crossed her path, for she was continually involved in drama, partly as a result of her husband's official position, partly because of her own dynamic personality. The abortive López revolution was only one of many instances of collaboration with Calhoun.

Toward the end of his life she watched Calhoun veer away from Senator Rhett. In his place rose the tall, spare figure of Jefferson Davis, whom he had picked as candidate for succession. Thus she saw the beginning of the feud between Davis and Rhett that was to hamper Davis in an hour of need.

Jeff had traveled to Natchez in 1845 and married Varina Howell, who was slow to warm to him at first and observed with some surprise: "He is refined and cultivated and yet he is a Democrat!" They established their home, Brierfield, in Mississippi, where Davis passed some contented weeks building and planning, watching wild geese flying past in flocks and white and blue cranes poising themselves among the lily pads.

The year of their marriage was also the year of his arrival in Washington as a Congressman. They found rooms, attended a congressional mess for meals, and soon Rose became conscious of Davis' growing

27

influence with Calhoun. She took careful note of the clever Varina, for new alliances were in the making. But the Mexican War swept Davis into the field and out of the social picture for a time. He came back full strength as President Franklin Pierce's Secretary of War. By that time they had a twenty-three-roomed house and Varina was a strong factor in the social scene. Although they were not mutually sympathetic, Rose and Varina regarded each other with respect, as did Rose and the more elderly Floride Calhoun.

In the closing days of his life Calhoun was again at Mrs. Hill's and in 1849 he wrote to his family that he was comfortably quartered on the ground floor, with Armistead Burt, a relative and fellow politician, along the hall from him. He had a large and barren room where he was able to receive guests, thus keeping in close touch with the political picture. He dined frequently with the Greenhows and was always Rose's most honored guest.

She was more amused than surprised to hear the gossip that Clay, still a dude at seventy-two, from sheer force of habit had snatched a kiss from Amelia Burt, Calhoun's young niece, when he encountered her in a dark corridor at Mrs. Hill's.

It so happened that Amelia was thrilled. "Just think, I've been kissed by the great Mr. Clay!" she told her uncle rapturously. A great many others by that time had shared the privilege.

"Amelia," said Calhoun, gravely studying his blooming young niece, "don't you put your trust in that old man."

By this time both Clay and Calhoun were in feeble shape, but were battling still for their convictions. The old flashes of hate ripped between Clay and Benton. As Varina Davis saw it: "Mr. Benton's mailed glove lay always before the Senator from Kentucky."

From the other side of the fence Calhoun, too, looked at Clay with mingled emotions, bitter over his compromise bills which would admit California as a free state, give New Mexico and Utah the power of self-determination on slavery, and reinforce the Fugitive Slave Act of 1793. As far back as 1812 Calhoun and Clay had been

28

War Hawks together, campaigning for war against Britain. Now the South Carolinian could not wholly forswear his mighty colleague. He had already summed up his feelings for Clay in paradoxical terms: "I don't like Clay. He is a bad man, an impostor, a creature of wicked schemes. I won't speak to him, but by God, I love him."

That was how things stood between them as they battled over the compromise that postponed but did not stop the war. Clay spoke early in February, holding his audience spellbound for the better part of two days. Once again that commanding figure, with musical voice and incisive mind, cut through all the inconsistencies, past and present, in a clear statement of policy:

I know no South, no North, no East, no West to which I owe any allegiance. I owe allegiance to two sovereignties, and only two: one is to the sovereignty of this Union, and the other is to the sovereignty of the State of Kentucky. My allegiance is to this Union and to my State; but if gentlemen suppose they can exact from me an acknowledgement of allegiance to any ideal or future contemplated confederacy of the South, I here declare that I owe no allegiance to it; nor will I, for one, come under any such allegiance if I can avoid it.

This was not the way Calhoun felt. It was not the way Rose felt. Calhoun's turn came a month later, when he dragged himself into the Senate on March 4, 1850, weak and swathed in flannels, too ill from a pulmonary infection to deliver his own address. Rose was there to hear the message that chilled the North. As he listened, Calhoun looked already like the specter of death, with his dense brown eyes sunken deep in their sockets, his thatch of shaggy hair frosted with silver, his mouth fixed in unyielding lines.

Rose listened attentively, with implicit belief in the words of her idol as he challenged the North. He pointed out that the number of states had increased from sixteen to twenty-six; that the nation's population was seventeen million, with two million more persons in the North than the South, and that the cry of "Union, Union—the glorious Union!" could no more prevent disunion than the cry of

29

"Health, health—glorious health!" on the part of the physician could save a patient lying dangerously ill.

Responsibility for saving the Union rested on the North, not on the South, said Calhoun, and the time had come for an "open and manly avowal on all sides" as to what should be done. It was the last chance to settle the question. At this point he cast the glove:

> If you, who represent the stronger portion, cannot agree to settle them [the issues] on the broad principle of justice and duty, say so; and let the States we both represent agree to separate and part in peace. If you are unwilling we should part in peace, tell us so, and we shall know what to do, when you reduce the question to submission or resistance.

> If you remain silent, you will compel us to infer by your acts what you intend. In that case, California will become the test question. If you admit her, under all the difficulties that oppose her admission, you compel us to infer that you intend to exclude us from the whole of the acquired territories, with the intention of destroying, irretrievably, the equilibrium between the two sections. We would be blind not to perceive in that case, that your real objects are power and aggrandizement, and infatuated not to act accordingly.

Webster came next, backing Clay on compromise. Salmon Portland Chase and Charles Sumner turned stony with anger, as they heard their ally giving ground. Within two years all three of these eloquent statesmen were dead. Each had repeatedly watched the Presidency go to lesser men. The first to go was Calhoun, and Rose was with him at the end. Robert was ill and could not leave his bed when the news reached F Street that their aged friend was dying at Mrs. Hill's. Rose ordered her carriage and drove to the familiar boarding-house.

Calhoun knew he was close to death but he was conscious of Rose, and of his son John, whom he asked to put away some manuscripts on which he had been working. Rose served as his nurse, wiping his lips and brow, listening attentively to his dying murmurs, which were all about the South. He passed in loneliness, a single tallow candle lighting his room, sounds of revelry echoing along the hall.

Congress convened on the day of his death. Slavery was again the burning issue before it. Rose sat in the Senate gallery, tears drenching her cheeks as she listened to the tributes paid to the man who had stirred up excitement among them for years. The official committee on arrangements assigned her a special place with his family for the burial.

Rose walked beside Daniel Webster, who turned to her as they left the grave, and repeated the words he had used in the Senate: "One of earth's princes hath departed—the purest, best and greatest man I ever knew!"

Calhoun was all of those things to Rose. His death was a personal grief, but more than that, for her it was also a challenge to sustain his political principles; to follow the difficult road he had chosen.

CHAPTER III

Golden Acres

Two months after Calhoun's death the Greenhows were installed in the lofty chambers of a dwelling on the Calle de Palmas y Plateros, the principal street of Mexico City, and Rose was glorying in the blaze of life, color and excitement that surrounded her.

The Treaty of Guadalupe Hidalgo, signed in 1848 at the close of the Mexican War, led to immediate confusion over land titles. The Rio Grande had become the boundary line, and California and New Mexico now were part of the United States. As the most informed man in Washington on the subject of boundaries Robert Greenhow went to Mexico City in 1850 to study the archives for the validation of land claims in California.

He was in poor health and Rose believed that the change of climate would do him good. She had been writing to Calhoun before his death about Robert's deep fatigue. He had worked uncommonly hard for a great many years, never sparing himself in the pursuit of obscure material. Now he was ready for a rest and a change of scene.

The white roses, daisies and marigolds which bloom incongruously in the Mexican spring were fading when the Greenhows reached Mexico City after an arduous journey from Washington. Almost at once Rose was deep in the worldly pleasures of the diplomatic set, attending balls, banquets, bullfights and cockfights. As she went about with Robert she was also perceptive of the people and their history.

Rose agreed with Frances Erskine Inglis, the Edinburgh-born wife of Don Caldéron de la Barca, the Spanish Minister, that in Mexico there was scarcely a connecting link between the "blanket and the satins, the poppies and the diamonds." With her own multiplicity of interests she was an asset to the parched society that confined itself to those of its kind, and to the few Mexicans who had traveled abroad.

One of her first and most significant encounters was with José Y. Limantour, who was brought to their home by M. de Joquet, Secretary to the French Legation. He was a Frenchman with a pronounced Breton accent, and he assailed the experienced Rose with such Gallic charm and persuasiveness that she lent an ear to the man who was to perpetrate the largest land fraud in American history.

Limantour had lived in Mexico for more than twenty years. He was a government contractor who dealt in arms. Since revolutions were of common occurrence in Mexico his wares were in great demand. He had considerable influence with the French and Mexican officials. His Spanish was poor and Rose did not consider him an educated man, but he was alert, persuasive and widely traveled.

In 1841 he had settled in the village of Yerba Buena, a region of brush and sand hills which three years before Rose's arrival in the West had acquired the name of San Francisco. There he met Eugène Duflot de Mofras, French author and traveler who was exploring the coast for Louis Philippe, and who predicted a golden future for this region. De Mofras urged Limantour to buy land at Yerba Buena.

Two years later Limantour met Governor Manuel Micheltorena in Los Angeles and sold him firearms. He later maintained that he received title from the Governor to the vast acreage he claimed, as part payment for his merchandise, along with an additional four thousand dollars. Micheltorena supported his story through much of the litigation that followed. The French Government gave Limantour support and countenance until he was exposed as a rogue.

33

Robert first looked at Limantour's titles at the Frenchman's home in Mexico City. Then José brought them to the Greenhow apartment for closer examination. Robert pored over them for hours in Rose's presence, and she learned that they represented immense land areas. Limantour claimed Yerba Buena, Alcatraz, the Farallones and Punta del Tiburona. In total his claims represented nearly one-half of what is San Francisco today.

Rose studied Limantour and listened attentively to what he had to say. After he left, Robert took a map and indicated various areas claimed by their guest, but Rose insisted years later in litigation proceedings that he did not trace the boundaries for her. In any event, her husband's aid was besought, both by Limantour and De Joquet.

Rose saw Limantour many times between May and October, 1850, dined with him twice at the French Embassy, frequently encountered him there at receptions, and listened to some of his lengthy conferences with Robert over the land titles. He was in high standing with his government at the time, and later correspondence between Rose and her lawyer suggest that diplomatic suggestion from Washington may have brought them together in the first place.

The upshot was that an agreement was reached by which Limantour would follow the Greenhows to California at the end of the year, where Robert would revive his old legal interests and take charge of Limantour's land claims. Thus Rose and Robert were unwitting aids in land operations that were to rock the nascent city, ruin many and reverberate in the courts for years, ending in the conviction and banishment of Limantour. He was a man of brazen deportment who, for a time at least, had his government persuaded of the validity of his claims, and even flourished the official seal of the French Legation on his documents, a use later repudiated by M. André N. Levasseur, the Minister, as being fraudulent.

Rose was to be plagued for years by this association and was to suffer from it financially when she, too, got caught in the general muddle created by Limantour. But while she was still in Mexico City the future looked promising. Daniel Webster was again Secretary of State and Robert was out of the State Department at last. They were facing a new way of living, and for the moment California, to which they were headed, seemed El Dorado to the Greenhows, as it did to many others.

Meanwhile, Rose explored Mexico City with all of her customary zest, dragging Robert away from his dusty archives for evening forays. Her imagination was stirred by the vigorous life surrounding her. She could overlook the abysmal dirt as she drove in a painted calèche to a ball, or joined the fashionable promenade along the Paseo at six in the evening. Here rows of carriages—some of them fine French coaches with liveried attendants—moved slowly along between the rows of stunted trees and oval spaces adorned with fountains and dusty statuary.

Rose was struck by the incongruity of the scene—the constant parade of splendor and the ramshackle, side by side. Parisian bonnets and dirty rebozos were always in juxtaposition, and fine blooded horses trotted along beside bedraggled mules. This interplay of abject poverty and great wealth was constant, but the vitality of the crowd caught Rose's attention at once, and she felt that a gambling fête champêtre she saw at San Augustin was nothing less than barbaric in mood. The distorted faces, clutching fingers, mountains of copper piled on the tables and ragged little boys running around with pulque, cast grotesque shadows.

She was startled by the savagery of the herraderos—the marking of the bulls with hot irons. Along with the other women of the diplomatic set she watched this week-long rite with some amazement. The roaring, the shouting, the music, the smell of singed hair, were robust even for her experienced taste. During this period of native fiesta they breakfasted in outdoor tents made of the boughs of trees intertwined with garlands of white moss. They ate meat cooked on stones and drank the native pulque.

35

Rose savored all these experiences to the full. She was in her radiant thirties, and nothing seemed an effort for her. She entertained her new friends with Washington gossip, and presented a distinguished appearance at a ball given by the British Minister at the Mineria. Robert was graying slightly but was still the handsome Virginian who had appeared at her side for years.

In her time Rose had attended notable parties under all manner of circumstances, but had never seen anything resembling this fête in the School of Mines at the University. The hall suggested a Greek theater, with lofty ceilings and noble pillars. The staircases were of classic sweep. The women from the legations stayed in the boxes and looked on instead of dancing.

Rose enjoyed the masked balls of Mexico City and the diplomatic dinners lasting for three and a half hours. She warmed to the tinkle of angelus bells; to cupolas gleaming in the dying sun; to the distant ridge of hyacinth-tinted mountains; to volcanic cones and dramatic sunsets. Unlike the Mexican women, who flouted tradition if they walked in the street, Rose strolled freely around the cathedral, the palaces and the great public square. She explored the Botanic Garden, the Museum and the Alameda.

This was a happy interlude for her, since Robert was relaxed and joined her in some of her wanderings. With his sure touch he primed her on the history of their surroundings. The palaces, the processions and religious fêtes, all had meaning for Robert. His fluent Spanish added to the ease and pleasure of their associations, for he was deeply interested in the ways of the people, and took Rose to market in the early morning to watch the light canoes come in laden with fruits, flowers, vegetables, maize and straw.

Wild duck and other game brought in by canal were displayed in the marketplace along with parrots on long poles, candied chestnuts, wax figures, bouquets of violets and a rich assortment of flowers and fruits, ranging from the fig to the passion fruit. Sharp-faced men in gold-tasseled hats and richly embroidered jackets sold calico,

36

hides, earthenware, baskets, ropes and matting. Rose watched their attitudes and chaffering trade with the liveliest interest.

By the end of October Robert had finished his work in the archives and they moved on to San Francisco, where he opened a law office at 145 Montgomery Street and they took quarters at 8 and 9 Montgomery Block. The city had just been chartered. It was young, lusty, sprawling and wild with the echoes of the Gold Rush. Rose, who had seen some of these elements in operation in Jackson's Washington, was much attracted by its vigor.

The population was fifty thousand and the streets were lively with miners who still brought gold dust in to the gambling tables, or assorted Forty-Niners who had failed to find their fortune and now were earning a living in any way they could—doctors turned barbers; lawyers working as waiters; merchants running lodginghouses. There were more than five hundred saloons in town, forty-eight dance houses and innumerable brothels. Rondo, roulette, chuck-a-luck and monte were played in every saloon. The lights flared. The pace was fast. The population was largely male and streetwalkers abounded.

Rose watched the promenade past their windows on Montgomery Street with the liveliest interest—noticing the Mexicans in serapes, the Chinese in coolie hats, the French in blouses, smoking black pipes; the miners in old flannel shirts and battered hats swopping gold dust for a night's diversion. The parade usually included a number of the more solid men of business who were intent on building up the city—bankers, judges, lawyers, stockbrokers, speaking in different accents, wearing the ruffled shirts, the highly polished boots and embroidered waistcoats of the era.

On a later visit Rose was also to catch glimpses of Lola Montez, who promenaded regularly on Montgomery Street, wearing a black velvet bolero over a flaring silk skirt. The waterfall of lace from her wide black hat half-concealed the magnificent eyes and white skin of this famous siren. She usually carried a riding crop, and the story was that she had snapped it at too bold a suitor in the street. Lola by that time was bored with life in America. She was tired of her journalist husband. She was getting ready to leave the tawdry city that was about to flower into true magnificence.

But in the meantime men talked of gold, of high stakes, of new strikes and lodes. The Mission Road was gay with huge candles and oil lamps, with folk dances and the silver harness of hitched horses whose owners were passing their time in the Spanish taverns. Building materials were scarce. Food was dear. Apples were a dollar apiece. Wooden cottages rented for one hundred and twenty-five dollars a month and Rose was quoted a price of one hundred dollars for a parlor and two bedrooms in a brick building.

There were a few neat homes in regional style, sent out from Boston, Germany, Belgium and France. The tiny acorn was growing into an oak. A square in Montgomery Street that had sold for twelve dollars five years earlier was now assessed at six figures. The Episcopal Diocese of California had just been organized and, although not of her faith, one of Rose's earliest friends in San Francisco was Bishop William Ingraham Kip, who headed it.

Robert automatically became one of the group of lawyers deeply involved in settling land claims. The confusion over titles was unparalleled and able lawyers gathered from different quarters to work on them. The validity of the titles, the extent of the claimed land, and its boundaries, were insoluble issues. Fistfights and brawls were an everyday occurrence. Passions flared as men battled for the acquired land, rich and still unprobed, held under Spanish or Mexican grants. Limantour's claims were the most fabulous and soon they were the most discussed.

Rose observed all this but lived apart from it, except for the echoes Robert brought in from his office. The Greenhows were drawn at once into the group of Southerners who were implanting their traditions on the raw surface of the infant city. They were cordially received along Stockton Street and in South Park, where a small group lived behind high iron fences and Southern traditions prevailed. Senator William M. Gwin, recently arrived in the West, entertained lavishly in South Park, which was laid out after the plan of London's Berkeley Square.

California loomed large on the national scene at the moment. Rose had seen the start but not the finish of the long wrangle over the Compromise of 1850. After leaving Washington she and Robert followed every subsequent move. They heard of the tears shed by Northerners and the angry mutterings as President Millard Fillmore signed the Fugitive Slave Law section of the compromise bills. Neither side was satisfied, but the war was postponed for another decade. And California was admitted to the Union as a free state.

Now Rose was on the spot to share in the excitement that followed this bitterly fought battle. She was not slow to see that California was destined for political greatness. She had the imagination to envision the riches it had to offer, and she was already won by its climate and its natural beauties. With strong Secessionist elements around her she cast out strings at once on behalf of her friend, James Buchanan. She knew how deeply he longed for the Presidency in spite of his protestations of indifference. He was in the thick of another political battle, which he lost to Franklin Pierce, however. He retired to Wheatland to lick his wounds and turned again to letter writing.

Just as he was addressing affectionate and revealing letters to Mrs. James Roosevelt in 1844, and to Miss Eliza Watterston in 1851, saying "I feel it is not good for man to be alone," he was in close correspondence with Rose in 1852 and she was reproaching him for being content to pass his time "ingloriously" in ease and retirement. Her letter to him must have been provocative, for he answered proudly and defensively, incidentally revealing his outlook on patronage:

Never have I been so contented and even happy as since I have lived at Wheatland. I find that a life of idleness or rather a life in which I can just employ myself as I please, is exceedingly agreeable. I no longer indulge

39

any ambitious aspirations. I could not if I would, have avoided being a candidate for the Presidency.

That is now past and gone & my defeat cost me not a single pang. Instead I felt it more on account of my friends than on my own account. It is a delightful privilege for one to have it in his power to bestow favors upon those to whom he feels himself indebted for acts of kindness. The power of patronage of the Government will now be wielded by the men of a younger generation; & it is the true policy of the "old fogies" to retire gracefully from the political arena before they are driven from the lists. Benton and Cass will, I have no doubt, hold on to the last.

But Rose was not deluded, nor did she lose hope that he might yet attain his goal, although he was growing old. She never missed an opportunity to work for him, as she had once done for Calhoun, Basking in the Californian sunshine it was easy for her to picture her friend at Wheatland, settled in comfort in the substantial brick building that stood on a slope, with a wide lawn twisting down to the road like a green banner. Oaks, elms, larches and evergreens shaded the house, and near by a wood began. It had little of the charm of Fort Hill, but was dear to the Greenhows, all of whom had enjoyed Buchanan's hospitality on many occasions.

Aside from their joint political interests, Rose and Buchanan had a close bond in the training of their young. Rose was educating Florence and Gertrude with the greatest care, and Buchanan was unconsciously preparing his niece Harriet Lane for the role she would one day fill with grace in the White House.

By the summer of 1852 Rose was back in the East and was visiting Warrenton Springs with her daughters. While there she received a letter from Buchanan in which he spoke of her "successful mission" and hoped that she was now "reposing on her laurels and receiving the homage of all persons of good taste" assembled at the Springs.

What was the successful mission? Did this refer to California and the Limantour interests?

40

Buchanan, too, was touring the Springs that summer. He had been at Saratoga, the favored spot for the Southern planters, and had found a "mob of fashionable folk" although not so many of the "dashers" as he had feared. He confessed to Rose that he had found Mrs. John Slidell the most gay, brilliant and fashionable lady at the Springs, "& as I am her admirer and attached to her party I am thus rendered a little more conspicuous in the beau monde than I could desire."

Buchanan escorted Mrs. Slidell and her friends to a concert given by Madame Marietta Alboni, the Italian contralto. He was much impressed by her voice, if not by her appearance. "She is short and thick; but has a very good arch, and benevolent countenance," he commented.

He went on to deplore the death of one of Senator Gwin's children, writing:

I was once very warmly attached to that man. We were on terms of intimate friendship & therefore at the first I felt his hostility very keenly. But this feeling has passed away, like everything else in this world & I would not, if I could, do him an injury.

Gwin had deserted Buchanan politically and the ice was thick at Wheatland when finally he called to try to heal the breach. In this same letter Buchanan wrote to Rose:

We shall all be most happy to see you here whenever you may be able to gratify us with a visit. After the excitement of Washington and the Springs, you may be able, as a variety, to pass some time with us, without ennui in tranquility and retirement. I trust you will not fail to make the experiment.

Rose returned to a gay winter in the capital. She was expecting her fourth and last child, but her health was perfect and she kept in the social swim. She was now a beauty in full bloom, an accomplished intrigant quite capable of molding men to her will. Although she no

41

longer had access to documents of state she was well informed from many different quarters, and she still had strong political opinions on all the issues of the day.

With the election of President Pierce the Southern influence was strong. Young, handsome and melancholy, he took office with the weight of his son's accidental death upon him. He promised to uphold the Compromise of 1850 but before his term ended he lent his support to the Kansas-Nebraska Bill, which virtually abrogated the Compromise. This infuriated his Northern friends but was pleasing to Rose, Mrs. Roger A. Pryor and other Southern hostesses who were in his counsels.

Rose was slow to warm up to the Pierces at first because of her bitter disappointment over Buchanan's defeat, but she realized that he, Lewis Cass, William O. Butler and Stephen A. Douglas had nullified one another as candidates. Although her favorite was again the loser, she floated tactfully into the Pierce inner circle, but was ever on the alert for Buchanan's interests.

Mrs. Pierce was so crushed by her family sorrows that her grief cast a pall over all functions at the White House, but the President, fond of liquor and fireside conferences with his cronies, drew in a strong Southern following. The dinners at the White House were stiff and formal during this administration. James Monroe's controversial gold spoons came into view again. The bouquets were huge wired effects.

The breach between North and South became crystal-clear at this time. The new political gods of the North were coming strongly into view—William H. Seward, Charles Sumner, Henry Wilson, Salmon Portland Chase. As one of the "Radical Whigs" who opposed the Fugitive Slave Act during Zachary Taylor's administration, Seward had now become a national figure.

Rose took stock of them all, as she circulated among the wealthy planters of the South, and attended the soirées where the fires of secession were well alight. She had a new and overmastering interest—

42

California. It had now become more than academic, for she had set her heart on a political appointment there for Robert. The uproar over land titles had caused Fillmore before going out of office to create a United States Land Commission for adjudication of these cases. The stories reaching Washington of pitched battles and bloodshed, of land grabs and fraud, had stirred the President to the need for law and order in the nation's great new acquisition.

On February 5, 1853, Limantour appeared before the newly appointed commission with his papers claiming extensive acreage in the San Francisco area. A month later Rose was importuning Buchanan to get Robert appointed to the commission. Buchanan was embarrassed. Like all the more scholarly statesmen of the day he admired Greenhow's abilities and was interested in his advancement, but whether for his own sake or for his family is conjectural. However, patronage was an old story to Buchanan. Rose was a dear friend. And although the commission was already manned, he thought he could find a loophole by having Robert admitted as an associate law agent for the government.

Buchanan wrote to Rose from Wheatland on March 21, 1853, pointing out that he had declined to recommend his own niece's husband for an appointment as naval officer at San Francisco because "I would not, a mere private as I now am, interfere in California's appointments." For the same reason he had refused to recommend the son of a "near and dear friend for an Indian agency in California, on the earnest appeal of his mother."

Nevertheless, he capitulated to Rose, indicating that he would have to help her husband in a roundabout way:

It may be said there is a distinction between that case and the appointment of Land Commissioners. Be it so, I am willing to adopt almost any distinction which will enable me to make the attempt to serve you; but I cannot write to the President on the assumption that he will remove three commissioners whom he has just appointed. I doubt very much whether he will do it; but when the deed has been actually done then I will adopt

43

my own mode of proceeding, without informing you of it, at least for the present.

But what did the next paragraph imply? Buchanan went on:

"If your good friend the Doctor should learn that I had recommended Mrs. Greenhow's husband after having refused to do this in favor of . . . a young gentleman named after myself, he would make the most of it."

Was Rose's good friend the Doctor her husband? Was she maneuvering to keep him in California? Or was it a question of Robert's health? In any event, her plan succeeded, and he was appointed associate law agent of the commission, which was backed by Gwin. Benton opposed the whole idea of the commission. He and Frémont considered this federal body a threat to the rights of the old Californians. They championed the Mexican grantees and urged the speedy confirmation of their claims. Both Gwin and Frémont had already battled this out and Gwin had won with the appointment of the commission.

Robert did not live long to pursue this work. Rose was in the East caring for her new baby, named after her, when she was shocked to learn of her husband's death. She had not even known that he was seriously injured.

On a February day in 1854 he was walking along Pacific Street when he slipped off a plank pavement and fell six feet down an embankment to the street, which was in course of being graded. He picked himself up and paid little attention to his injury until his left leg became paralyzed. He suffered acute pain for six weeks, but did not send for Rose, since he had no idea how serious his injury was. Moreover, the long journey, with her new baby just getting started in life, would have been difficult for her, and Robert was always considerate.

He died six weeks later, and although many good friends and all the more important members of the local bar attended his funeral, his beloved wife was not present. His death notice in the *Daily Alta*

California described him as a "man of great industry and very varied attainments . . . universally respected among his acquaintances, of singular purity, uprightness and singleness of character and purpose."

To all outward appearances the Greenhows were an exceptionally happy pair to the end. Rose may have overshadowed Robert by sheer force of personality, but he preferred to pursue his scholarly aims, leaving most of the social moves to his energetic and ambitious wife. His chivalry to Rose was constant, whatever complications she may have brought into his life. Her intimate friends viewed her as a well-informed and cultured woman who was an ideal mate for Robert. Her enemies called her a political meddler.

With the break-up of winter she traveled west, a widow in heavy mourning. She left her baby Rose in the care of her sister, Mrs. Cutts. Leila was a growing girl in school. Gertrude was deep in her teens and frail in health. She closely resembled her mother in looks but lacked her strength and vitality. Florence was a young belle, enjoying the diversions of the Pierce administration.

The isthmus route had become fashionable as a relief from the swaying and jolting of the cross-country stages. It seemed easy to Rose after some of her early journeyings with Robert. She had rocketed around in Ben Holladay's coaches and had watched covered wagons go by, drawn by oxen yoked with rawhide harness. Now Congress had passed a bill allowing thirty thousand dollars for a camel corps, and they had just been bought, although the first caravan was not to reach Los Angeles until 1858, a grandiose scheme that petered out from its own unsuitability.

Although a lover of the luxurious life, Rose stood up well to exigencies. Her health was excellent. Her muscles responded to every challenge. Always an excellent rider, she could handle mules with little difficulty. She had often amused her dinner table companions with racy accounts of sandstorms, snowstorms and miring up to the hubs. She had been known to help the men shove a stage up a steep grade.

Pillaging along the highways was an old tale to Rose, and she was apt to dwell on the meals served at some of the stagecoach stations or taverns as she dined on the epicurean feasts supplied by the Southern hostesses in Washington during the 1850's. She remembered some with relish—rainbow trout, venison, white raspberries, thimbleberries, tiny wild strawberries and huckleberries brought in by Indian women in heavy baskets swung on their backs. Actually Rose was one of the more traveled women of her day, knowing her own country singularly well although, unlike many of her friends, she had never been abroad.

On this occasion she rested and did some deep thinking about her future as she sailed south past Cuba, San Domingo and the bold coast of Jamaica. She was keenly aware of the tropical landscape—the coconut trees with tufted tops, the blaze of white and blue and gold, the luxuriant gardens fringed with cacti, and the dark-faced women with bright turbans on their heads, who coaled the ship or moved majestically along the wharf with baskets of fruit on their heads.

Saddened though she was, Rose was too gregarious to isolate herself from her fellow passengers. Soon she was spotted as an entertaining conversationalist with vivid tales of life in Washington; of Clay, Calhoun and Webster, all recently gone from the national scene; of Dolly Madison and other Presidential wives; of the growth and expansion of her native land, in which she was always intensely interested.

Rose paced the deck with businessmen traveling for the first time toward the Golden West. She watched the dolphins play, the sharks pursue, the breakers roll, as they moved south at the rate of ten knots a day. Sometimes she played eucher in the lounge, or read and wrote, two of her favorite occupations. She was charmed by the harbor of Aspinwall, with its forests rolling down to the cerulean bay, its ramshackle wooden hotels and picturesque settlement.

The Panama Railroad ran only twenty-five miles of the way across the isthmus at this time. The eleven passenger cars clanked along

46

between coconut, palm and date trees, heavily draped with flowers and vines; through densely forested lands and stretches of oozing marsh. At intervals they ran by the banks of the Chagres River and Rose had a chance to study the thatched huts and tiny villages.

They left the cars at a hamlet between Barbacoas and Gorgona and were poled up the river for hours through rugged scenery by boatmen who sang as they pushed the boat against a heavy current. Rose sat under the wooden canopy and watched the parrots and monkeys being driven away by pistol shots.

She passed the night in a filthy wooden tavern where a partition ten feet high separated men and women. Scores slept in tiered bunks, with dim lanterns hanging from the beams. Brandy was consumed in quantity as the night wore on. There were no beds or pillow cases, and the Express mules arriving in the night with the baggage added to the bedlam raised by roistering men. The click of castanets from a fandango in a near-by house added to the night's disturbance, and fiddles whined in the distance.

The next stage of the journey was by mule, and this became an endurance test even for Rose, as she whipped on her stubborn beast hour after hour. The old Indian path across the isthmus was rough. It had been used by the Spanish conquerors to bring their Peruvian treasures on muleback for shipment to Spain, but the paving stones they had used were now displaced and stood on end, making the way more hazardous for the mules.

Rose's beast scrambled up shelving rocks, then down the other side with the slip and thud of falling stones. Sometimes she closed her eyes as they skidded down an incline. She was splashed with mud and water, but from past experience she had learned to wear a resistant riding costume. Occasionally the path leveled out in a small area of cultivation, with native huts or a place of refreshment. As they approached Panama they left the mountains, traveling through open country and past the massive ruins outside the city.

Her friends rallied around her as she went through Robert's papers

47

and effects. She took the unfinished book on which he was working and later asked Jared Sparks, who had just retired from the presidency of Harvard, to edit it. He gave her advice and a few copies were issued.

Rose entered suit for damages against the City of San Francisco and by late August the Board of Aldermen awarded her ten thousand dollars for the death of Robert. With this she returned to Washington, sold the family home and settled in Brown's Hotel with her daughters, while she looked for a more modest place. She sought Jefferson Davis' help in finding a suitable house and eventually settled at 398 16th Street, which was to become in time espionage headquarters in Washington for the Confederate States.

CHAPTER IV

Buchanan at St. James's

WHEN President Pierce sent James Buchanan to London as Minister for the United States, Rose entered on a transatlantic correspondence with her friend that amounted to a political interchange on current affairs. Both happened to be gifted and diligent letter writers.

Relations between the two countries were strained, and the courtly Pennsylvanian was thought to be a sage choice, but he found himself in trouble almost at once. Echoes of these complications ran through his correspondence with Harriet Lane, Rose and other women friends.

Friction began with a minor social battle over what to wear at court. This became a cause célèbre. Jackson had repudiated court dress, and William L. Marcy, a man of rugged manners, had decreed that United States representatives abroad should appear in the simple dress of the American citizen. Marcy was Buchanan's chief as Secretary of State. The newly appointed Minister was much upset over his predicament. He was also stubborn, and took note of the fact that Stephen A. Douglas had appeared at the Russian court in his everyday clothes.

Ultimately he decided to dress according to Stuart's portrait of George Washington, saved by Dolly Madison when the White House was burned. He merely added a black-hilted sword to his own customary black coat, white waistcoat and cravat, black pantaloons and dress boots. Buchanan was more than six feet tall, broad-shouldered and inclined to be portly. His long face was bland, pink and smooth-complexioned. At this time he had an abundance of silky white hair. One of his eyes was blue; the other brown. They focused unevenly, and his head was invariably cocked slightly to one side. But the general effect he created was one of dignity and intelligence.

Buchanan's manners were impeccable, so that it was something of an ordeal for him to approach Queen Victoria in his unconventional dress, after all the uproar the matter had created. But he observed that "an arch but benevolent smile lit up her countenance; as much as to say, you are the first man who ever appeared before at Court in such a dress."

"I must confess that I never felt more proud being an American than when I stood in that brilliant circle in the simple dress of an American citizen," he wrote. But the London papers viewed things differently. *The Times* commented that "the American Minister sat unpleasantly conscious of his singularity." The *Morning Chronicle* blamed Pierce's republican ill-manners and American "puppyism" and added: "There is not the least reason why Her Majesty should be troubled to receive the 'gentleman in the black coat' from Yankee land!"

Since Buchanan had hoped to pour oil on very troubled waters between the two countries, this was an annoying complication at the beginning of his term. However, he weathered it after some preliminary ill-will, and as time went on, got along well with the British, although he found the ducal homes dirty, London gloomy, expensive and inhospitable, the people in general "very far behind our own in almost every respect." He thought the English girls more robust and healthy-looking than their American counterparts, but deficient in that "delicacy of beauty for which our countrywomen are so distinguished."

His own niece, Harriet, was built along healthy lines. She was a tall, fine-looking girl with blue eyes and fair hair verging on chestnut.

50

Her manners were dignified and she was richly endowed with tact. Although the British were suffering from their losses in the Crimean War there were ceremonial parties, and Harriet frequently danced the nights away after joining her uncle in London.

Queen Victoria openly approved of the substantial and intelligent Miss Lane, and Rose's growing daughters read with interest of their friend's adventures in London. Ailing Gertrude, in particular, enjoyed the letters which told of Mr. Buchanan's niece wearing pink tulle and apple blossoms at a drawing room, or dining with Queen Victoria and her consort Albert at a table graced by twelve golden candelabra, while a band played military tunes and Harriet quaked a little before the Lady of Windsor.

When the Emperor and Empress of France visited London in the spring of 1855, Harriet had a long talk with Eugénie. She had no fear of this elegant lady, who looked "striking and graceful" in green silk flounced with white lace, a matching mantel and a white crêpe bonnet with feathers. But she was disappointed in the Emperor. He was short, with weak shanks, and was not imposing in appearance.

Harriet and her uncle dined with the Archbishop of Canterbury and Buchanan received an honorary degree at Oxford. They all discussed Harriet Beecher Stowe's *Uncle Tom's Cabin* at the home of the Duke of Newcastle, Secretary for the Colonies, and Buchanan observed: "I did not mince matters, but spoke right out, evidently to the satisfaction of a majority of the company."

After the visit of the French rulers Buchanan wrote to Rose, as usual expressing himself frankly to her on political questions:

In the case of Louis Napoleon, fact is stranger than fiction. Whilst in London as an exile, he was never appreciated to be a man of talent. Now he is "the foremost man" of all Europe, & at the present moment possesses more extensive and real influence than ever did his great uncle. All the Powers of the Continent except Russia pay court to him as well as fear him, & England is his ally. His armies in the Crimea have covered themselves with glory. They & they alone have captured the Malakoff. I confess

51

the feeling for my own race is so strong that I wish the English arms had shared in this exploit. Whilst we cannot approve, on the contrary we must condemn, the means by which Louis Napoleon has acquired imperial powers, yet the French people seem now to be entirely satisfied with the manner in which he has employed it; and this is a question for them & not for us. . . .

I am anxiously looking out for the next Liverpool steamer from the United States. By her, we shall hear the counter-blast from our country, to the blast so unnecessarily raised in this country. I hope the storm will pass away without any serious damage. A war between the two countries would be highly detrimental to both. I ardently hope it may not become necessary. Please do give my love to Gertrude & Florence, though I know not where the latter is. With sentiments of sincere regard, I remain as always, your friend

(Signed) JAMES BUCHANAN.

By this time Buchanan had been forced to cope with a series of political complications, not the least of which was the Clayton-Bulwer Treaty between the two countries providing that neither should have exclusive control over any interoceanic canal in Central America. He was now breasting the storm raised by the Ostend Manifesto of 1854, in which he played a leading role. Buchanan, John Y. Mason and Pierre Soulé, three American ministers to European capitals, had met in Ostend at President Pierce's request, to consider the filibustering attacks on Cuba aided by proslavery leaders, an issue in which Rose had taken a hand.

The manifesto proposed that Spain sell Cuba to the United States. Failing that, it recommended that the island be taken by force as a measure necessary for the protection of slavery. Violent reactions raged over this in two factions already deeply stirred by Senator Stephen A. Douglas' success in pushing through the Kansas-Nebraska Act.

Rose was a responsive audience for Buchanan's outpourings on his political troubles. He in turn delighted in her letters and complimented her on her "graphic and glowing description of California and of her travels through the interior." He wrote that he often used facts and impressions from her sparkling letters to liven up his dinner table conversation in London, and to diffuse information about the United States.

The shadings given events by clever Rose must have permeated Buchanan's thinking over a period of years. By favoring the annexation of Texas and promoting the Ostend Manifesto he had become known as a proslavery man. Although a Pennsylvanian he was constantly in the company of Southern women. Rose in herself was a notably persuasive force, whether she wrote or spoke of the terrors and beauties of crossing the Continent; of the discernible spread of civilization and the growing number of states; of foreign entanglements and their effect on political thinking; of the industrialization of the North; or of the quenchless issue of slavery, viewed against the wide canvas of a nation slowly dividing within itself.

Buchanan knew that Rose was a listening post and a quotable force in the diplomatic world. Men of affairs took note of her opinions even when they were highly charged and colored by emotion. Since she had a genius for getting around and collecting facts, she was unfailingly well informed. Moreover, she could diffuse her knowledge where it counted. Only observers of the most tempered judgment saw her as the ceaseless advocate of a given set of principles.

By the end of 1855 Buchanan was weary of his post and longed to get back to America. Moreover, siren voices were calling him again in the direction of the White House. John Slidell, the political leader of the Southwest whose wife was a favorite of Buchanan's, kept whipping up his Presidential aspirations. So did Rose, with great subtlety and persistence. In December Buchanan wrote from London to Slidell that no desire lurked in his bosom for the office. He conceded that he had hoped for the nomination in 1844, again in 1848, and even in 1852, but by this time he professed indifference. "Now I would hesitate to take it," he wrote. "Before many years the

53

Abolitionists will bring war upon the land. It may come during the next Presidential term."

On a November day in 1855 he wrote to Rose:

It is long since I have enjoyed the pleasure of writing to you; but you need not be assured that my sincere friendship & regard for you still continue undiminished, & I feel the most perfect confidence that you still think kindly of your old friend. The truth is that I have heard so confidently of your intended marriage I scarcely knew by what name or where to address you.

I had hoped to meet you ere this . . . at Washington; but the existing relations between the two countries rendered it improper for me to abandon my post. I shall leave as soon as duty may permit; because I am heartily tired of my position. I do not say this because I have any complaint to make of the manner in which I have been personally received & treated in this country. Far, very far from it. But because at my age one almost necessarily loses the relish for those scenes of fashion & gaiety which I found highly agreeable in former years when at the Russian court.

Who was the man to whom Rose was reported engaged twenty months after Robert's death? Was it Colonel Erasmus D. Keyes, the handsome widower who was later to describe her as the most persuasive woman ever known in Washington society, and as one who had worked hard to tip his interest toward the South as war drew near? Keyes was from Massachusetts. Spare, bearded and aquiline in feature, he was a wit, a gallant and a man of worldly wisdom. He had served for several years as General Winfield Scott's aide-de-camp and was to return to Washington as his military secretary in 1860. In the meantime he was stationed on the Pacific coast off and on between 1851 and 1860. His first wife, Caroline, died in 1853, the year before Dr. Greenhow's accident. He was to marry Mary Bissell in 1862 when Rose was behind the bars of Old Capitol Prison, but in the intervening years he passed much time in her company during her frequent trips to San Francisco.

Although Rose disappeared for a time from the social scene after

54

Robert's death, and missed many of the angry debates on the Kansas-Nebraska Bill that kept the capital stirred up during 1854, she was soon back in the public eye. Her keen, clever face, framed in rustling black silk and net, was on view again in the Senate gallery, alive with interest as she followed every move, much as she did in the days of Clay and Calhoun. But now she was carefully appraising the mounting tension. More and more the stern voices of the North were drowning out the soft Southern accents on the floor.

Douglas was much in the forefront during this period, and Rose observed with consternation that her niece, Rose Adèle Cutts (known to her family as Addie), had developed a strange and unaccountable passion for the Little Giant. She did not underrate this romance, knowing how formidable Douglas could be when he wanted anything. Rose knew a great deal about him, since she had watched him from the days of his political emergence in 1835. He was not one of her favorites, and to Rose he seemed no match for the young and beautiful girl who had grown up with her own daughters, and who had been wooed by many young and desirable suitors.

After his first wife's death Douglas plied an erratic course, and one of her friends wrote to Harriet Lane on April 3, 1855: "What do you think of *dirty* little Douglas dancing and flirting with all the girls? He was quite attentive to Ellen Woodbury, he will not have to ask her twice." Ellen was one of the attractive daughters of Judge Levi Woodbury, New Hampshire jurist who gave strength to the forces of democracy in New England.

Later, after Douglas had persuaded Addie to marry him, she was to turn her back on Harriet Lane with a chill foreign to her gracious and warmhearted nature. She had sworn to make Douglas' enemies her own, and Buchanan was one of them, for a number of different reasons. In the end both Rose and Mrs. Cutts accepted the marriage. Addie had five extremely happy years with Douglas, which ended with his death from typhoid fever in 1861. They were together through the fierce storms of the prewar days and were among the first

55

to welcome and back the Lincolns. But Rose never warmed to Stephen, nor he to her, and her relations with Addie chilled off from their earlier closeness. She no longer regarded her as she did her own daughters.

While Addie was preparing to marry Douglas, Rose was concentrating all her forces on promoting his rival, Buchanan, for the Presidency. She worked quietly and powerfully for him behind the scenes, while Jessie Frémont staged a more open campaign for her husband. There were many points of similarity between Rose and Jessie, much as they disliked each other. Both had married pathfinders—pioneers who had spent months in the wilds and had helped to chart the boundaries of American territories. Both were women of wit, charm and literary ability. Both were involved in land scandals in the West. Both were charmers of men and good linguists. But they had little in common in their outlook on life.

Rose had watched Jessie grow up as the spirited daughter of Senator Benton, and had noted with interest her marriage to the Pathfinder in 1841 against her father's wishes. As a small boy in Richmond Robert had taken dancing lessons from Frémont's father, Charles. He was familiar with the tale of the French émigré schoolteacher's elopement with Mrs. Ann Whitney Pryor, his flight to Savannah, and his subsequent efforts to earn a living teaching French and dancing.

General Frémont's military and exploratory expeditions, as well as his court martial and fluctuating popularity, were of the utmost interest to both the Greenhows. Jessie went west in 1849 to join her husband and live the frontier life. She knew what it was to ride a buckboard, to sink in drifts of ashy earth, to suffer from the glare of sun and sand, to be pillaged along the highway, to rough it at lonely taverns, to ford a river, to fall ill at Panama, to cope with primitive conditions and to lend strength and support to the temperamental man she had married.

The General was filled with enthusiasm for his Mariposa property in the Sierra foothills when Rose first met him. He had established

56

his claim during his first military sojourn in that area and it was promptly confirmed. He told her later that he longed only for the primitive life he had marked out, and "confessed himself utterly unsuited for the part he had been appointed to play upon the world's great stage—in which opinion I heartily concurred," Rose added.

The prospect of being a ranchero was inviting when the hundred-pound bags of gold dust from the Mariposa mines were pouring in. They enabled him to buy extensive property in San Francisco, to live on a generous scale at Monterey and to develop his Mariposa property. The grant to this area represented immense interests, since it was one of the few that covered gold-producing land. But Frémont had little luck with it, and eventually lost the mines and all his Mariposa property.

Rose was scathing about the Frémonts' tour of Europe to raise money for this venture, and of the rare emeralds from Mariposa proceeds that were handsomely set for Jessie. "The Monte Cristo of Dumas creation was not the possessor of such countless riches as was this agent of a wholesale swindling firm," Rose wrote while the Civil War raged. "The Mariposa humbug exploded, and Frémont was dropped by the party who had temporarily used him, and suffered to relapse into poverty and obscurity, until the revolution again brought him upon the surface."

But the Frémont-Benton influence was still strong in California as Rose worked hard through her Western friends to further Buchanan's interests there. One of the more potent local figures was her friend and lawyer, Edward Jenkins Pringle, a Scotch-Presbyterian from Charleston, who had practiced law in New York before going west and setting up partnership with the brilliant Charles B. Felton.

Many of Pringle's letters to Rose were seized at her home after her arrest. They gave strong proof of her Secessionist activities, implicated her in Limantour's affairs, and also illustrated the kind of intellectual bond that she was able to establish with men of affairs. This was not a romantic association but one of joint working and

57

political interests. All of Rose's seized letters from prominent men suggest their high regard for her knowledge and capacity.

She traveled to California in the summer of 1856 to bolster the Buchanan column in the West but was back in Washington as the leaves fell. On October 18 Pringle informed her by letter that the Black Republicans were betting against Buchanan in California. "But I don't give up the ship," he added. Two weeks later he wrote triumphantly: "I suppose we may say Hurrah for Buchanan, for we send him without doubt the vote of California, and the same influences that have given him this State must have given him a handsome vote at the East. . . . I hope you will not forget to enlighten me sometimes upon passing events in the world."

Rose was so identified with Buchanan by this time that she was actually receiving congratulations on his election. She was jubilant. This was the fourth and the fortunate try. It started her on an era of open power and prestige. She could not have foreseen that she was also headed for ruin. For the time being she had become the most powerful woman in Washington, since Harriet Lane, handsome, tactful and gracious, refused to involve herself in political affairs. Rose never hesitated to pick up a challenge and this was one in which she gloried. Her political influence reached its zenith between 1856 and 1860.

The New York *Herald* summed it up when war broke out:

In those gay secession circles which ruled the Court and Cabinet at our Federal city under the diluted rose-water administration of Mr. Buchanan, Mrs. Greenhow was a bright and shining light.

Actually her influence with the bachelor from Pennsylvania reached back to 1845 when he became Secretary of State and Robert's chief. Buchanan's interest in women was not matrimonial, although he courted them with frequency and devotion, and kept up a lively correspondence with a number on a half-affectionate, half-literary basis. He had a facetious and gallant touch with the very young, and

58

cherished a lifelong halo of romance over the death of his early love, Anne C. Coleman.

Buchanan preferred promenading to driving, and Rose walked openly with the tall, foppish President whose white stock, tilted head and courtly manners were the trade-marks of an ambitious, studious and bewildered man, who was to go down in history as a vacillating leader in a moment of historic crisis. He deplored the influence of women in politics, particularly on the slavery issue, yet was continually surrounded by Southern belles who used their wits as well as their wiles upon him. The cleverest of these was Rose.

Her closeness to the new President had long been a matter of gossip. Now that Buchanan occupied the White House their friendly rather than romantic relationship took on new significance and Rose became a focal point of observation. She did not mind; indeed, she rather enjoyed the role. Buchanan was by no means the first President to seek her out, enjoy her conversation or profit by her political *savoir-faire*. She was still a good friend of Van Buren's.

Rose was stately at the inauguration ball. Diamonds sparkled in her black hair and around her white throat as she danced in a make-shift hall under a white cloth ceiling studded with golden stars and surrounded by the flags of many nations. Although well advanced in her forties her dash and animation overshadowed the attractions of younger and fresher women. Wherever she went her voice, with its alluring intonations, was listened to with attention.

Rose watched Buchanan with concern that night, believing that an attempt had been made on his life when he fell ill from acute poisoning at the National Hotel a few days before his inauguration. She was never to give credence to the explanation that infected rats had fallen into the tanks that supplied the hotel with water. To Rose his illness was the result of an abolitionist plot to get rid of Buchanan and his party leaders.

In her memoirs she insisted that arsenic was used. She outlined all the ramifications of an involved plot which she said was vouched for

59

by Attorney-General Jeremiah S. Black. According to Rose, he told her that Buchanan would not permit further investigation because of the "startling facts it would lay open to the world, and that he shrank from the terrible exposure."

Whether the poisoning incident was accidental or deliberate, Buchanan felt ill for some time afterward. He told Rose that every day he had "to drink several tumblers of unadulterated brandy to keep himself from entire physical exhaustion." She reproached him for not pushing the investigation, believing that he showed weakness in taking this stand.

But he had deeper worries the moment he took office. The Kansas issue was still a raging bonfire, and the Dred Scott decision reached his desk immediately after the inauguration ball. The antislavery group went into action at once and he was tossed about between discordant elements, seeking the pacific road but being heavily swung to the South through his friends.

He had been in office little more than a year when Rose had to journey again to California to testify on behalf of her old acquaintance, Limantour, whose name by this time was notorious throughout the country. The Land Commission, dissolved in 1856, had rejected his claims for outside lands, such as the islands, but had confirmed his titles in the San Francisco area. This had invoked a heavy run on these lands. While the building boom that followed the Gold Rush was at its height, Limantour quickly rolled up three hundred thousand dollars from settlers eager to put up homes in this promising area.

But complications followed. His documents were attacked as forgeries. All kinds of experts were called in to invalidate them. Governor Manuel Micheltorena's right to deed any of these lands was questioned. A clerk who lived in Limantour's house gave damaging testimony of faked records. Rose's old friend, M. Levasseur, said that the official seal of the French Legation was fraudulently used by Limantour. Handwriting, seals and the type of paper used in his

60

titles, all served to confound Limantour's claims, as experts denied their authenticity.

Although Governor Micheltorena and a number of prominent citizens backed up his cause Limantour was arrested for forgery and perjury. He furnished bail of thirty thousand dollars and fled to Mexico. But he returned later to battle his accusers in the civil courts. The litigation ran on for years, with the government taking an active part, since the Presidio and other federal properties came under the Limantour grants.

Grown bold and reckless, he was now appealing in the United States District Court for the settlement of private land claims not approved by the Land Commission. The islands cited by Rose were involved, and she was the star witness called by the claimant.

She was not averse to traveling West at this time, for not only would she see Colonel Keyes, but her oldest daughter, Florence, was at the Presidio as the bride of Captain Treadwell W. Moore, a youth from Ohio whose appointment as quartermaster had been pushed through by Buchanan.

By this time Rose was deeply involved in Californian politics. She had made a deal with the Western politicians by which they would support Buchanan for the Presidency if he would write a letter in support of the Pacific Railroad. He balked at this, fearing he would lose the support of Governor Henry A. Wise, of Virginia, and other Southern Democrats who did not favor spending Federal funds for a transcontinental railroad. But even after his mind was made up against it Rose called on him and talked to him so persuasively that at the last moment he wrote the letter. It was published in the West just before the vote was taken, with California giving him its support. It was read with some bitterness in the South a day or two later. Rose was at all times an advocate of the Pacific Railroad bill, and followed its fate to the last ditch through her friend, Senator Henry Wilson, of Massachusetts.

❨ CHAPTER V

An Ageless Belle

O N A July day in 1857 a stifling courtroom in San Francisco was filled with fashionable citizens who had come, not so much to follow the Limantour proceedings, as to see the famous Mrs. Greenhow, Buchanan's favorite.

The younger set who danced and flirted at the Presidio had been making bets on Rose's age. They were sure she would have to reveal it in court. Among those intent on settling the matter was Mrs. Amelia Ransome Neville, bride of Captain Thomas J. Neville, of the British Army. In 1851 her father, Colonel Leander Ransome, had established Mount Diablo as a base point for government surveys in California and now he had moved his family west from Connecticut.

When she came to write her memoirs, Amelia recorded the impression created by Rose:

One delightful lady at the Oriental unconsciously afforded us much entertainment, discreetly concealed. She was Mrs. Greenhow, of Washington, who had come West to visit her daughter, the wife of Capt. Treadwell Moore, of the Presidio. Mrs. Greenhow had known Washington society for many years and could talk of events back in Dolly Madison's reign, and other remote periods, until we wondered how old on earth she must be! She looked fifty, or seventy. Her age became a matter of wide speculation and bets were made on it but they remained unsettled.

62

Rose looked neither fifty nor seventy when she took the witness stand, fanning herself briskly. She might have passed for thirty-five. The handsome young creatures in summer flounces leaned forward expectantly, watching her.

"She will have to tell her age now, they grimly gloated," wrote Amelia, in recalling the incident.

"How old are you, Mrs. Greenhow?" counsel asked.

The courtroom was still.

Rose looked around without concern, and then with dignified finality answered, "Of sufficient age to testify."

The bets were never paid.

James H. Wilson, who was later to become a strong Lincoln supporter and to fight as a general with the Union Army, was counsel for Limantour on this occasion, and questioned Rose. He was one of the men originally appointed to the Land Commission by President Fillmore. He had staked his character and reputation on the validity of the claims, a stand which he was to regret and finally abandon, pulling out of the case.

Rose was asked to tell in detail how she and Robert had first met the claimant and what had transpired. She described their interviews in Mexico City, the establishment of their relations through the French Legation, and observed: "When I speak of 'us' I mean my husband and myself. Mr. Limantour's visits were to Mr. Greenhow, not to me; I dined with him twice at the French Embassy, and met him often."

Questioned specifically about boundaries Rose recalled that when Limantour left after his first visit, Robert took a map and indicated the lands and islands to which he laid claim, but without defining the actual boundaries for her benefit. He showed her the position of San Francisco on the map, and indicated Goat Island and Cedros in lower California, both of which were claimed by Limantour.

Rose could give no further help in the matter, although her appearance on the stand was one more stimulus to a sensational case. The sequel to this hearing was a flat rejection of the appeal by Judge Ogden Hoffman on November 19, 1858. He spoke of the "distinguished witnesses" who had appeared for Limantour and condemned the "unscrupulous and pertinacious obstinacy" with which the claims had been pursued. The cases were without parallel in the judicial history of the country, Judge Hoffman commented.

In this he was adding his verdict to that of Attorney-General Black, an old friend of Rose's. In the previous April he had denounced the Limantour claims in sweeping fashion as "the most stupendous fraud—the greatest in atrocity as well as in magnitude ever perpetrated since the beginning of the world." And that same year, Edwin M. Stanton, sent west to act as special investigating counsel for the government in land fraud cases, with particular emphasis on the Limantour claims, had found "irresistible proof of an organized system of fabricating land titles" carried on for a long time in California by Mexican officials.

The Limantour litigation was long-drawn-out, and even after the outbreak of the war Rose and Pringle still were trying to straighten out one particular claim in which they had an interest. It involved two square leagues of land at Point Lobos, part of which was included within the limits of the Limantour grant.

Prodded on by Pringle, Rose used all the influence she could in Washington during Buchanan's time to salvage this piece of property. She had often ridden out by wagon or horseback through oak woods to visit Point Lobos, the extreme eastern tip of San Francisco, and had watched the sea lions playing on the rocks. She had also seen the telegraph station at the summit of the hill in San Francisco being linked by wire to the lookout station at Point Lobos, a matter of much interest at the Presidio.

Although she did not particularly relish being a court witness for the notorious Limantour, and by this time had lost all faith in him, Rose enjoyed her visit to San Francisco. The Oriental Hotel, where she stayed on this occasion, was a gay gathering ground for the Southerners. It was a two-story frame building on Market Street with long galleries stretching across the front. Building materials were so scarce that the walls between the rooms were mere layers of stiff stretched linen covered with wallpaper.

On other occasions Rose had stayed at the Brannan House, a fashionable boardinghouse conducted by Dr. Oliver M. Wozencraft, the pioneer who laid the foundations for the Palo Verde irrigation system which ensures the Imperial Valley productivity in California today. One of her fellow guests in this establishment was the notorious Mrs. Désirée Fleury.

But although an interested and alert observer, Rose wasted no time with the more raffish elements of the rapidly growing city. She now had many substantial contacts in San Francisco. With every trip west she was amazed to see the rapid changes. This time she was aware of a sharp business decline. The collapse that followed the Gold Rush was now apparent. Many firms had gone bankrupt. Unemployment was widespread. Only half as much shipping had arrived in the port as in 1853.

Rose noticed that some of the wildness was subsiding, too, as the Southern element made headway against the gun-toting Forty-Niners. Although gambling, drinking and carousing still were widespread, there was a strong drive for a more seemly way of living. Soirées and promenade concerts were pushed, not always successfully. New hotels and cafés were opened up, but the emphasis still was on entertainment. However, the honky-tonk was giving way a little to the Strauss waltz, and the Barbary Coast was not yet in the making. More women were arriving from the East, and the trollops were less in view. There were polka cotillions, and the Southerners lived much like their kin in Washington.

The wooded tracts of the Presidio stretched from Lobos Creek to the rim of the Golden Gate, and Rose became as familiar with the officers there as she was with her husband's legal associates in San

Francisco. Some were to be her friends and some her foes when war broke out. Among the generals she met at the post were Irvin McDowell, William T. Sherman, Albert Sidney Johnston and Winfield Scott, a warrior whom she had known for many years.

At this time Rose was seen continually in the company of Colonel Keyes. They met at the Gwins and at the home of Judge Matthew Hall McAllister, who had moved west from Savannah in 1850 and practiced law with his two sons, Hall and Ward. Mrs. McAllister was arbiter of the social life of San Francisco during this period as her son Ward later was to set the pace in New York. He had moved east by this time but Rose had met him on earlier trips. As the first U.S. Circuit Judge in California, the elder McAllister made many decisions affecting the land grants.

All the reigning wits and beauties of California gathered at his home, and the McAllister Christmas and New Year parties were famous. In old-fashioned parlors, lit by candlelight, the guests danced Old Tucker and the Virginia Reel, or raced through Fox and Geese. Cutler McAllister usually led the merriment and sometimes Mrs. McAllister sang. They played charades and Blindman's Buff, sang carols and made merry with scores of guests.

Although Rose circulated freely in the social life of the young city she steered clear of Jessie Frémont. The Frémont fortunes were definitely on the decline while she was making this last visit to California, although the General was to come briefly into view again when war broke out. At the moment Jessie was living with simplicity in a ranch house which she had decorated with much ingenuity.

Since large window panes were not to be had, she had used innumerable small ones to create a Queen Anne effect in the desert. Her floors were solidly covered with Turkey-red carpeting. Her full, straight curtains, contrary to fashion, were topped with deep frills. Tapers of beeswax decorated with gold leaf adorned her dinner table. Wood fires burned and the smell of cedar pastilles pervaded her rooms. At Christmas she used wild rose haws for berries, and hung ground pine wreaths. Her piano, her books, her friends, her daughter, were life to Jessie at that particular moment.

She reveled in the violent contrasts of the seasons in the Mariposa area—the dark timber belt, the deep ravines, the snow on the Sierras, the golden pheasant in flight, the honeysuckle, azaleas, forget-me-nots, the pervading smell of vanilla, and—as her friend Bret Harte saw it—the sudden rush of spring, when "every creek became a river and every river a lake" and one was conscious of "rushing water, crashing trees, crackling timber and darkness."

The Washington to which Rose returned was also a city dancing to gay tunes but, underneath, the fires of disruption burned hotly. None knew this better than politically conscious Mrs. Greenhow, who never doubted that the nation was heading into desperate trouble. The stern prospect was always in the back of her mind as she moved about the capital. While all the discordant elements formed into a threatening pattern, the social round went on without a break. The German had come into vogue as a change from the quadrilles and cotillions of the Pierce administration. Fashions were picturesque. The frail gossamer tulle and flounced effects of the early 1850's were giving way to heavier materials. Hair was wound around the head in braids, coronet fashion. The garlanded belles danced with rosetted slippers, short white gloves, fans and the bertha neck popularized by Harriet Lane. Pond lilies, violets and trailing vines draped their gowns and hair. Hoops were spreading out.

The feasting was substantial, with many French chefs and fine Negro cooks busy in the capital kitchens. Wild turkey, prairie hen, partridge, quail, reed birds, terrapin, oysters and lobster were served with champagne, sherry cobblers and fancy confectionery. There was high living all along the line, particularly in the planters' homes, and at some of the legations. Rose was a favorite at the French Legation, both with the Minister and his New England wife. But her most intimate ambassadorial friend at this time was Gabriel Garcia y Tassara, the Spanish Minister.

She usually attended Mrs. Slidell's evening receptions, if not her matinee dances. The wife of the Senator from Louisiana, who was Marie Mathilde Deslondes of New Orleans before her marriage, was the sister-in-law of General Pierre G. T. Beauregard. She wore handsome Paris clothes and was gay, charming and popular. Rose was to be one of Beauregard's most loyal supporters, even against Jefferson Davis, and she was always close to Mrs. Slidell.

Another favorite was Mrs. Clement C. Clay, who had been brought up in Alabama to take pride in "her name, her blood and her section." Her husband was to be one of Davis' last supporters, and to suffer imprisonment, but at the moment she had an inexhaustible zest for parties and drove around in a carriage lined with amber satin and drawn by blooded horses. Her velvets were woven in Genoa.

All of the women were slightly afraid of Mrs. James Chesnut, a traveled and worldly observer whose husband owned a thousand slaves and great plantations in South Carolina. She was the only child of Governor Stephen Decatur Miller of that state and she had always had her own way in everything. Rose was to figure a good many times in the sharp entries Mary Boykin Chesnut made in her diary, but she could easily hold her own with any woman in Washington, when it came to spirited comment.

The year 1858 was known as that of the "court days." Harriet Lane presided with dignity, introducing a formal touch that was much commented on. The White House was freshened up with new furniture, portraits and silver. More ceremony was introduced, and all of Harriet's arrangements were marked by a stately austerity at a time when some of the parties around the capital verged on extravaganzas. Harriet was a poised and tactful hostess, and did credit to the long course of instruction she had endured from her Uncle James. Common sense came first and she moved the household to Soldiers Home in summer, away from the miasmic poisons of swampy Washington.

Rose thought that Buchanan stood as immovable as the "bronze statue of Jefferson in front of the Executive Mansion" before all the blandishments of the attractive women who careened around him. Mrs. Clay, Mrs. Chesnut, Mrs. Slidell and Mrs. Roger A. Pryor, all had his ear, but Rose was his cherished adviser. Behind a worldly exterior, political prescience came first with her. Buchanan was glad to have her back in the East. He welcomed her counsel as well as her conversation, and she brought him a fresh and buoyant picture of the newly acquired areas. The Oregon Settlement and the Mexican War had added eight hundred thousand square miles of American territory to the fast expanding nation.

In the spring of 1859 Buchanan was worrying about the isthmus region, and shortly after Rose's return from the coast he wrote to Lord Clarendon:

The little Frenchman, although repudiated by his Government, has made these silly people believe that he is going to dig a Ship Canal for them between ocean and ocean, a work which all the money in Paris would not accomplish. His plan is a subject of ridicule among capitalists both in England & this country; but the Nicaraguans venerate him as a perfect prodigy.

British interference with American merchantmen suspected of carrying slaves was causing much ill-will at this time. Buchanan, who felt with justice that he had allayed some of the suspicion between the two nations during his term as Minister, was deeply interested in binding up this sore. Instead of leaning on his Secretary of State he preferred to handle the diplomatic negotiations personally, because of his intimate knowledge of the British statesmen involved. When Lord Napier, the slender, light-haired Scot who had made himself popular in Washington, was on his way out as Minister, and Lord Lyons was headed in, Buchanan wrote to Lord Clarendon:

Your mission here ought always to be filled by a first-rate man whose character is known in this country & whose acts & opinions will command respect & influence in England. Above all things, he ought to be instructed not to interfere on one side or the other in our party politics.

69

Lord Napier is personally a very agreeable & well-informed gentleman; & Lady Napier is charming. No lady ever made or in my opinion deserved to make a more favorable impression on the society of this city than she has done.

Buchanan was devoted to Lady Napier and he hated to see this couple go. Seward, too, was her slave, and Rose considered the pious and elegant Lady Napier "one of the most ideal-looking persons" she had ever known. They met frequently in Buchanan's presence.

While in England he had pursued his light flirtations, the Duchess of Somerset being one of his favorites. When the Napiers were appointed to the Washington post in 1854, she wrote jestingly to Harriet Lane that she hoped Lady Napier would not "cut her out with Mr. Buchanan." Now, as the Napiers prepared to leave, the Duchess wrote again to Harriet: "Oh! be kind to dear Lord Lyons. He is a most amiable, and excellent young man and feels his father's ever-to-be lamented death very severely."

Harriet was kind and courteous to all the diplomats, but she made a special effort with bluff Lord Lyons and the report soon spread that she would marry him. But Rose had his ear on official matters, and soon Kate Chase, the brilliant daughter of Salmon Portland Chase, would push the Northern interests with Lord Lyons as persistently as Rose worked for the South. The new Minister was exposed to a heavy battery of fire between these three, but maintained his balance and came out of it bland and untroubled, although the impression prevailed that in the beginning he leaned far to the South.

Rose got on as well with Lord Lyons as with the Napiers. Mrs. Chesnut took note of this in a diary entry which later became part of her published memoirs. She wrote of Rose:

In Washington, they said Lord Napier left her as a legacy to the British Legation, and they accepted the gift—unlike the British nation, who would not accept Emma Hamilton and her daughter, Horatia, though they were willed to the nation by Lord Nelson.

70

The farewell party for the Napiers and a fancy dress ball given in the spring of 1858 by the Gwins were the two last great routs before the war. Addie Douglas was dressed as Aurora at the masquerade, "radiant in the pale tints of morning." Mrs. George Ellis Pugh, the handsome brunette wife of the Senator from Ohio, was her opposite number as Night. Mrs. Jefferson Davis appeared as Madame de Staël. Senator Gwin strutted as Louis Quatorze.

Buchanan attended the ball but not in costume. His relations with the California Senator had been somewhat patched up. Soon Gwin would be arrested for espionage and Rose would be climbing the Gwin stairs under military guard for a hearing. But all was magnificence at the ball. The costumes were long remembered. And Rose was the uncrowned queen of the occasion. She chose simplicity in the midst of extravagance and appeared as a "most comely Housekeeper of the Old School." But the New York Times commented that the "ésprit of the wearer made her glorious as a diamond richly set."

Among the guests, looking sulky and handsome, was Philip Barton Key, dressed as an English huntsman in white satin breeches, cherry velvet jacket, with lemon-colored high-top boots and a silver bugle. Within a matter of weeks he was dead—shot by Daniel E. Sickles, a friend of Buchanan's, who startled all Washington by killing Key for his attentions to his young Italian-born bride, Theresa Bagioli.

Sickles had been Secretary of the Legation in London and Buchanan was attached to him. When he entered Congress in 1857 he rented the Woodbury house on Lafayette Square and lived in high style. His coaches and dinners were of the sumptuous order. Mrs. Clay had called on his wife a day or two before the murder. She found her looking naïve and charming in a painted muslin gown with yellow crocuses in her dark hair.

Stanton defended Sickles and his acquittal was followed by a number of parties to celebrate the occasion. Buchanan was glad that "Dan got off." Rose followed this case with the deepest interest, knowing everyone involved. The murdered man was a native of her own state and she was always loyal to Maryland. He was the son of Francis Scott Key, the lawyer who immortalized himself by writing "The Star Spangled Banner." But her sympathies were divided, for she was a friend of Sickles too.

Rose now used her time to the best advantage, concentrating on men of influence. She played her cards with the greatest care, keeping up all her Northern contacts and circulating freely on the social scene. As the drift of the South took shape she became more openly partisan, and she followed the Lincoln-Douglas debates with close attention. She appraised the angry sessions in the Senate, and added fuel to the hot discussions in Southern homes and at the favorite messes. She listened attentively to the gossip at Brown's Hotel, a focus for Secessionist activity. Many of her impressions made background for the President's outlook on current affairs.

Rose still consorted with the men and women of the North at a time when most of her Southern friends were showing their feelings openly and cutting them dead. But she did it all with a purpose, deliberately cultivating the strong antislavery element. She was as likely to have Seward at her dinner table as her particular favorite, W. W. Corcoran, the handsome widower whose art treasures, exotic plants and Johannesburg wine were distinctive features of his hospitality.

By this time Jefferson Davis was firmly entrenched with the Southern group. He was less popular than many of his fellow Senators but by 1859 he had moved deep into the Southern ring, although never wholly part of it. His cold, haughty exterior and imperious ways, his taut manner and soldierly reserve, were chilling to men of more genial mold. He treated Rose with respect. Although she never warmed to him as she did to Calhoun she was his ally to the day of her death.

Colonel Keyes, who was Rose's devoted slave at this time, wrote of Davis after the war: "As a rule there was a mannerism in all his

72

public discourse by which he endeavored to appear in loving harmony with his audience, although he was obstinate and selfish by nature, and his heart was as cold as a stone."

No hostess in Washington viewed the social scene in the prewar months with more perception than Rose. She had been in the capital almost continuously through four decades of changing modes, fluctuating tastes and successive politicians. Her wit by this time was faintly acid. She knew where danger lay, where men were susceptible to persuasion, where old feuds had left cold ashes.

Her time had come to drive through the streets with queenly assurance and invite whom she wished to her table. She was besought for favors because she was close to Buchanan. Her correspondence ranged across the country. She was the power behind the throne and none knew better how to make use of influence. Always interested in writing, she sent James Gordon Bennett letters of social comment, which he printed in the *Herald* as coming from *Veritas*.

CHAPTER VI

Abigail versus *Rose*

O N A winter day in 1859, when Christmas greens were reflected in the dangling crystal prisms of her dining room, and passions flared over the hanging of John Brown, Rose picked up a challenge from a noted guest at her dinner table and hotly argued the slavery issue.

She had brought together Mr. and Mrs. Charles Francis Adams and some of her Southern friends, a daring experiment in the prevailing atmosphere of Washington. Alone among the capital hostesses, with the exception of Mrs. Pryor, she still freely crossed the boundary lines between North and South.

Seward, just back from Europe, was present, and enjoying Rose's Madeira and wild pigeon. He was still one of her admirers but regarded her with increasing wariness. She flattered him at every opportunity and her later astute appraisal of the Senator from New York supplies the key to her relations with him. Rose wrote that Seward,

who in the morning is the most reticent of men in the world . . . is, after supper and under the influence of the generous gifts which the gods provide, the most genial and confidential of men. I have often had occasion to admire the confidingness of his nature on these occasions, and wondered if the judgment of the world was correct in ascribing to him the character of a subtle schemer and tortuous intriguer.

Abigail Adams, stern, self-assured and well endowed with argument, bluntly broached the topic that was taboo between North and South. Addressing herself directly to Rose, this daughter of the wealthy New Englander, Peter C. Brooks, embarked on a spirited analysis of the John Brown case. She defended him eloquently and called him a "holy saint and martyr."

Rose sparked back without an instant's hesitation. She had a deep and alluring voice and when she wished she could command attention with it. She did so now. A hush enveloped the table. "I have no sympathy for John Brown," she announced. "He was a traitor, and met a traitor's doom."

The encounter was electric, because of the high tension surrounding this topic. Feeling on the subject was so violent that John Brown was nothing less than martyr or devil. Rose turned to Seward, who squirmed as she told him in the same unequivocal way that he had shown good taste in a recent speech in repudiating all connection with John Brown.

Seward smoothly replied that he had met him only once. On that occasion Brown had struck him as being a "wild and visionary man, erratic in his ways, and singularly striking in his appearance." Then, with Mr. and Mrs. Adams both within earshot, Seward hastened to add that Brown had impressed him also as being a bold, truthful and honest man. However, he considered him eccentric to a degree "bordering on an unsettled state of mind." The raid had merely confirmed his original suspicion that John Brown was mad.

Colonel John Bankhead Magruder, a Winchester friend of Mrs. Lee who was soon to serve as a general with the Confederate Army, was present. He took Rose's side, quibbled with Seward, and hammered a few more nails in John Brown's coffin, saying he was guilty of prevarication, intimidation and theft.

Seward, the ever canny diplomat, steered the conversation into safer channels. Rose professed relief. "I should have shrunk from the most distant allusion to these incidents, had they not become

75

matters of public notoriety," she commented later, apologetic for what at that time seemed to be a breach of manners at her dinner table.

Adams, on her other side, sat through it all, impassive and noncommittal. But Rose had not heard the end of this encounter. The picture of two such formidable characters as Mrs. Adams and Mrs. Greenhow in conflict at the dinner table made an intriguing item of gossip. Buchanan heard of it with some dismay. He brought up the matter, half in jest, half-reproachfully, next time he saw Rose. One did not fool with an Adams of New England, and certainly not with Abigail.

"Do you keep spies in my household?" Rose protested, and then, with unwonted humility, added that she was much vexed about the incident. It had never occurred to her that the gatherings of "so humble an individual" as herself would have come to his attention.

"How you talk!" jested Buchanan. "I have heard it spoken of by five or six persons, who all greatly commended your spirit and independence."

Seward told her a few days later that in writing to their mutual friend, Lady Napier, he had pointed out that in all Washington only Rose had the independence to give a "mixed" dinner party. But Rose now felt that the matter had lost grace. She told Seward that she would not repeat the experiment. At the moment she was swinging away from the Senator, although still quite ready to use him for her own ends. After years of friendship and a mild degree of after-dinner conviviality, she had come to the conclusion by 1859 that he was a weakling who would not face an issue squarely.

Their relations were to get steadily worse, although Seward continued to pay her lip service until the day of her arrest. But none was to be more indifferent when she landed in jail, except in so far as her revelations embarrassed him.

Senator Henry Wilson, a stalwart antislavery man from Massachusetts, told her that the Republicans blamed Mrs. Adams for raising the John Brown issue, and thought the demonstration on her part "very ill-timed." In actual fact Wilson, like Seward, was critical of John Brown's raid, which had the backing of the extremists.

In the months that followed, Rose came into close association with Senator Wilson and he was believed to be her lover. All through the winter of 1860-61 he appeared to be suffering excruciating pangs of love for her, if the notes seized at her home after her arrest, and destined to be filed eventually with the War Department as "*Love Letters (Supposed to be) from Henry Wilson, U.S. Senator from Massachusetts,*" were authentically his. Handwriting experts have challenged them. But it is a matter of historical record that Rose and Wilson were intimate friends and saw much of each other in the months before war broke out.

Rose had the notes romantically tied with ribbon. She had attached a notation on yellow paper in her own bold handwriting: "Letters from H not to be opened—but burnt in case of death or accident." This was a gesture of protection for the mysterious H. They were not letters that the puritanical and respectably married Wilson would have wished the world to see, yet the evidence is strongly suggestive that they may have been his. One was written on Senate notepaper. Another referred to the Pacific Railroad bill in which he was interested. All expressed the same note of passion, frustration and even a touch of desperation. They implied a series of love encounters with Rose, and great pressure on her part to bring him to her side.

There were ten in all, signed for the most part by the single initial H. In one instance, where the first name was written out in full, everything but the H had been snipped off. All of the notes convey the impression that Rose kept importuning H, and demanding assurances of his love, in spite of the difficulties entailed for him in getting away from the Senate and keeping appointments. Only one was dated, but they seem to run in close continuity:

You know that I do love you. I am suffering this morning; in fact I am sick physically and mentally and know nothing that would soothe me so much as an hour with you. And tonight, at whatever cost, I will see you

This was followed by a more cheerful note next day:

I am happy to say that I feel particularly well this morning; and can well account for the favourable change. We are in the act of entering on the consideration of the Pacific R R Bill. I will not fail you tonight and will bring with me the thing of which we spoke last night. Bless you always Yours.

Several of the notes were lines obviously scribbled in great haste such as: "*I will come up this evening—I will be busy until then. H.*" And again:

If fate is not against you I will be [with] you this night. I long for your sympathy—for I need it. I am exhausted. I have been labouring hard and incessantly. My love is all yours & only yours. H.

A third read: "*I do love you and will be with you tonight and explain why I did not come last night.*"

Three more notes indicate how importunate Rose must have been in her demands; how desperate her lover was to meet them; yet how difficult he was finding the situation. The first read:

Your note caused me pain because when I read it I realized how much you had suffered. You wish me to say whether or not I will be with you tonight and also to say that I love you—I *do* say both. I am thankful to you for not doubting me. I am sick and suffering. Yours.

The second was another gasp of pain from H:

I am in receipt of your note. If you knew how I suffered last night, and am still suffering you could find it in your heart to forgive me. I had a burning fever the whole night. I am now only able to sit up because I must be here. But sick or well I *will* be with you tonight—and then I will tell you again and again that I love you; as I now do and that too most truthfully. Ever your H.

78

The third was further assurance to doubting Rose that H did indeed love her:

I feel conscious that you can scarcely forgive me—and yet I feel this because I know that you cannot know what I have had to encounter for some days and nights past. Indeed I am nearly exhausted. Tonight, unless *providence* has put its foot against me I will be with you—& at as early an hour as I can. That I love you God to whoom (*sic*) I appeal, knows. H.

As the correspondence continued, a new and anxious note crept into H's love notes—the thought that he and Rose were being spied on. The most specific of his communications on Senate notepaper, conveyed this information:

United States of America
Thirty Sixth Congress
Washington City 30th Jany. 1861

Your note is recd. Believe me or not you cannot be more wretched than I am. I cannot now explain. Let it suffice until we meet that for the last few days every movement and act of mine have been watched with hawk-eyed vigilance. For your sake more than my own I have been compelled to be cautious. But tomorrow at 10 a.m. I will see you at all hazzards. (*sic*)
Yours ever

(Signed) H

The fear that spies were on his trail tinged another apologetic note:

I fully intended to come at the hour appointed this morning—but was not up until nearly the time—and then found three or four gentlemen waiting to see me on important business. You well know I love you—and will sacrifice anything on my own account. I have feared bringing you into trouble—for I repeat to you that spies are put upon me but I will try to elude them tonight and once more have a happy hour in spite of fate. H.

Evidently the pressure on H mounted as the railroad bill was pushed through. His notes became hectic:

I will come tonight but at what hour I can't say. This is the last night of the session and we will sit late. We are making one last effort to get up and pass the PRR bill. But I *will* come I repeat. Yours always.

This was followed up with:

At 10 o'clock tonight precisely expect me. I have but one moment. The Pacific R.R. bill is now being voted on & you may know that I am all anxiety. Yours. H.

Wilson was not a romantic figure. He was a forceful, broad-beamed man, tall and sullen in appearance. The features of his florid and clean-shaven face were heavily molded and brooding in effect. He was the self-educated son of a New Hampshire farm laborer, and had changed his name from Jeremiah Jones Colbath when he left home at the age of ten. He often said: "I was born in poverty. Want sat by my cradle. I know what it is to ask a mother for bread when she has none to give."

By the time Rose met him he had become a wealthy shoe manufacturer, and was known as the Natick cobbler. He had been in turn a Free-Soiler, a Know-Nothing and now was a strong antislavery figure. He was uncompromising in the same fashion as Charles Sumner, but he lacked the rhetorical grace of that Apollo. However, he was a useful party man, solid and reliable. He had helped to shape the Republican policies and was a leader in Senate debates. As a member of the Senate Military Committee, both before and after the outbreak of war, he was unusually well informed on matters that interested Rose.

He followed Jefferson Davis as chairman of the committee. Thereafter he was a key figure for espionage purposes. The evidence is strong, if not battle-proof, that the puritanical Henry Wilson was fighting his more primitive instincts with the importunate Mrs. Greenhow at a crucial moment in his country's history. But although it is an indisputable fact that he was seeing a lot of her, there is no convincing evidence that he betrayed his political trust. The country

80

was not yet at war when the love notes, whether his or not, were written.

To all outward appearances Wilson was devoted to his wife, the gentle Harriet Malvina Howe of Natick, and if Rose impinged on this New England idyl, the scars were not discernible. His marriage, like his political career, seemed untroubled to the end. His political fortunes rose steadily, and in 1873 he became Vice-President in the Grant administration.

Although Wilson seems to have been an important figure in Rose's life for a brief period, he stood for almost everything that she most detested, including moral bigotry. When she came to write the story of her months in prison she treated him with hostility and strongly implied that he had poured strategic secrets into her ears of his own volition. No echo of past tenderness is detectable in her narrative.

Wilson was only one of several men on whom Rose cast her spell during this significant period in the nation's history. All were men who could serve her purpose in a political or military sense. The genial Colonel Keyes, by this time serving in Washington as General Scott's military secretary, was less in evidence as Henry Wilson came to the forefront. But he made no secret of the skill with which Rose had tried to ensnare him, and although he later made light of their relationship in his memoirs, few who knew them doubted that she had entangled Keyes romantically.

After Rose's arrest Jessie Frémont made capital out of her association with the Colonel, which had stirred up talk on the coast, as well as in Washington. She wrote that his love letters were found among her possessions, that they held up the dashing Keyes to ridicule, and that Rose had set a price on them. "As a U.S. officer she found him valuable for information, their old relations being confidential," Jessie commented.

Nothing appears in the Pinkerton or War Department records to substantiate the claim that letters from Keyes were among those found in Rose's seized correspondence. In any event, the Colonel

pulled away from her completely. He also annoyed General Scott b
resigning abruptly as his military secretary on April 2, 1861, an
donning the uniform of the North almost the instant war was de
clared. Keyes fought stoutly, if not always successfully, with the Arm
of the Potomac. He commanded a brigade at Bull Run, showed
gallantry at Fair Oaks, and in 1864 resigned from the army an
returned to California.

The Colonel, by his own admission, was most susceptible to the
opposite sex. During his stay with General Scott at Wormley's, where
they had a private table and attracted much attention, he was con
tinually exposed to their fascinations. Rose by no means held the
field. He was much enamoured of a "Mrs. Bass, a tall handsome
widow from Mississippi." And when Corcoran introduced him to
Mrs. Slidell he wrote that as he conversed with the beautiful South
erner he thought more of "lutes and bowers than of guns and drum
and camps." He indulged in gallantry also with her daughters and
with Harriet Lane, the Magruder and Loring belles, Reverdy John
son's daughter and other members of the younger set.

Commenting facetiously on this group of feminine charmers
Colonel Keyes jested that their sectional rancor was administered to
him tempered with soothing conditions. They promised him that i
he were wounded and captured they would bring him comforts in
prison. "Some of the matured Southern dames and dowagers appeared
to hate the portion of earth where I was born, unconditionally," he
noted.

Colonel Keyes' memoirs, *Fifty Years' Observation of Men and
Events*, published in 1885, give the most precise and enlightening
view available of the Greenhow technique:

I found great delight with the Southern damsels, and even with some
of the matrons, notwithstanding the incandescence of their treason
Although I now consider myself far enough along in years to be out o
danger, it is my solemn opinion that beautiful women ought to be con

sidered as contraband of war, and captured wherever found, and detained till after the fight under the guard of old persons of their own sex.

Mrs. Greenough, who was reputed to be the most persuasive woman that was ever known in Washington, after expatiating on the injustice of the North, tried to persuade me not to take part in the war. Among her other arguments, she dwelt upon the sickliness of the Southern coasts in summer; but she showed her woman's weakness by prescribing to me remedies against the deadly miasma. I reported the temptations to which I was exposed to a patriotic Northern lady, who, if she lacked some of the peculiar accomplishments of Mrs. Greenough, was more beautiful, and equally eloquent on this particular question.

The latter encouraged me to hasten to the conflict, and told me that nothing but a bullet could kill me. Although I was never in the least danger of being diverted from my purpose, yet I well remember how often I was lured to the brink of the precipice, and I am convinced that under the slave regime few men could have boasted of their ability to withstand the blandishments of Southern ladies. It would have been idle to deny that in society they were the most attractive women in the world. The extinction of slavery has dimmed their brightness.

Rose's interest at this time extended also to Senator Joseph Lane of Oregon. Robert's work in the West had brought her into touch with this curious character and eventually she helped to maneuver him toward a Vice-Presidential nomination on John C. Breckinridge's split party ticket.

A decade earlier he had led a little band through the Rocky Mountains in winter, spending five "weary and desolate months amid the gorges, defiles and snows of the mountains." He reached his goal on a bitter March day and became Oregon's first territorial Governor. His feat was compared by enthusiasts to Napoleon crossing the Alps. President Pierce was his friend and patron. Buchanan considered him a man "who had proved himself a gallant soldier in war, and a true statesman in peace."

In Washington Joe was known to be reckless, hard-working and erratic, but endowed with much personal charm. He was an independent thinker, spoke well in public and was one of the vivid characters of the West. His record there was controversial. He was a storm center in Oregon. His enemies accused him of cheating the Indians, of enriching himself in war, of being drunk and disorderly in the capital.

He had an on-and-off devotion for his illiterate wife, Polly Pierre, who stayed in the backwoods while Joe paid court to Rose and received some crumbs scattered from her munificent table. Polly was the mother of ten, but Joe reproached her on one of his visits west: "If you had taken the trouble to learn to read and write they would be getting their letters at home, the way others do." But Polly knew how to be tender and forgiving, even though she could not read or write.

Lane was inordinately proud of his family line, which he traced back by intricate stages to the Crusades. Oddly enough, his genealogy was found in Rose's library when she was arrested. So were Joe's crudely penciled love notes. They were hurried scratches, suggesting less passion and more reluctance than H's. Rose was using the same technique with Lane—importuning morning or evening calls.

One, undated, read:

I have had the pleasure of receiving your note and would go up and see you this morning, but I am obliged to be with the Committee on Military Affairs at 10 this morning, and may not be able to leave the Senate till late this afternoon, and of evenings you are crowded with company. I hardly expected to find you at home last eve. It was only a quarter after ten when I left. I could not sit long alone naturaly (sic) impatient restless and almost reckless. How could I stay alone? I will see you before many days shall pass by.

On another occasion he would have been happy to have been with Rose but "My dear, you see how it is"—Senators Pugh, McLane and Robinson were with him. What could he do? Again he wrote reproachfully to Rose from the Senate chamber:

84

⟨[Abigail versus Rose

Your note has been read. I would be glad to see you, but you must bear in mind that the Senate meets at 11—committees meet at 9—and of an evening you are surrounded by admirers, and to meet them affords me no pleasure, and besides I have no desire to be in the way of any one— understand me I have no complaint to make, but don't like to meet those above referred to. I may however call and see you at 9 this eve (not certain however).

Was Henry Wilson the figure in the background whom Lane did not wish to meet?

Rose kept putting pressure on Lane for her own ends, and he wrote abjectly:

You can hardly imagine how feeble I am, and how unable to be on my feet. Still, if you insist, I will go. Believe me, my dear, I am not able to move about as a young man should. Please answer. Your Lane.

Lane was a tired fighter as war approached. Rose's political drive wearied him. She was urging the ailing and bibulous politician to pull himself together for the Democratic Convention in Charleston in the spring of 1860. Stephen A. Douglas loomed as the likely candidate for the Presidential nomination, but Robert Barnwell Rhett, Jefferson Davis and William L. Yancey were out to circumvent him.

Colonel Keyes described this particular convention as being made up of elements as "various and incongruous as the ingredients of the witches' caldron." It came to grief, and in the midst of the hectic proceedings, while surrounded by an angry, split-up group, Lane remembered that his first allegiance was to Rose.

On April 24 he dispatched two messages to her in quick succession. One read:

The convention has divided . . . conciliation hardly probable, should they hold out as now, a Southern man will be nominated, then we will have a triangular fight, result doubtful. My room is crowded. Will see you before long. Yours Lane.

The other made it clear that Douglas could not be nominated.

85

Both his name and Lane's had been stricken off the list. Lane recorded the final break-up when the representatives of the cotton states walked out rather than support Douglas, thus tearing the Democratic party asunder and paving the way for the emergence of Lincoln.

Out of this split came the separate convention at Baltimore, at which Breckinridge was nominated for the Presidency, with Joseph Lane his running mate, a ticket pleasing to Rose. The Northern Democrats nominated Douglas and the party moved forward against the Republicans, divided in strength.

The success of Breckinridge and Lane would have meant the continuation of Rose's influence at the White House for another four years, since she was a good friend of the Senator from Kentucky and had real power over Lane. But she had little hope of the split party carrying the country. Nor was Rose one of those who foresaw the election of Abraham Lincoln. Seward, for whom she had grudging admiration as a politician, seemed to her to be the inevitable choice.

With the defeat of the Breckinridge-Lane ticket Rose tried hard to get Lane the brigadier-generalship that he coveted. Pringle, her lawyer friend from San Francisco, was in the East and worked with her on this, but without avail. Lane sent her a final note saying the application had been decided "straight out" against him. There was no appeal and so he would "go out on his own hook."

After the election Lane faded completely from the Greenhow picture and returned to the West and Polly Pierre. He reached Oregon on the steamer that brought word of the fall of Fort Sumter. Like Rose, he considered disunion inevitable, although in the course of his stump speeches, he denied that he and Breckinridge were Secessionists. Oregon, which he considered his personal masterpiece, gave its support to Lincoln. But it was the one Northern state to give Breckinridge a lead over Douglas.

Lane lived until 1881. His life was tumultuous from beginning to end. He was eighty-one when he died, and he left no record of his

86

feeling for Mrs. Greenhow, other than the love notes found in her library. But their friendship did not pass unnoticed in Washington. From the days of Jackson, Rose had shown a fondness for frontier pioneers.

But that year she had other and deeper worries. Gertrude's health was failing noticeably. She coughed, grew thinner and ran a fever. She was in decline and no power available could arrest the course of her disease. In August Rose took her to Atlantic City, which was not yet known as a resort.

Pringle wrote to her from New York saying he had heard that she was in "some out of the way place called Atlantic City." He teased her for being so friendly with Mrs. James Gordon Bennett. "Do write to me to New York Hotel to say how you and Miss Gertrude are . . . and give me all the news to date, political, personal, scandalous . . . and have Atlantic City put in the next geography book."

On September 23, just before leaving for the West, he wrote significantly to Rose:

I applaud your heroic resolution in resisting the tempter but with some misgiving, as I begin to fear that a fortune via Point Lobos will be long in coming. I have kept our compact with equal sternness and have resisted much. Goodbye to you and my friend Miss Gertrude. . . . Goodbye once more—all kinds of good luck to you.

What was the compact between Rose and Pringle? What had Rose been offered? Did it have some bearing on the Limantour affair? The fact that Pringle also was involved would suggest that this may have been the case. Or did it have political implications?

While Douglas was still a Presidential possibility Pringle opposed him strongly in California, and usually Pringle and Rose worked hand in glove on political issues. On his return to California he wrote to her that he was amazed at the strong showing Douglas was making in the national field. But he assured Rose that if he should get the nomination he would never be elected. Rose was singularly and consistently antagonistic to Addie's husband. It is likely, too, that Douglas, familiar with Washington society and knowing the barroom gossip, had his own opinion of Addie's distinguished aunt. Her political maneuvers would be all too transparent to a man of his experience.

But Pringle soon wrote dismally of the Lincoln sweep and the Breckinridge débâcle:

What is to become of this forlorn country? I do believe that Lincoln has carried California. He is now 1300 votes ahead of Douglas and nearly 100,000 votes counted and Breckinridge nowhere. Of course the East has done likewise and elected him. What a breaking down in Washington! What nausea to you and to all our friends.

It was indeed nausea to Rose, but she scarcely needed her lawyer's prodding "to make friends with the Mammon of Unrighteousness— cultivate Seward and Adams, but oh! not Sumner." Pringle constantly sought Rose's advice or asked favors, and had boundless faith in her capacity to pull strings at the capital. That summer he had urged her to get Joseph Holt, who was then Postmaster-General, to see Cornelius Vanderbilt about starting a daily overland mail service. Pringle complained constantly of the slow communication when he wished to put something across in Washington through Rose.

With the change of government the Limantour interests again came up to plague them early in December. A fresh suit was filed and Calhoun Benham, newly appointed United States Attorney for the District of California, promised to press it. Pringle urged Rose to let him know at once if Buchanan should decide not to sign Judge Ogden Hoffman's bill adverse to the Limantour interests, adding significantly: "Make Buchanan help his friends a little before going out of office."

He advised Rose to tell Attorney General Black nothing except that zeal for his new office had made Benham stir up the matter, and that he had no knowledge of what had occurred earlier "between you, and the French Govt. and the Department." They would be less disposed to act, said Pringle, if they knew of its commencement. Again the strings led back to Rose's early encounters with Limantour in Mexico City, and the likelihood that his negotiations were tied up in some way with the French Legation in Washington.

At this point Pringle gave her specific legal guidance. He told her that she was to try to work through their old friend Black, but with discretion. She was to aim for a discharge of the Limantour bond, or instructions to the District Attorney that in case an appeal was not taken in the civil case, proceedings should not be pushed on the bond issue. "*Must leave it to your generalship,*" Pringle concluded, with complete faith in Rose's efficacy at the seat of government. "It is of immense importance not to try it this term."

On December 20, 1860, he wrote again to Rose, combining the political and personal outlook with candor and significance:

What is to be the end of all this? Can you give me any hope for the preservation of the Union? If not, if South Carolina and Georgia and Mississippi and Florida and Texas are to go out—shall the rest of the country go on and defeat our Point Lobos cases and collect our Limantour bonds?

What right has this Federal Government, now that South Carolina forms no part of it, to hold its court and take away the title to my property, I, a South Carolinian? And if I am to pay up $35,000 for José's delinquencies, why should I pay it up to the fragment of a Government, wherein my own state, that must be in sore need of friends, has no part?

Seriously, what is to become of the country? Bad enough for you in Washington, who used to be in the midst of a gay society where a Black Republican was a rare sight and now will be left alone to pay court to Mrs. Lincoln and Mrs. Hamlin. . . . I despair of any solution. I sit and await the result as I do the result of the Point Lobos case and the Limantour Bond. The latter we will fight as desperately as we can if we get no aid from you.

By this time Rose was thoroughly tired of Limantour and all his affairs. She was intent on the grim drama going on in Washington, and on her daughter's health. The balance of power was shifting.

The last social events of the Buchanan administration involved the Japanese emissaries and the visit of Baron Renfrew.

Gertrude, no longer well enough to go to parties, heard through Harriet Lane many inner details of his stay at the White House in October. Harriet dismissed the future King Edward VII summarily as a "charming little fellow, full of fun and jokes and wonderful in the admirable manner of conducting himself upon all occasions."

But she deplored the fact that "*dignity* is a sad obstacle in the way of *pleasure*" when he urged her to go to New York with him and open the ball to be given in his honor at the Academy of Music. When Harriet declined, he begged her to accompany him to Philadelphia and at least attend the opera with him. But Harriet could not break the bonds of convention, even for a prince. He passed out of her life, an engaging memory, and Queen Victoria wrote warmly to her uncle of the reception he had received.

Colonel Keyes found him a "polished young gentleman of good abilities" who rode, bowled and played tenpins with the young officers at West Point. He bowled with Keyes for a dollar a strike and won three silver coins which were later strung on his watch guard.

All this was of interest to Rose but she no longer responded so readily to conventional social stimulus. She was too deeply stirred by the political developments of the moment and was filled with foreboding. One night, toward the end of the year, she retired to her library and expressed her feelings in verse, an old custom of hers when profoundly moved:

> There is a feeling of the heart
> A dreary sense of coming evil
> That bids all mirthful thoughts depart
> And sends enjoyment to the d——l.
>
> A cloud that bodes the coming storm
> And partly wraps the heart in sorrow
> And bids our feelings bright and warm
> Prepare a shroud upon the morrow

([Abigail versus Rose

When all is sunshine to the soul
It turns its brightest hour to sadness
And grief with misty clouds will roll
Above the sunniest scenes of gladness.

This was to turn up among Rose's seized papers, along with the footnote:

No misfortune of my life but has been foreshadowed by a presentiment. Its warning at times disregarded, but ever recurring when the thunderbolt has fallen.

The thunderbolt was imminent and Rose's days were filled with brisk effort. Letters reached her from all parts of the country deploring the Lincoln victory, seeking her judgment on future events, and detailing Secessionist activity at large. Secretly convinced that nothing now could stop the drift to war, her maneuvers took definite shape. A parade of politicians and uniformed men almost jostled one another coming and going at 398 16th Street, the house later described by Provost-Marshal William E. Doster as the "favorite rendezvous of Secessionists" during the last days of Buchanan's administration and the start of Lincoln's.

Rose cultivated army and navy men, and kept close to all her friends in the inner political circle. Among the men in Lincoln's councils two if not more were her admirers. But the romantic element was only incidental to the deeper plans of this clever widow. With Lincoln's election, time was running out for the Southern beauties who had long adorned the capital and helped to influence legislation. Not the least of these was Mrs. Greenhow.

She prepared herself for open battle with all the weapons in which she was specially skilled. For her the fight was just beginning, but the groundwork was laid. There had been years of preparation. Now the hour had come.

CHAPTER VII

"Secesh Dame"

N○ ○NE knew better than Rose that her influence would decline with the retirement of the courtly James Buchanan, who had been her cavalier and friend. The man from Illinois whom she called the Mammon of Unrighteousness represented a complete turnover in government, and Mrs. Greenhow was one of the "Secesh dames" to Lincoln.

The closing days of 1860 and the early months of 1861 were charged with excitement. Rose attended many of the Secessionist gatherings as the Southern states began to break away. She bolstered the weak even while she shed tears over departing friends.

Rose stayed close to the vacillating Buchanan while he prepared his last message to Congress, delivered unhappily on a glum December day. He and Davis were at odds on the legality of secession. In modifying the first draft of his message, the President infuriated the Senator from Mississippi. His reasoning was puzzling to his powerful Southern claque and gave cold comfort to the extreme wing of the Republican party. Rose had often disagreed with him on political issues, but on this occasion she heard him with sympathy, although much that he said went against her grain. She acknowledged the truth of his statement that a sense of security no longer existed around the family altar and agreed that for "five and twenty years the agitation by the North against slavery has been incessant." A

92

poor prophet in a moment of crisis, Buchanan expressed the belief
that the slavery question "had reached and passed the culminating
point." He went on:

The fact is, that our Union rests upon public opinion, and can never
be cemented by the blood of its citizens shed in Civil War. If it cannot
live in the affections of the people it must one day perish. Congress
possesses many means of preserving it by conciliation; but the sword was
not placed in their hand to preserve it by force.

But may I be permitted to invoke my countrymen to pause and deliberate, before they determine to destroy this, the grandest temple which
has ever been dedicated to human freedom since the world began. . . .
It is not every wrong—nay, it is not every grievous wrong—which can jus-
tify a resort to such a fearful alternative. This ought to be the last desperate
remedy of a despairing people, after every other constitutional means of
conciliation has been exhausted.

A chill pervaded the White House on New Year's Day, 1861.
Callers were few and the President looked unhappy. The inner guard
rallied around him, but many Southerners from the seceding states
were missing, and the Northerners had declared a boycott. "It is not
lucky to talk of the Girondists' feasts on the eve of a revolution,"
murmured one of Rose's friends.

Knowing Buchanan well, she thought him a man to be pitied
rather than blamed. In the moment of crisis he stood confused and
uncertain. She viewed him as a lost leader, but she retained a fondness for him that she accorded few of the men who failed in any
degree to share her devotion to the Confederate cause.

She stayed close to her dying daughter on the day of Lincoln's
inauguration but she learned later that Buchanan looked careworn
and haggard as he rode beside his unique successor. Yet she knew
he was glad to be giving up office. Much as he had coveted the
Presidency he had found, in his own words, that "whoever embarks
on the stormy ocean of politics must calculate to make a shipwreck
of contentment and tranquillity." He had often told Rose that with

the blessing of God he could enjoy himself under his "own vine and his own fig tree." Better than most, he knew what Lincoln faced. Rose's final comment on her friend took into account the obvious fact of his age:

He was full of honours as of years, and unfit to grapple with the terrible events which crowded upon the closing period of his Administration. He would, I believe, have sacrificed his own life to have averted the doom of disruption, and sought, at least by a negative policy, to stay its progress. By a fatality of birth, he was thrown on the wrong side when the sectional division came. But he nevertheless carries with him to the retirement of Wheatland—where I have spent many happy days—the affectionate remembrances of many of his old friends.

Davis viewed him many years later as the man who had best fulfilled the European conception of chief of state since George Washington's time. He recalled him as "dignified, polished, reticent, and suave; fond of lady-gossip and an atmosphere of intrigue, a stickler for the ceremony of power."

Rose, handsome in heavy silk trappings, her graying hair smoothly arranged in a waterfall, wept openly in the gallery when Mississippi seceded early in January and Jefferson Davis bade farewell to the Senate. The sword now flashed openly between North and South.

Rose encountered Varina in the Senate cloakroom which was so crowded that they could scarcely push their way through the crinolines. Varina commented that the bright faces of the ladies resembled a "mosaic of flowers in the doorway." Davis felt ill that day. He had not slept all night, but had talked to his wife of war, famine and bloodshed to come. Both set out in the morning feeling "blood in the air."

Davis' thin face was taut as he rose to speak, at first in low tones, then in what Varina described as the melodious note of a silver trumpet. She saw him through wifely eyes: "Unshed tears were in his voice, and a plea for peace permeated every tone. Every graceful gesture seemed to invite to brotherly love."

94

Rose listened attentively as he paid tribute to Calhoun—"a great man who now reposes with his fathers"—and drew the distinction between nullification and secession:

Mr. Calhoun advocated the doctrine of nullification, which he proclaimed to be peaceful, to be within the limits of State power, not to disturb the Union, but only to be a means of bringing the agent before the tribunal of the states for their judgment. . . .

Secession belongs to a different class of remedies. It is to be justified upon the basis that the States are sovereign. There was a time when none denied it.

I am sure I feel no hostility to you, Senators from the North. I am sure there is not one of you, whatever sharp discussion there might have been between us, to whom I cannot now say, in the presence of God, I wish you well . . . it only remains for me to bid you a final adieu.

Davis bowed to his fellow Senators and turned away, headed for a leading role in the ultimate tragedy of civil war. There were shouts, sobs, applause, the rustle of men picking up portfolios, the flutter of handkerchiefs in the galleries, then dead silence.

Four years later, writing to Mrs. Clement C. Clay from Fortress Monroe, at a time when he thought he faced death, Davis said that he had not changed his opinion as to the sovereignty of the states or the right of a state to secede. "I only regret that we did not defer the evil day or prepare longer, better maintaining our independence," he added. "I still think we might and would have maintained it, with more wisdom in council and in the field, and with more virtue among our people."

Rose was deeply moved by Davis' speech. She considered him the standard-bearer for Calhoun, although they had disagreed on nullification. As she watched the exodus of her Southern friends she opened wide her own salon to the invaders, for she was now working with intensity and purpose. The Washington Rose knew quickly closed its shutters. Her old associates dismantled their homes, led by Mrs. Benjamin Ogle Tayloe whose mansion, the ghost-haunted Octagon, like Corcoran's, resembled a museum. Chandeliers, mirrors and bric-a-brac were swathed in protective wrappings. Paintings were covered up. Mahogany was encased in clumsy linen dusters. Coaches rumbled out of town laden with the trappings of a brilliant social era. Clothing, jewels, silver, blooded horses, soon were on their way south.

A fresh era was being ushered in. Rose had lived through many, but never one without Southern names. Now new hostesses took over. Belles with harsher accents but equally lovely forms and faces appeared on the scene. The cuisine was less exotic. There was less grace in the salon. Brisker manners became good form. A sterner, more austere spirit prevailed, but the social whirl went on with little interruption. The music scarcely missed a beat.

Rose had little patience with her few remaining Southern friends who still talked peace and harmony. She sadly watched Buchanan fumbling along with the Peace Congress, and believed that her old Kentuckian friends, Joseph Holt and John J. Crittenden, were swung over to peacemaking by being "bribed with the same bait—a seat on the Supreme Court bench."

According to Rose, Crittenden actually told her that he expected to receive the appointment, but when she tried to confirm this through Wilson, the Senator from Massachusetts said: "I rather think not, but we will hold out the bait to them until they can't retreat."

One of Crittenden's sons was to fight for the North, one for the South. Holt was to be the Judge Advocate General who would try the conspirators in Lincoln's assassination. He would also sit in judgment on the various individuals figuring in the espionage activities surrounding Rose.

"How are you in these times that try men's souls?" Pringle wrote to her when Stanton was appointed Attorney General. He confessed he was still worrying about the Limantour bond case, as well as the state of the country, and he believed Stanton might be harder to beat

96

on this issue than Black. Both men were familiar with the land grant squabbles and had strong opinions concerning them. Both men knew Rose well. Pringle told her bluntly that if things came to the worst, they must trust to the new administration. He believed that both Black and Stanton were deeply prejudiced against the "figurantes in our Point Lobos Drama."

"Perhaps after all, thanks to Seward and Wilson, you may do more with the incoming than the outgoing powers," he wrote, surprisingly. "We must be Bohemians in politics and get what we can out of anybody whom we can prevail against."

Evidently Rose met with some small measure of success, for on January 20, 1861, Pringle wrote: "Bravo! for [Judah P.] Benjamin's victory over Black and the postponement of the Point Lobos case. In these trying times it is a drop of comfort to have succeeded in one thing."

Rose evidently reached Lincoln, too, before he was inaugurated, because Pringle wrote to her on March 10, 1861, from San Francisco, mentioning casually that Lincoln or Seward "would be able to tell her always whether Wilson was in Washington." This was James H. Wilson, who had served on the Land Commission and had represented Limantour in the hearing at which Rose had testified in 1857. Never doubting her capacity to make her way, even with the new regime, Pringle wrote:

We have great hopes of getting a dismissal under the present Administration, with your assistance. (I am glad to see you have made friends of the Mammon of Unrighteousness.) General Wilson, our venerable ally in the case, is a personal friend of Lincoln's and a big Republican. He is in Washington now and has promised to do his best in the matter. Still he is not personally interested, and besides that is probably not as familiar with all the facts and equities as you have made yourself in your learned and eloquent advocacy of the case. I wish you would see him, if he is in Washington at any time, and cooperate with him. I think you and he together will be able to do anything. . . .

In this same letter Pringle confessed that he was not a disunionist *per se* and still believed reconstruction possible. His own state, South Carolina, would not go back, for a time at least, he believed, but the others might soon return "on a good compromise." However, he felt uneasy about war. If it broke out he planned to return to the South and help his "natural friends" in South Carolina.

Pringle enclosed two hundred and fifty dollars for Rose from her Plank Road stock, which was one of her sources of income at this time. She was having financial troubles, and so was he. The winter had been a bad one for him financially. He said he hoped things would soon be easier for both of them, although by this time he feared that Point Lobos was "a bubble burst."

Rose had investments in New York as well as in California, but he warned her against Eastern holdings with the country in such turmoil. Moore, a youth of means, was always ready to finance his mother-in-law. He remembered the many kindnesses she had shown him when he was courting Florence. All existing letters from Rose's children suggest that they held her in the deepest respect and affection.

She, in turn, was much attached to the vigorous, ambitious and generous youth who had married her eldest daughter, but who seemingly had little inkling of her Secessionist sympathies. At the moment he was doing well financially. His mining interests were running up to a fortune, and he wrote affectionately to Rose:

You must certainly feel by this time that I look upon you, dear Mama, as if you were indeed my mother and that everything I have is given as freely to you and yours as if they were my own, so do not let any false delicacy keep you from letting me know your condition and prospects for the future. . . . Should the mines turn out as I expect I will be well enough off to permit us to live comfortably, Union or no Union. This is of course for yourself alone and should not be repeated.

No sooner was Lincoln well established in the White House than Moore wrote saying he was for the Union "right or wrong," and he

98

hoped Uncle Abe would be firm and use force with the Secessionists where necessary. "I will do all in my power to support the Government as long as there is one state remaining to represent the Confederation," Moore added, with a conviction that was disquieting to his mother-in-law. She had not counted on this development in her immediate family.

Rose must have suffered as she read to Gertrude, her dying daughter, Moore's lighthearted request that she come out west, where he could supply her with two fine horses and eight to ten young officers to ride with her. Gertrude died in the middle of March and all else was forgotten by Rose for the time being. She vowed she would never again wear anything but black.

But in the midst of her sorrow Pringle arrived from the West and drew her out of her lethargy and grief with a sharp summons to action. On March 29, he wrote to her from Charleston, where he was visiting his sick mother: "We must be ready to go to work. Prepare all your Batteries. Get your arms in order." He refused to stay at her house, since "it would not suit his bachelor habits."

Then came a brisk shower of notes showing that Rose and Pringle had indeed gone into rapid action, well before the fall of Fort Sumter. "Do send me that memorandum you had yesterday to go to Senate with," Pringle wrote to Rose, as soon as he reached Washington. And again: "Do send me the map. I have just met Black . . . and had a long and rather satisfactory talk. Phelps has gone to send Toucey to him, so you had better not try him today. . . ."

What were Rose and Pringle hatching up at this point? Rose had been importuning Isaac Toucey for a morning call. He was Secretary of the Navy and was suspected of disposing of the naval forces in 1860 to the best advantage of the South.

In his next note Pringle urged Rose to look among her papers for the letter from the "Engineer Department to the War Department which gave a description of the Government Reserves." "We *will*

*take that letter and the map (which I believe you have), with us at
six o'clock,"* he added.

The war had not yet begun. Whatever their rendezvous it was
obvious that Rose and Pringle were tinkering in military and naval
affairs. Rose's closeness to Wilson was strongly implied in Pringle's
next communication, undated, but marked Tuesday:

> I would rather you send one to Wilson today. He is of the Committee
> and that is the first thing to be attended to. We will send one to Seward
> as soon as we fix the Committee.
>
> I left you yesterday from motives of delicacy, not liking to interfere
> with an agreeable tête-à-tête. I am glad it so happened that I missed your
> distinguished Black Rep—friend.
>
> I am going to try to see Black today (without Stanton) and I'll give
> Chesnut one of my documents. We must press on. If you will write a
> note to Wilson and enclose a Document I will make William carry it
> to him.

This would suggest that Rose was having intimate meetings with
Wilson in the week preceding the fall of Sumter and the declaration
of war. Was she scouting for information on military and naval
matters? In her memoirs she frankly admitted that her efforts with
the strong men of the North had started early and been quite
deliberate.

Seward might not have been so grateful to her for the social
countenance she gave him, Rose wrote, could he have fathomed her
real motives. At this point she outlined her plan of action in a most
revealing way, indicating the ruthless deliberation with which she
courted the men of Northern sympathies long before war broke out,
using both seduction and forethought in achieving her ends:

> I saw forehadowed what was to follow, and I desired to obtain a
> thorough insight into the plans and schemes of these who were destined
> to become the prominent actors in the fearful drama, in order that I might
> turn it to the advantage of my country when the hour for action arrived.
> To this end I employed every capacity with which God has endowed

100

me, and the result was far more successful than my hopes could have
flattered me to expect. I had verbatim reports of every caucus, of every
Cabinet Council, beginning with the hasty conclave convened on the
morning of Lincoln's unexpected arrival in masquerade at Willard's Hotel;
with piquant additions of private anecdotes of the distinguished pair, in
which Mrs. Lincoln was described as boxing the ears of a buxom chamber-
maid who inclined too amiably to receive the salute of her illustrious
spouse.

Although Rose did not hesitate to consort with the Northern element to serve her own ends, it irked her that Addie and Stephen
Douglas should have joined forces so enthusiastically with the Lincolns, and that her niece should have become Mrs. Lincoln's strongest
defender in face of the snubs and insults that were already the fate
of the President's wife.

Rose was scathing over Seward's conciliation speech. She called it
his "bitterest pill coated with sugar." She scoffed at his social maneuvers during this transition period, making the point that he was too
new in the role of "diplomatist to disregard so important a concomi-
tant of success." Charles Francis Adams, too, had made a conciliatory
speech at the end of January that had lost him the support of
Sumner. Rose saw little use in these gestures of amity.

As the weeks went on she observed with disdain the women who,
with few exceptions, "were not of a class to shed much lustre on
the Republican Court; for the refinement and grace which had once
constituted the charm of Washington life had long since departed,
and, like its former freedom, was now alas! a tradition only."

She considered the show of military strength in the capital at this
time a farce. It seemed to her a grave mistake to have called in
General Scott, who had been "resting uneasily on his laurels." The
presence of military companies in the capital, and of ammunition
vehicles "sounding through the streets as if a foreign enemy were at
the door," was an insult to the people of Maryland and Virginia—
a sure way of strengthening the Secession movement in these states.

Buchanan had deplored this rattling of the sword while former President Tyler struggled along with the Peace Congress, but Scott broke out enthusiastically on Washington's birthday with a big parade.

Rose knew the General well, thanks to old associations and to her more recent friendship with Colonel Keyes. She was aware that he believed war to be the natural state of man; that he was widely read and easily bored; that he liked travel, blooded horses and chess; that he chewed tobacco and disliked strong liquors; that he was gluttonous, impatient, vain, jealous and ironical; that he might be a hero to the public but not to his military secretary.

Scott had always been gallant to Rose, as he was to all of her sex. Like Buchanan, he liked women's conversation, although he was never swayed by it. Since he was not a man whom Rose had been able to influence, he did not count greatly in her calculations. Colonel Keyes, on the other hand, may well have been one of her deliberately chosen victims, although she appears to have been fond of him too. She deplored his rush to join the Army of the Potomac—a good soldier lost—and she considered General Scott a traitor to Virginia. She had nothing but contempt for Seward's efforts "with Jesuitical skill, to prop up that mighty ruin in their way."

In a letter written to one of her political friends during this period of breathless waiting, Rose summed up her view of the current scene in her usual impassioned style:

"Illinois first" may now be recorded of these United States. The old Confederation is rapidly crumbling to pieces. . . . Section division is widening, sectional hate growing stronger. The feeling, the language of the dominant, the aggressive party from the sterile coast of Oregon to the granite hills of New Hampshire is insulting and hard to bear. Coercion at the point of the bayonet or the cannon's mouth—or unconditional surrender are the mild alternatives offered us. . . .

Surrender forsooth this heritage of which the Gods might be proud, to the Puritans, the wooden nutmeg maker, the Yankee pedlers of New England. Every feeling of honor, every feeling of humanity cries no. Then

102

do you wonder that the South with the alternative of national degradation before her should choose the least of the two evils—and that the cry to arms should resound from the mouth of the Chesapeake to the Gulf of Mexico. That we should "hold up our national flag and guard it as sacredly as the masters of old fighting for the Sepulchre of Christ. . . ."

Rose regularly sounded out politicians on their views and she tackled Senator Edward D. Baker of Oregon in advance on the subject of Fort Sumter. She had known him as an able lawyer in California before he moved to Oregon in 1856. Now he was a close adviser of Lincoln's, and she quoted him as saying: "It is true, a great many lives may be lost, and we may not succeed in reinforcing Fort Sumter. But the President was elected by a Northern majority, and they are now becoming dissatisfied; and the President owes it to them to strike some blow by which he will make a unified Northern party."

Among the lives lost was Baker's own, six months later. He commanded the first regiment of California Volunteers and died at Ball's Bluff.

The actual outbreak of war in April was no surprise to Rose. For her the die was cast when South Carolina seceded in December, 1860, and Mrs. Roger A. Pryor conveyed the news to Buchanan as they all attended the wedding of Mary Parker and Congressman J. E. Bouligny. Church bells rang then in Charleston, and cannon roared. Palmetto flags fluttered from windows. All business was suspended. A group of youths went to Calhoun's tomb and formed a circle around it, vowing to devote "their lives, their fortunes and their sacred honor" to the cause of independence.

Now the reality had come to pass and Rose's thoughts must have turned back to Calhoun as all Washington blazed with the first excitement of the nation at arms, then sank into a hush of apprehension. Stanton wrote to Buchanan on April 12: "We have the war upon us." In the capital, he added, many believed that the effort to reinforce Fort Sumter would be a failure; that in less than twenty-four hours Captain Robert Anderson would have surrendered; that

103

in less than thirty days Jefferson Davis would be in possession of Washington.

Within two weeks after the outbreak of war Rose had committed herself irrevocably and officially to the Confederate cause, and had become a central figure in the espionage system established by Colonel Thomas Jordan before he doffed the uniform of the North to serve as General Beauregard's adjutant-general.

Jordan was a bluff and handsome soldier in his forties with calm, cold eyes, a wide forehead and dark beard. He was a native of Virginia and had roomed at the United States Military Academy with William T. Sherman. He was to play a significant role as Beauregard's right-hand man. At the close of the war he was also to write an article for *Harper's New Monthly Magazine* that aroused much discussion, since it was sharply critical of Jefferson Davis, calling him censorious, imperious and narrow.

When Jordan called on Rose he made wary approaches at first, but he found her a willing accomplice. He gave her a simple cipher that he had devised himself and told her to address her communications to Thomas J. Rayford, the alias he had selected for himself. What more likely than that Jefferson Davis had personally nominated Rose as the person best equipped to extract secrets from the Black Republicans? No woman in Washington knew more statesmen, diplomats, officers and businessmen, both of the North and South. Moreover, her family was firmly entrenched in official circles. And she was known to be fiercely committed to the Confederate cause.

Rose went to work at once, "employing every capacity with which God had endowed her." It was really only an extension of what she had been doing for years, in subtler, less closely applied ways. She was merely shifting her political maneuvers from amateur to professional status. She had always consorted with the diplomats more consistently than any other woman in the capital. Her stately manners, linguistic skill and old associations in the foreign field through Robert, had endeared her to a succession of foreign envoys who had

104

her spotted as a valuable ally. Mrs. Greenhow was a sophisticate who was always worth her salt to them.

With the most casual skill she now charmed young lieutenants, government clerks, secretaries and aides, as well as their masters. They talked freely to the brilliant Mrs. Greenhow as they toured defenses with her, responding to her interest in Union affairs, and divulging details that she quickly absorbed and put to specific use.

Anything for the Confederacy, Rose had always said. In the North her course spelled cold treason. In the South it was the red-hot fire of patriotism. She was never in any doubt that she had chosen the right, the inevitable, the only course, as the War between the States became a reality.

In the next few months she pulled strings in all directions, so that Provost-Marshal Doster later wrote of her that although she had lost much of her beauty and vivacity, and the society which she had charmed had passed away, still her "masterly skill at managing affairs and turning them to her own account, or to that of her friends, her experience in parlor diplomacy, and her knowledge of all the forces which reigned at the Capitol, made her still very formidable for good or evil." Colonel Doster believed that she loved notoriety and wished to become a Southern martyr—"to gain that applause for heroism which was now denied her beauty."

No sooner had Rose moved from unofficial to official status as a Southern agent than she found herself awkwardly placed where her son-in-law was concerned. It was bad enough to have the Cutts family rallying around Abraham Lincoln, and her nephew, James Madison Cutts, Jr., Addie's brother, joining the First Rhode Island Volunteers, but now Moore asked her flatly to use influence on his behalf for a colonelcy with a volunteer Ohio regiment. He thought she had merely to reach up and pull the golden apples off the tree, as in the time of Buchanan.

This must have been a poser for Rose. But when Florence added her pleadings she decided to write to Salmon Portland Chase, Secre-

105

tary of the Treasury, and an implacable antislavery man. As former
Governor of Ohio, and something of a god in his own region, she
asked him to grant her this favor. However, Rose did not overlook
the opportunity to get in a few licks for the South. She told him just
what she thought of the conflict.

Two stout warriors had met in correspondence. The situation was
charged with irony. But the ever-courteous Chase snapped right back
on May 30, 1861:

MY DEAR MADAM:

Your letter, asking for the promotion of Capt. Moore, is just received.
It will be a gratification to me to promote his wishes, if in my power. I
am sure he is deserving of the promotion he desires. I regret, however,
to observe that you regard the war, which the Government is compelled
to wage against those who have conspired for its destruction and that of
the Union, as a "war against our kindred and friends." It seems to me
rather a war for the rescue of kindred and friends and of our Country—
that sacred name which includes all the Charities—from ruthless
despotism.

> With very great respect,
> Yours truly
> (Signed) S. P. CHASE.

Moore went further. He had come out strongly and unmistakably
for the Union and was just as politically conscious as his mother-in-
law. Without a qualm he asked Rose to get President Lincoln's
assurance that he would not lose his commission in the regular army
by switching to the Ohio volunteers. Did Rose tackle Lincoln on this?
It is altogether possible that she did. In any event, Moore did not get
his heart's desire. Chase wrote another courteous note to Rose, saying
that all officers' commissions had already been handed out.

Moore was bitterly disappointed. Florence wrote to her mother
with an attempt at diplomacy:

Poor Moore is almost beside himself at having to remain here inactive
whilst so many are earning laurels. But I thank God for it. Of course he

106

will fight for the Union. And although of course, dear Mamma, all my warmest feelings are enlisted for the Southerners rather than the Yankees, still I do think the Union should be before all small state feeling, and do think Secessionists a little like traitors. Still I most earnestly pray Moore may not be engaged in this terrible Civil War.

By this time another quarry had come into view. William Howard Russell had arrived to represent *The Times* of London and, incidentally, to influence greatly the British view of the war. Mrs. Jefferson Davis was to label him the "storm bird of battles." To Mrs. Chesnut he was always the "licensed slanderer." Rose's close ties with the British Legation brought him quickly within her ken and he was indeed to prove an asset to the South.

Rose had been playing the dangerous game of espionage for less than two months when rumors of her activities must have reached Florence at Moore's post in Utah. He had been assigned to Fort Churchill when trouble broke out in that territory.

Florence wrote:

I am so much worried about the last news from Washington. They say some ladies have been taken up as spies. I so dread to hear of some of my friends. Dear Mamma, do keep as clear of all Secessionists as you possibly can. I so much fear everything for you all alone there.

Florence warned her mother not to say anything on behalf of the South when she wrote to Moore, since "he believes that all Southerners should be hanged." By the same mail Moore warned Rose not to do anything that might compromise her "even should her inclinations be for the South." At the same time the practical Moore added: "Keep a bright lookout to my interests."

He was still eager to get in the midst of the fighting, and chafed over his inactive role in Utah. He kept writing to Rose that he was better suited for line than staff duty in time of war, since "all his instincts were for active service." Failing the Union Army, could she get him moved back to San Francisco?

107

Rose must have read with mixed feelings a letter in which he expressed regret that Lincoln had not called up five hundred thousand soldiers right at the start to crush out the rebellion, which "might now go on for several years." Florence, too, was bored with the dull life in Utah after the gay days of the Presidio and the excitement of her earlier years in the capital as Mrs. Greenhow's oldest daughter. She was rapturously happy when a friend sent her a box of violets by express. "They are the first flowers I have seen, as none grow in this barren desert," she wrote to her mother. "They took me back to Washington at once."

Florence had been threatened with a miscarriage from the shock of Gertrude's death, but was now expecting a baby. By this time both she and Moore were beginning to understand that Rose's power in Washington had waned. On July 20 she wrote that she was sending a youth with an introduction, and she hoped that Rose could help him, but she had told his mother that "you have now no political influence whatever." This was indeed a change in the life of the Greenhow girls, who had grown up to believe that anything their mother wished for could be had.

Rose had watched every move made in the South from the February day on which Jefferson Davis was elected President of the Confederate States. He was making rose cuttings in his garden at Brierfield when word reached him of his new role. She noted that in his inaugural speech he said that a well-instructed and disciplined army was needed in the South, and a navy for the protection of "our harbors and commerce on the high seas." With absolute realism he wrote to Varina at that time: "We are without machinery, without means, and threatened by a powerful opposition; but I do not despond, and will not shrink from the task imposed on me."

Varina closed their Washington home and traveled South to Montgomery by way of New Orleans, where great bouquets of violets were thrust into her arms and she was greeted along the way like a visiting celebrity. She found the capital swarming with statesmen, lawyers, congressmen, planters, merchants and all manner of men seeking government commissions. Few battled for rank, in Varina's opinion. They were there for service. Among them were such old friends of Rose's as James M. Mason, William L. Yancey, Pierce Butler, William C. Rives and James Chesnut.

Then, when war came, "the fury of the North was met by a cyclone of patriot enthusiasm that swept up from the South," in the words of Varina Howell. The government was moved from Montgomery to Richmond. Agents were sent abroad to buy small arms, guns and ships. Niter beds were established. Old arms were altered. Railway and transportation companies offered the free use of their lines and resources for the conveyance of troops.

Men flocked to arms from all quarters. The South soon blazed with uniforms, gold fringe, glinting arms, the strains of "Dixie," the last waltz, the lovelight in the eyes of countless girls, and the heaped-up fires of patriotism. The suffering was yet to come. Rose knew it, if Mrs. Lee was slow to see it. The war brought these two women together again and they kept up an underground correspondence for months. They had drifted apart after Robert's death but now were drawn into intimacy again through their mutual interest in the South.

When Jordan first called on Rose and showed her in specific terms what she could do for the Confederacy, Rose was tentatively considering joining Mrs. Lee in Winchester. She was still grieving over Gertrude's death, and the stand taken by Florence and Moore distracted her further. Nearly all of her friends had left the capital by April. But Florence wrote urgently to her mother by Pony Express warning her not to go to Winchester, since Virginia and Maryland would undoubtedly be the focus of warfare.

It had taken Mrs. Lee a long time to accept the fact that war was inevitable. She felt sure up to the last moment that the North "would concede." But her neighbor, James M. Mason, who was later to serve as Confederate Commissioner to Britain, and have much to do with Rose, held no such hope. He was deeply depressed, and all the horrors of disunion appeared inevitable to him from the beginning.

Mrs. Lee urged Rose to bring her daughters and join her at any time. She did not then know that Rose was committed to the dangerous business of espionage. A spirited character herself, Mary Lee was to defy the Federal soldiers at every point, smuggle letters through when she could, hide food and medical supplies, and refuse to leave her home.

When there was panic in Winchester early in the war, and talk of sending away the women and children, she and a "few other strong-minded women who were not easily frightened, turned the current and everyone is now bright and cheerful," she wrote to Rose.

In another letter smuggled north by her Negro manservant, Henry Nicholson, she commented on the change that had come over the Southern men. They were like the knights of old going forth to victory or to death. They were electrified with a spirit she thought "had died with the Cavaliers of old." Young men raised in the most luxurious style now gloried in the hardships of military life and chafed only under inaction.

Mrs. Lee urged Rose to tell "that traitor General Scott" that there were eighty thousand armed men in Virginia, besides companies of volunteers not yet called into service. She grieved over Maryland's laggardly stand, but said she was infinitely proud of Virginia. In this same letter, written on May 20, Mrs. Lee observed: "Do write to me as often as you can; are you keeping up the correspondence with a dignitary to which you alluded in one of your letters?"

Was this Henry Wilson again?

Rose, too, was deeply concerned over the plight of her native state. Wilson angered her with his observation that his party would enforce its principles at the point of the bayonet, and would put the iron heel on Maryland, crushing out its boundary lines. He forfeited the

110

last shred of her good-will by saying the country had been ruled long enough by the Southern aristocrats.

They had an angry interchange in which Rose quoted Wilson as saying that few of the Union men would return to the North. They would have homesteads given them in the conquered country. Congress would apportion the land into quarter sections, and they would settle there and marry Southern girls.

"Never, sir," Rose snapped back. "But our Negroes will go north and marry yours, as far more fitting helpmates."

Rose worked hard over her old friend, Reverdy Johnson of Maryland. He was calling on her in June, when she was moving heaven and earth to stir up resistance in her native state, and he was doing what he could to keep it in the Union. On June 15 she wrote to S. T. Wallis, of Baltimore, who was arrested four months later for insurrectionary operations: "Those who run may read the destiny reserved for Maryland. To make her an integral part of the North—and if her citizens resist to raze her cities and blot out her boundary lines." She referred to Maryland as that "once proud little state which is now only a military department." She bemoaned the fact that she was only a "poor woman at this crisis—but heart and soul I am with this cause and with all my poor ability will I serve it."

As the country moved deeper into war, Rose's correspondence, which was to be used later against her, shed considerable light on her associations, and also gave a cross-section of opinion. Garrick Mallory, Jr., wrote bluntly that although a conservative Democrat and friend of the South through maternal blood and interest, he regarded the Secession movement as without excuse or good motive, deserving only the name of treason with its penalties.

Edmond Goold, an old friend, wrote from New Orleans that the people there cared little for Lincoln or his Cabinet, or how the Northern states were governed. They were engaged in attending to their own business. David S. Turner wrote from San Francisco on

111

May 20 that Gertrude had been "spared much suffering from cold and heartless humanity by dying when she did." He added:

I will not endeavor to combat your opinions for I know you have been educated to them. But oh! how sadly I feel the mistakes of the South—I do not deny the North has also made mistakes—and may continue to make them—but the North, now fully aroused—and conscious of her power—will never desist until her object is accomplished.

Turner recalled that on one of her trips west Rose had influenced him in the selection of his political party when the Whigs were breaking up. Another vote for Buchanan! Now he believed that if "every shred of the Union disappeared California would go with it."

Although Rose's power faded with the rise of Lincoln, she was still besought for political favors. Once a potent figure in the division of patronage, a system warmly fostered by Buchanan, she was flooded with letters long after the outbreak of war. An appointment to the Supreme Court bench, a cadetship at West Point, an architect's commission to work on the new Post Office Building in New York, an introduction to the American Minister in England "since she was so well acquainted with Mr. Seward," the post of melter and refiner in the California Mint, were only a few of the favors sought through Mrs. Greenhow.

CHAPTER VIII

Beauregard Forewarned

R<small>OSE</small> always considered Manassas something of a personal triumph. Jefferson Davis and General Beauregard both gave her credit for the valuable service she rendered with three messages that forewarned them in their preparations for the first great battle of the war. It was undoubtedly a substantial coup in the history of wartime espionage and she never matched it again. To the South the battle was the victory of Manassas. To the North it was the rout of Bull Run.

In the months that followed she subtly spread the impression that Henry Wilson was the source of her advance information. But seized Confederate papers point more convincingly to young John F. Callan, a clerk of the Senate Military Committee whom no one had suspected of complicity. She was gratified when she heard that Wilson was questioned by his political peers after the battle was fought and lost by the North.

Before General Irvin McDowell's men moved away from Washington on July 16, 1861, with three days' supplies in their haversacks, Rose had seen their marching orders and had given specific warning. A few days earlier she had sent a young and beautiful courier into Virginia with the more general message that the advance was planned for the middle of the month.

Betty Duvall, the Maryland girl who bore the first message, later

113

dropped from sight, but her one known act of aid was significant. She rode out of Washington by way of the Chain Bridge, a country girl in calico bouncing along in a farm produce cart. Rose may well have chosen her disguise. She was an experienced hand at helping her daughters and Addie Cutts dress for masquerades. Once in Virginia, Betty called on friends, picked up a horse and riding attire, and galloped off for Fairfax County Courthouse, a young lady of fashion with a heavy crop of hair.

General Milledge L. Bonham, the South Carolinian Congressman fresh to army life who held the picket outpost with an observation unit of three thousand soldiers, was surprised to see so handsome a girl approaching him with quiet purpose and an air of caution. He commented later on her looks. She was "a brunette, with sparkling black eyes, perfect features, glossy black hair . . . a fine person of medium height . . . with the glow of patriotic devotion burning in her face."

Betty told him that she had a message for General Beauregard, who was then holding twenty thousand men at Manassas Junction, a vital railroad point approximately thirty miles from Washington. She wished to make sure that it would get right through to him. Later recalling this incident General Bonham wrote: "Upon my announcing that I would have it faithfully forwarded at once, she took out her tucking comb and let fall the longest and most beautiful roll of hair I have ever seen. She took then from the back of her head, where it had been safely tied, a small package, not larger than a silver dollar, sewed up in silk."

Rose had ciphered the message. Rose had sewn it in silk. Rose had obtained the information. The message was rushed to Beauregard, who sent Colonel J. S. Preston with it to Jefferson Davis at Richmond, along with a request for reinforcements. It gave Beauregard a chance to deploy his forces to the best advantage behind the banks of Bull Run Creek, and to plant his batteries strategically for defense. The plan was to overwhelm the Confederate forces in a surprise

114

Mrs. Rose O'Neal Greenhow in her thirties

Robert Greenhow, Jr., Richmond boy who became
Rose O'Neal's husband (Painting by St. Memin,
owned by Hall Park McCullough, courtesy Frick Art
Reference Library)

Senator Joseph Lane, first Governor of
Oregon (Courtesy Library of Congress)

Cave Johnson, of Tennessee, Postmas-
ter General in President Polk's Cabinet
(Courtesy Library of Congress)

Dolly Madison at 72 (Crayon by East-
man Johnson, given to Daniel Webster
by Mrs. Madison. Courtesy The Essex
Institute, Salem, Mass.)

Mrs. Charles Francis Adams (Painting
W. M. Hunt from the original Charles
Adams collection)

liam H. Seward, Secretary of State in
President Lincoln's Cabinet

President James Buchanan

Mrs. Stephen A. Douglas, niece and namesake of Mrs. Greenhow (From Brady Collection. Courtesy L. C. Handy Studios)

Mary Boykin Chesnut

Peggy Eaton (Portrait by Henry Inman. Courtesy Ladies' Hermitage Association, Nashville, Tennessee)

Jessie Benton Frémont (Portrait T. Buchanan Read in the Sou west Museum, Los Angeles)

Senator Henry Wilson of Massachusetts, antislavery politician (Courtesy Library of Congress)

John C. Calhoun (From the portrait by G. P. A. Healy. Courtesy of the Virginia Museum of Fine Arts)

These letters, signed "H," were found in Mrs. Greenhow's house. They are now in the National Archives with the notation: "Love letters (supposed to be) from Henry Wilson, U. S. Senator from Massachusetts."

Allan Pinkerton, who arrested Mrs. Greenhow as a spy on August 23, 1861 (From *The Photographic History of the Civil War*)

Old Capitol Prison (From *The Photographic History of the Civil War*)

Mrs. Greenhow and her eight-year-old daughter Rose in the Old Capitol Prison (Courtesy Library of Congress)

Cipher used by Rose Greenhow to communicate with Colonel Thomas Jordan (Courtesy the National Archives)

Jefferson Davis, President of the
Confederate States

General Pierre G. T. Beauregard

Colonel Thomas Jordan,
General Beauregard's Ad-
jutant General (From *The
Photographic History of
the Civil War*)

Matthew Fontaine Maury, a commander in the Confederate Navy
(New York Public Library)

The second Earl of Granville (Painting by Emery Walker)

Lord Lyons, British Minister in Washington during the Civil War

ames M. Mason, Confederate Commissioner to Great Britain

Colonel Erasmus D. Keyes, General
Winfield Scott's military secretary
(From The Photographic History of
the Civil War)

Rose O'Neal Greenhow shortly before her death

Mrs. Greenhow's grave in Oakdale Cemetery, Wilmington, N.C. (Photograph by John Kelly)

A page from Mrs. Greenhow's address book (Courtesy New Hanover Museum, photograph by Harold Ludwig) attack with superior numbers, drive through their lines and proceed to Richmond.

Colonel Jordan sent George Donellan, a Confederate soldier who had worked in the Department of the Interior, back to Rose for further information. The young man introduced himself by showing her the phrase *"Trust Bearer"* in the Jordan cipher.

Donellan returned on July 16 with the vital message that McDowell with 55,000 troops "would positively commence that day to advance from Arlington Heights and Alexandria on to Manassas, via Fairfax Court House and Centerville." He had hidden this message in the heel of one of his boots and had journeyed down the Maryland shore of the Potomac by horse and buggy until he reached Indian Head. There he had ferried across to Dumfries, on the Virginia side, where cavalry couriers met him and galloped off to Jordan with the message.

Donellan waited for a reply for Rose. When it came it was signed by Colonel Jordan:

Yours was received at 8 o'clock at night. Let them come. We are ready for them. We rely upon you for precise information. Be particular as to description and destination of force, quantity of artillery, etc.

In the morning General Beauregard telegraphed to Davis: "Send forward any reinforcements at the earliest possible instant and by every possible means." The Confederate President was jolted into fast action. Bonham had been alerted but by this time the Federal troops were pushing back his picket line, and Fairfax Courthouse was abandoned in a flurry of haste, and without resistance.

Davis ordered General Joseph E. Johnston, whose twelve thousand men were guarding the gateway to the Shenandoah Valley, and General T. H. Holmes, who had a small force at Aquia Creek Landing, to move in to the support of General Beauregard.

On the seventeenth Rose had a third message ready for Donellan. She had learned of the plan to cut the Manassas Gap Railroad leading into the valley, in order to prevent Johnston from joining forces

115

with Beauregard. Forewarned on all counts, the Confederate command was ready as McDowell's forces closed in. Some of General Johnston's men arrived on the nineteenth and next day he appeared personally with another detachment.

Bull Run Creek was the line of defense. The surrounding terrain was heavily timbered and intricate for maneuvers. Although Johnston was Beauregard's superior in command he deferred to the Creole General's judgment because of his greater familiarity with the wooded region and the disposition of the troops. There was to be much debate in the months that followed over whose victory it was, but for the time being there was solidarity of purpose, and there never was any doubt that the troops themselves were the victors.

After preliminary gains by the Federal forces, the main battle was fought on the twenty-first. McDowell had expected to cope with a force of 20,000. Instead he found 32,000 troops well deployed, and the last detachment of Johnston's men cutting in on his flank turned the battle into a rout. By the time Jefferson Davis arrived from Richmond, Manassas had been won.

Johnston's support had saved the day, and Rose had hastened its coming. General Beauregard later reported that from sources "treasonable to the Union, and in other ways, he was almost as well informed of the strength of the hostile army in my front as its commander." He wrote of the "reliable and regular information which he had from Washington through a perfect spy system organized by Colonel Jordan."

Rose followed the battle at long distance and with considerable anguish of spirit. Immediately after delivering her last message she left for New York to put Leila on a ship for the first stage of her journey west to join the Moores in Utah. Rose had long considered this move, and now that she had embarked on delicate espionage operations the moment had come. Florence had promised to have Leila educated with the greatest care, and to see that she was schooled in all the fashionable accomplishments. In addition, Leila would be

116

company for her older sister, and Washington had become an uncomfortable spot for Secessionist families.

Friends were chaperoning Leila on her trip west, and Rose was obliged to see her off. Otherwise she would not have left the capital at this crucial moment. She had many friends in New York and it was her usual custom to stay at the New York Hotel or the Astor House, receive guests in the daytime or shop, and dine at night in fashionable homes or go to the theater. But she avoided her customary haunts on this occasion and was incredulous when the early word came through that the North was winning. She refused to accept it as final, even though there was rejoicing in the streets. "My heart told me that the triumph was premature," she wrote. And she was right. On Sunday the twenty-first the Battle of Manassas was fought. To Rose it was as "memorable in history as that of Culloden or Waterloo."

Having bade good-by to Leila, she traveled back to Washington with considerable elation. She noted "the craven fear of the Yankees manifested everywhere." At Philadelphia most of the women left the train, and she was urged to join them, since the "rebels of Baltimore would rise, in consequence of the rout of the Federal Army."

Among those who tried to persuade Rose to ensure her own safety in this way was Lieutenant Henry A. Wise, who was married to Charlotte, daughter of Edward Everett. She knew him well. He sprang from a Delaware family and had been reared in Virginia. His wife and mother were Northerners. He wrote under the name of Harry Gringo. Governor Wise, of Virginia, was his cousin.

"I have no fears," Rose told Henry. "These rebels are of my faith. Besides, I fear, even now, I shall not be in time to welcome our President, Mr. Davis, and the glorious Beauregard."

Obviously Rose could not be silent, even though her situation was precarious. She found Washington in chaos. Black Monday had dawned with its toll of dead and wounded, its demoralized soldiers, its wrecked equipment, its shaken people, moving through thick clouds of alarm. She found the "very carriage way blocked by its panic-

117

stricken defenders who started at the clank of their own muskets."

A message awaited her at her home. She read it with pride. It was to be one of her most prized possessions. Jordan had written:

Our President and our General direct me to thank you. We rely upon you for further information. The Confederacy owes you a debt.

The Greenhow house was filled with Southern friends, welcoming Rose back with full details of the "glorious victory." They leaned against her rosewood piano, sat on her striped damask chairs, and even lounged on the floor. Her own first impulse was to throw herself on her knees and offer up "tearful thanks to the Father of Mercy for his signal protection in our hour of peril."

Rose heard from her friends that the heat, the dust, the confusion and the panic of the battlefield were indescribable; that the roads were strewn with discarded accouterments of all kinds; that the flower of the Union Army had panicked, while their officers bolted. The Senators and officials who had ridden out with refreshments to watch the battle, as if it were a medieval tournament, had been caught in the mêlée. Their carriages had added to the confusion.

After breakfast and a hurried change from her travel attire, Rose characteristically went up to the Capitol to appraise the havoc she had helped to create among her friends on the Hill. The plumes of woe drooped heavily at the seat of government. There she quickly spotted the "crestfallen leaders who but a few days before, had vowed death and damnation to our race."

She went at once and without any qualms to Henry Wilson and Senator Zachariah Chandler, both of whom had ridden out to watch the battle. She listened skeptically while they told her what they had done to bolster up the fleeing troops. Rose decided that they were all trying to snatch a stray laurel from an utter débâcle. She bluntly told them that if they had not "good blood" they certainly had "good bottom," for they had run remarkably well. She noted

118

that handsome Colonel Ambrose E. Burnside, who had needed two orderlies to carry the flowers showered on him by the women of the North as he left, returned without his hat or shoes.

She deliberately sought out Seward. Little suspecting the part she had played in the defeat, he assured her blandly that she could tell her friends there was nothing to worry about—all would be over in sixty days. Was Seward being sarcastic with Rose? Or did he mean it? Since it was morning and not the convivial after-dinner hour, she took him at his word and gibed: "Well, sir, you have enjoyed the first fruits of the 'irrepressible conflict.' "

Rose had taunted Seward so often with the much discussed phrase, that on this occasion he turned on her with the exasperated admission that if only "Heaven would forgive him for stringing together these two high-sounding words" he would never repeat the offense. Certainly Rose would neither forget nor forgive.

Seward had used the phrase in a speech on the slavery issue delivered in Rochester in 1858, saying: "It is an irrepressible conflict between opposing and enduring forces, and it means that the United States must and will, sooner or later, become either entirely a slave-holding nation, or entirely a free-labor nation."

Rose would soon have another of Seward's pat phrases with which to taunt him. As she and her fellow agents were being rounded up in quick succession he told Lord Lyons: "My Lord, I can touch a bell on my right hand and order the arrest of a citizen of Ohio. I can touch a bell again and order the imprisonment of a citizen in New York. And no power on earth except that of the President can release them. Can the Queen of England do so much?"

Rose was to harp on the tinkling bell as she did on the irrepressible conflict. Seward always got under her skin, for she could not help but admire his political capacity in some respects. In the meantime she was a dedicated woman, exhilarated by her success, and determined to push on to further participation. She was urged by

119

friends to leave the city, as many other women, particularly those with Southern sympathies, were doing in the days after Bull Run. She was offered an escort south, but resolved to remain, whatever the peril, conscious of the "great service" she could render her country, her position giving her "remarkable facilities for obtaining information."

This was not overstating the case. Old friends had become Cabinet officers. Quondam dinner guests now ranked high in army and navy circles. Jurists and diplomats were at her beck and call. Some of Rose's invitations had the quality of summonses. The newspapermen and bankers knew her well. And she did not hesitate to use the lower echelons when the top figures showed signs of drawing away. She invariably knew to whom to turn for information.

At this time her brother-in-law, James Madison Cutts, was in the Treasury and worked with Chase. His brother, Richard D. Cutts, was with the U.S. Coast Survey. Her nephew, James Madison Cutts, Jr., had joined the First Rhode Island Volunteers. He was a lawyer by profession and the brother of Addie, who was close to the Lincolns, Seward and Chase. All of the Cutts family now grew wary of Rose; yet the ties of blood were strong and they continued to see her.

The house that had been known as a gracious home was suddenly starred as a place of intrigue; of visitors coming and going at all hours of the day and night; of generals, Senators and diplomats calling on Mrs. Greenhow; of clerks and young lieutenants ringing her doorbell. The flow was so constant that it is hard to believe much secrecy could have been preserved at any point.

Although figures of name and reputation loomed in the background, Jordan kept sending Rose new agents and couriers—clerks and junior officers, and good-looking women of uncertain status. A number of scheming damsels were at large at this time in the capital, haphazardly picking up information and playing the dangerous game of seduction in exchange for wartime secrets. Their parlors were softly lighted with fringed hanging lamps or flickering candles. Wood fires

120

blazed. Port and Madeira were served, with cozy suppers of venison, cold duck and lobster.

Jordan had set up an intricate network, and directed it with considerable success from his post close to Beauregard. He kept one agent in ignorance of what the others were doing, and fed out rope to Rose quite slowly in the beginning, since he did not wholly trust her. Her impetuous nature was indeed a hazard in the field of espionage. But after Manassas she was singled out as his star performer, and the entire network depended in the early days on her intimate connection with the inner social, political and military life of Washington.

Her work was so effective that General McClellan, who had stepped into McDowell's shoes after the defeat of Bull Run, was finally pushed into saying bitterly of Mrs. Greenhow: "She knows my plans better than Lincoln or the Cabinet, and has four times compelled me to change them." She boasted of having the Senate Military Committee map with the red dotted lines of the army's route to Richmond, and of sending it to Manassas "thinking it might serve as a lesson to the Confederate engineers."

The discovery of a haul of papers and maps after the flight from Fairfax County Courthouse, all credited to Mrs. Greenhow, caused consternation in Washington. The New York *Herald* commented pointedly on the "mystery of those important government maps and plans" and added: "We are at liberty to guess how Beauregard was so minutely informed of this advance and of our plan of attack on his lines, as to be ready to meet it at every single point with overwhelming numbers."

Rose rarely underestimated her own prowess. Her wartime memoirs show a boastful spirit, but in a rare moment of insight she put what might well be a sound valuation on her own powers when she wrote that McClellan gave her credit sometimes for having more information than she actually possessed. She confessed, with a touch of realism:

121

I was, of course, a close observer of the smallest indications, and often drew accurate conclusions without having any precise knowledge on the subject. I was in Washington, as the Indian savage in the trackless forest, with an enemy behind every bush. My perceptive faculties were under a painful tension, and every instinct was quickened to follow the doublings and windings of the ruthless foe who was hunting my race unto death; and, of course, no word or indication was lost upon me.

Rose had a certain degree of admiration for McClellan, and often "looked on with sickening heart, at the energy and talent displayed by him" as he reorganized the army. She believed that he labored hard to make it "the best appointed, and best disciplined in the world." She appraised the component parts of the Army of the Potomac with some discernment in the early days of the war and made notes in her diary on the fighting spirit and outward appearance of the assorted regiments.

The antics of the agile Zouaves were distasteful to her, and she was particularly scornful of New York's famous Seventh Regiment, whose millionaires "took more pains to prepare white gloves and embroidered vests for 'the balls' to be given in their honor at Richmond than in securing cartridges for their muskets."

Since Rose frequently had access to the minutes of McClellan's private consultations, and seemingly obtained extracts from his notes, she had considerable insight into his operations. In her opinion he never underrated the Southern forces. On the contrary "he magnified our force and capabilities beyond what our modesty would have allowed us to claim on our own behalf." She also thought that he properly evaluated the morale of his own men; knew that his only hope of success in invading the South was by overwhelming numbers; and was alive to the need for artillery operations instead of "bayonet charges and hand-to-hand collision with dare-devil Southern chivalry and men born to the use of arms."

Rose considered McClellan unsophisticated as a man, and quite susceptible to the hero worship so bountifully offered him. She viewed McDowell, whom she had known on the coast, as a scholarly gentleman, and she had no word of blame for him in her memoirs. The other warriors of the North fared less well at her hands. She likened General Scott at the end to Cardinal Thomas Wolsey—left in his extremity to the mercy of his enemies. She thought that the old hero who "had borne himself loftily on a hundred battlefields had sullied the glory of his proud heels by ranging himself under the Abolition banner."

Rose was fully persuaded that artillery operations would win or lose the war. She was much interested in the subject and at a time when Henry Wilson received authority to raise a regiment in Massachusetts, with a battery of flying artillery attached, she wrote to Senator Daniel S. Dickinson suggesting that the whole army be changed to "flying artillery," with ample appliances. She proposed that the men wear shields, since she had learned from reading Herodotus that in his time breastplates were worn even by persons of the "most inferior condition." This idea came up less than a month before Rose was seized as a spy. Wilson was out of town on August 23 when the blow fell and she was taken into custody.

Her progress in espionage was marked by the utmost candor. She functioned openly as an *agent provocateur* and almost came to blows in the Senate gallery with a young officer who listened to her uninhibited discourse in the seat behind him. He bluntly accused her of treason. She retorted in kind.

Some months later this same youth was to watch her being marched in to a commission hearing as a prisoner, and to grin at her in a vengeful way. But Rose, remembering Joseph Balsamo and Marie Antoinette, gave the moment a Cagliostro touch by zipping her finger across her throat and crying "Beware!" No whippersnapper could flout Mrs. Greenhow, even though she was figuratively in chains at the time.

The smoke from campfires across the Potomac gave her further opportunity for sarcastic comment as she stood on a balcony with

Northern sympathizers. But when she was seeking specific information, she changed her tactics and functioned with more discretion, parading around with junior officers, flattering them with her worldly charm, listening attentively while they poured out their fresh army lore. Rose had had years of practice in inciting men's intellectual interest, as well as in stirring their emotions. She had a quick and thorough grasp of detail when it came to a map or a document, and her memory was crystal-clear. She obtained the dimensions and other characteristics of the new Navy gunboats while they were still in the early blueprint stage.

Was it her fault if men talked, she demanded, when finally called to account before a war commission. Where was their patriotism? She was doing her part with the best of motives. One of these tours with an officer of the Provost-Marshal's office proved rewarding. From this encounter Rose later obtained the plan of defense in full, should the capital be invaded.

She promptly organized a counterplan. With the help of fellow Secessionists, working under cover, arrangements were made in case of invasion to cut all telegraph wires connecting military posts with the War Department, and to spike the guns of Fort Corcoran, Fort Ellsworth and other important points of defense. Rose topped this with the imaginative notion that General McClellan and others of the high command should be taken prisoner from within, "thereby creating still greater confusion in the first moments of panic." By this time she and her fellow Secessionists still in Washington were raising relief funds, and were quietly organizing themselves as an inner core of rebellion within sight of the Capitol.

Immediately after the Battle of Manassas a number of Confederate prisoners passing Willard's Hotel were pelted with stones and missiles. Some were wounded. A company of army regulars was called out to accompany them to Old Capitol Prison. Rose was indignant when she heard of this. She hurried to see them, along with Miss Lily Mackall, a close relative of Assistant Adjutant-General W. W.

124

Mackall, of the Confederate forces, who was later to serve as chief of staff of the Army of Tennessee. Theirs were the first friendly faces on the scene.

Rose at once encountered Superintendent William P. Wood, an official she was to know well before long. He was a former model maker, a stern and stubborn Abolitionist, and a man whom she soon found to her sorrow she could neither wheedle nor impress. She now caught him earnestly telling the prisoners that they would all be hanged unless they took the oath of allegiance to the Federal Government. Or this was how it sounded to Rose. She listened attentively; then, when he had turned his back, she assured the men that this was only an idle threat. She told them that their government would "fearfully retaliate any violence against them."

"This satisfied them, especially the younger portion, and each refused the Yankee pardon on the terms proposed," Rose noted with satisfaction.

She had worked her spell again. She took a list of their immediate needs and along with Southern friends, such as John C. Breckinridge, who had funds for this purpose, she supplied them with clothing, food, wine, beds and bedding. Soon grateful young soldiers were writing notes to Rose, thanking her profusely, but telling her that the ardent spirits she offered were denied them, except medicinally.

Some days later an order was issued to exclude all visitors. Rose was specifically named. It took her no time at all to protest to General Joseph K. F. Mansfield, and to report that one of his subordinates had been grossly impudent to her. The General succumbed to the extent of giving her a permit to leave clothes at the entrance of the prison. However, she was not permitted beyond that point. But bigger things were in the wind for Rose. "Soon after, I passed into other hands my share of this good work; for more important employment occupied my time." She let it go at that.

Among her milder activities was the preparation of comforts for soldiers. Rose was an expert with the needle. The few "Secessionist dames" who remained in Washington continued to use her home as a sewing center, as well as a distribution and gossip emporium, when deeper plans were not afoot. Shortly after Manassas Mrs. Chesnut recorded in her diary:

It gives a quaint look, the twinkling of needles, and the everlasting sock dangling. A Jury of Matrons, so to speak, sat at Mrs. Greenhow's. They say Mrs. Greenhow furnished Beauregard with the latest information of the Federal movements, and so made the Manassas victory a possibility. She sent us the enemy's plans. Everything she said proved true, numbers, route and all. . . .

Had Rose actually managed to hold her tongue in the knitting circle and not boast of Manassas? Mrs. Chesnut's entry suggests that her information came from outside sources. Rose at the time was stuffing her files with newspaper clippings bearing on the battle, including copies of *The Times* of London with stories by her friend Russell.

Like the other Southern ladies Rose was scathing about the Washington scene under Republican auspices. Her own set "had disappeared entirely from the surface of society," and after their long reign it was now apparent that department vacancies, government contracts and invitations of all kinds would be denied those with Southern sympathies. Rose felt that in their "insolent pride of conquest" the newcomers had effaced every landmark of civilization. She found them as "distinct and marked in their characteristics as any barbarian race that ever overran Christendom."

Washington was changing fast, whether viewed through Union or Confederate eyes. Forts bristled on the hilltops. Tents ringed the city. Soldiers stood guard at every gateway and swarmed through the streets. An infantry brigade was stationed on Capitol Hill. Bands played and muskets cracked. A quartermaster's depot was set up in the White House grounds. Corcoran's Art Gallery had become a clothing depot, Senator Gwin's house the headquarters of the military governor, and the Old Capitol a rebel prison. General Scott's home was now a boardinghouse, and every corner of the city was jammed with jostling humanity.

Saloons, gambling houses and brothels flourished. Commission merchants appeared in the wake of the army. Pickpockets, crooks, tricksters, vendors and adventurers of all kinds showed up. Circuses, bear shows and sundry forms of entertainment were offered to the soldiers. The population of seventy-five thousand when war broke out was to swell to two hundred thousand by 1862.

Hospitals increased in number. The wounded were brought in after every fresh engagement. The death toll was heard more often in the streets. Ammunition wagons, caissons, vehicles of all kinds rattled along the roadways. Northern and Southern women knitted, sewed, pulled lint and visited the hospitals. There were dances, flag-raisings, soirées and parties of different kinds for the men in uniform, but every engagement was followed by a lull in entertaining, and a fresh drive in effort.

Rose took a dim view of it all. She observed "thousands of drunken demoralized soldiers in the streets, crowding women into the gutters, shouting obscenities." The public squares had become the "chosen places of debauchery and crime." Schools had been closed. And Negro servants were so busy riding and driving with Yankee officers that they could not perform their services, according to Rose.

Every scrap of gossip that she could round up about the unfortunate Mary Todd Lincoln was spread on wings. In this she was not alone. Kate Chase and other Republican women were equally uncharitable to the sad woman in the White House. Rose chose to refer to the Lincoln menage as "High Life Below Stairs." The White

House was now like a hotel, "filled with a crowd of common people."
But Rose had known it also in Jackson's time, when muddy boots
and uncouth manners were not unknown in the East Room.

By her own admission she had encountered Mrs. Lincoln only
once, and then merely as an observer. She was returning from market
with some flowers and shrubs on a hot summer morning in 1861 when
she saw the "imperial coach, with its purple hangings and tall footmen
in white gloves" standing outside a little shop. She went in out of
curiosity and found a small woman bargaining for black cotton gloves.
Rose thought that the saleswoman seemed disgusted with Mrs. Lincoln as she moved over toward her more impressive self.

"Who is that?" Rose innocently inquired.

"Only Madam Lincoln," was the reply.

Rose made a trifling purchase and then took a good—and unfavor-
able—look at Mary. She thought her dress much too pretentious for
the occasion. It was of rich silk, embroidered with showy flowers. The
Point Venise collars and sleeves were edged with pink ribands. Her
white hat was trimmed with flowers, feathers and tinsel balls. Her
white parasol had a pink lining. A supermantle of black lace and
white gloves completed her costume.

This, said Rose meaningfully, was Mrs. Lincoln's shopping toilette,
and was not the sort of costume that Mrs. Davis or Mrs. Lee would
have worn for the occasion. Added to this was the dismaying picture
of Mary herself, as viewed by Rose: "She is a short, broad, flat figure,
with a broad flat face, with sallow mottled complexion, light gray
eyes, with scant light eyelashes, and exceedingly thin pinched lips;
self-complacency, and a slightly scornful expression characterize her
bearing, as if to rebuke one for passing between the 'wind and her
nobility.' "

Mrs. Lincoln's opinion of Rose is not on record. She may not have
identified her on this occasion, although the Greenhow features were
familiar enough to the older inhabitants of the capital. There is little
doubt that many of the tales of Mary's treatment of servants, her

128

vulgarity, her extravagance and her tempers, were whipped into brisk circulation by Rose, who could be wonderfully eloquent on any subject close to her heart.

She got much of her ammunition on the Lincolns from her friends in the diplomatic set. The items were trivial, and some may well have been apocryphal, but they gathered malice as they were passed around. Rose criticized Mrs. Lincoln's handling of the first diplomatic reception, which should have been "second only to a presentation at St. James's or at St. Cloud."

Instead, the guests thought they were looking at a servant when the "small, dowdy-looking woman, with artificial flowers in her hair" appeared on the scene, quite late and without apologies. Another gaucherie reported by Rose was the message conveyed to Madame Mercier, wife of the French Minister, that Mrs. Lincoln was studying French and would be able to converse with her in her own language by winter.

Rose conceded that the President was a "little less bizarre in his ministerial reception," although it was noted that when asked which wine he would take at an official dinner, he turned to the servant with the "most touching simplicity and said: 'I don't know: which would you?'" Much was made of the fact that he spilled a cup of tea on a guest's gown on another occasion. Rose quoted one of the diplomats as saying of the Lincolns: "He is better than she, for he seems by his manner to apologize for being there."

But by this time the Lincoln administration was taking careful note of Rose. In the days preceding her arrest she lived zestfully and with concentrated purpose. Her glance was bright with defiance as she walked the streets of Washington with all the assurance that seemed to be her natural birthright. She wore deep mourning, and set forth on the hottest days in thin black ruffled net, modishly cut, for Rose had always cared intensely about her appearance. Leaving her little daughter with a trusted maid, Lizzy Fitzgerald, she promenaded according to fashion, bought flowers in the market, went up to Capitol Hill to watch the new men in action, and in all respects was part of the life of the town.

By August detectives were hot on her trail—a luxury that she enjoyed. It amused her to lead them astray—to disappear in a friend's house, or walk up a side alley with Lily Mackall, then double back in her tracks and confront her pursuers. At first she did not take this shadowing seriously. She thought it was "private enterprise" designed for her protection. Rose was slow to believe that even "the fragment of a once glorious government could give to the world such a proof of craven fear and weakness as to turn the arms . . . against the breasts of helpless defenseless women and children."

She walked toward capture, head on, enjoying the experience to the full. As she recalled it in her wartime memoirs:

Day after day I waited for the warning's fulfillment. It was very exciting. I would be walking down the avenue with one of the officials, military or state, and as we strolled along there would pass perhaps a washerwoman, carrying home her basket of clean clothes, or, maybe, a gaily attired youth from lower Seventh Avenue.

But something in the way the woman held her basket, or in the way the youth twirled his cane, told me that news had been received, or that news was wanted—that I must open up communications in some way. Or, as we sat in some city park, a sedate old gentleman would pass by. To my unsuspecting escort the passerby was commonplace. But to me, his manner of polishing his glasses, or the flourish of the handkerchief with which he rubbed his nose, was a message.

Rose warned several of her friends to leave the city on the eve of arrest. When she received a note from a friend in Georgetown saying that one of McClellan's aids had disclosed that Rose and William Preston, Buchanan's Minister to Spain, were about to be arrested, she warned Preston. He returned to his native state of Kentucky and a month later joined the command of Albert Sidney Johnston, serving on his staff until the General's death at Shiloh.

Breckinridge changed the tone of his final speech, described by

130

Rose as the "last cry of freedom" to be heard in the Senate, when she warned him that he would be arrested for treason if he gave the slightest excuse for it in what he had to say. When she told him who her informers were he "at once recognized his peril, and so reworded his speech as to avoid the threatened danger, at which the Abolitionists were greatly chagrined."

From whom had Rose obtained her information in this instance?

When it came to arrest, she had no fear on her own account. Either she was prepared to face the ultimate from patriotic motives, or she was too sure of her own power to believe that her imprisonment would be sustained. Her later statements suggest that she did not really think the authorities would touch her. Her air to the end was defiant. She casually exchanged words with a fellow agent right under the eyes of the men she knew were waiting in the street to arrest her. This gives some conception of the boldness and devil-may-care spirit with which Rose operated, even when she must have realized that the jig was up.

There were those who believed that she gloried in the role of martyr. Addie Douglas, a tolerant and intelligent woman who must have understood her aunt's character better than most, was among them. Colonel Doster, a sharp observer, cynically observed that he considered the day of Mrs. Greenhow's arrest the happiest of her life, as "her object was to be made a Southern martyr, to gain that applause for heroism which was now denied her beauty."

This may or may not have been a just appraisal of Rose's motives. Her own writings, accepted at face value, strongly suggest that the spirit that stirred and drove her to extreme measures was her absolute and unflagging belief in the Confederate cause.

131

Part Two

CHAPTER IX

Pinkerton on the Doorstep

WASHINGTON steamed with heat and war fever on August 23, 1861, the day on which Mrs. Greenhow was arrested as a spy at the door of her house. She accepted her fate with composure, swallowed a cipher message while still in the street, and treated her captors with queenly displeasure and sarcasm.

Her arrest was the climax to a long and exciting chase. The tendency had been to pass off the maneuvers of the Secessionist ladies as misplaced patriotism, and to let them alone. But the War Department now meant business. After Bull Run, chivalry gave way to vigilance. The steady flow of information into Richmond had Lincoln's Cabinet and the army leaders baffled. Too often the trail led back to Mrs. Greenhow.

Allan Pinkerton, the Scot who ran a detective agency in Chicago and had guarded Lincoln on his trip east, was assigned to organize the secret service department of the Union Army, working with Thomas A. Scott, Assistant Secretary of War. He had orders to watch the Greenhow house, to proceed with caution, but to trail all visitors and arrest any who might attempt to pass through the Union lines. Rose was not to be interfered with until there was evidence in hand.

She was an important catch, from every point of view. A good deal of unrelated knowledge existed about her operations, but because of

135

her status in the community and her powerful family connections, the approach was wary. Seward may well have initiated the chase. None knew better than the new Secretary of State the tenor of Rose's thinking, or the boldness of her methods.

She made one grave mistake in showing her hand to Mrs. Martha Wright Morris, wife of Robert Hunter Morris, who was on Seward's staff. After a round of social calls together, Rose offered to transmit a letter to Mrs. Morris' sister, whose husband was on General Beauregard's staff.

"I'm a personal friend of Beauregard, and if you will bring me a letter, I will see that your sister receives it," Rose volunteered. Underground correspondence was commonplace to her at this time.

When Morris heard of this, he warned his wife to have nothing further to do with Mrs. Greenhow. Some time later Stanton sent for Mrs. Morris and, according to her diary notation, remarked: "My dear little woman, we wish to thank you for the great service you rendered your country, and the possible escape you had, by not sending a letter to Richmond."

It is unlikely that Mrs. Morris was more than another straw in the wind, but a straw that had settled in Seward's inkwell. She later confessed to being quite overcome by the knowledge that she had figured in Rose's arrest. According to Mrs. Morris, President Lincoln said to her: "We will give you a souvenir from her skirt—a pearl and ivory tablet on a silver chain—but be careful in future how you make acquaintances, for the city is full of spies."

On the day of Rose's arrest Mrs. Lincoln was in Long Branch, waltzing at a grand hop given in her honor at the Mansion House. Dodsworth's band played and firecrackers spurted over the ocean. But even at the seashore she was under attack as being difficult and self-important. There were malignant stories that she, too, having Southern blood and relatives in the Confederate Army, was a spy and traitor.

Before effecting the capture of Confederate Rose, Pinkerton ran

himself into a ludicrous situation and was held in custody for a
night. Taking several of his assistants with him, he went to the
Greenhow home to make personal observations at night. A summer
thunderstorm burst with great violence after a threatening day. Rain
pelted down and the wind blew wildly for August. One of the detectives named Pryce Lewis, a tall affable young Englishman with side
whiskers and a brisk sense of humor, proposed a trapeze act to permit
Pinkerton to do some spying through Rose's front parlor window,
which was well above street level.

Pinkerton removed his boots and straddled the shoulders of two of
his fellow detectives. Rose's blinds were drawn but both front and
back parlors were lit. The detective quietly raised the window sash
and turned the slats, so that he could view the interior. He was
impressed with what he saw: "The furniture was rich and luxurious,
valuable pictures hung upon the walls, and several pieces of statuary
and objects of art were arranged about the apartment."

When an army officer tramped briskly up to the entrance Pinkerton and his assistants scrambled under the stoop. The visitor's features
were indistinguishable as he entered, but when Pinkerton returned to
his post and saw him in the lighted room, he recognized him at once
as an infantry captain in command of one of the Provost-Marshal's
stations.

He was a handsome fellow, about forty years of age, looking the
"veritable ideal soldier" as he flung off his cloak and moved forward
eagerly in his blue uniform to welcome Rose when she walked into
the room. Pinkerton, on the alert for betraying signs, thought that
his face lighted with pleasure when he saw her. His findings from
this point on become rather inferential, for the storm blew so gustily
that little could be heard.

However, Pinkerton saw enough to make him feel like rushing
into the room "to strangle the miscreant where he sat." For he had
taken a map from the inner pocket of his coat and was holding it up
before the light for Rose to study. Pinkerton came to the conclusion

that it was a plan of the Washington fortifications, coupled with a "contemplated plan of attack." Since Rose undeniably supplied the Confederates with this material at about the same time, he may have been right in his deductions. On the other hand, his later knowledge of the seized papers may conceivably have influenced him when he came to write the book in which he made these disclosures. He referred to the officer as Ellison, which admittedly was not his true name.

Rose's information on the defense plans was known to have come from one of the Provost-Marshal's aides. Ellison may well have been the culprit. They consulted back and forth for some time, constantly referring to the map, as if to settle particular points. Another interruption from the street sent Pinkerton and his assistants scurrying back under the stoop. When they resumed their acrobatic stand the room was empty.

According to Pinkerton, it was a full hour and more before they reappeared, walking arm in arm. Again the watchers were driven under cover by passers-by. Soon the front door opened and the captain emerged. Through the wind and the rain Pinkerton thought he heard a whispered good-night, and "something that sounded much like a kiss."

Ignoring the fact that he was still in his stockinged feet, with one of his assistants he followed the captain "as stealthily as a cat." When they reached the Provost-Marshal's station Ellison walked in and the detectives were confronted suddenly by four men with fixed bayonets. This was an awkward moment for Lincoln's chief secret service agent. He did not wish to disclose his identity, so he trumped up a tale that he had been out late at night and had lost his way. Ellison went upstairs and returned with a revolver. Pinkerton believed he disappeared to get rid of incriminating papers. Both detectives were questioned exhaustively and then were ordered to the guardhouse for the night.

"One might more readily imagine that I had been fished out of the Potomac than that I was the chief of the secret service of the government in the performance of duty," commented Pinkerton later, acknowledging that he looked a spectacle. He was soaked to the skin. His hat was bashed down over his face. He had no shoes. He was covered with mud from his vigils under the stoop. The room was so chilly he "shook like an aspen, and his teeth chattered like castanets." Early in the morning he scribbled a note and bribed a guard to deliver it to Scott, suggesting that he be released in a manner guaranteed not to arouse the suspicions of his captor.

This was accomplished and the station commander was promptly summoned before Scott. When asked for particulars on the arrest of Pinkerton he said he had gone to visit some friends on the city outskirts. Believing himself to be followed by footpads, he had ordered their arrest.

"Did you see anyone last evening who is inimical to the cause of the government?" he was asked.

Flushed and nervous, the Captain glanced at Pinkerton, then said: "No, sir; I have seen no person of that character."

He was told to surrender his sword. His arrest followed. Incriminating papers were found among his effects and he was imprisoned in Fort McHenry. There is evidence that "Ellison" may have been Captain John Ellwood, who got into further trouble and cut his throat with a penknife some months after Rose's arrest. She does not identify him in her memoirs; nor does Pinkerton in his.

Pinkerton used two pseudonyms—Major E. J. Allen and T. H. Hutcheson. Rose was to know him as Major Allen and to view him with contempt. But he was now hot on her trail. He reported to Scott that a number of prominent gentlemen, including Senators and Congressmen, were received by the fascinating widow. They were men whose loyalty was above question and who were presumably "in entire ignorance of the lady's true character."

Scott promptly declared that Mrs. Greenhow was becoming a "dangerous character and must be attended to." This led to action

139

a few days after Pinkerton's storm-tossed night. She was trailed when out promenading with a member of the diplomatic corps. On her return home she bade him good-by at the house of a friend across the street whose child was ill. There she stopped to inquire for the little one, and was told that her house was being watched and that a guard had been posted around it all night.

Her neighborly mission accomplished, Rose walked boldly into the street and spotted the men at once. One of her agents was hanging about, no doubt by prearrangement, since she obtained a great deal of her information from diplomats, and may well have received from her promenading escort some word that she wished to pass along. She whispered to the agent in passing: "I think I am about to be arrested. Watch from Corcoran's Corner. I shall raise my handkerchief to my face if they arrest me. Give information of it."

Rose had a "very important note" which apparently she had intended for the agent. Instead, she slipped it into her mouth and swallowed it. The man went whistling on his way. Rose walked with an "air of conscious authority" past her house to the end of the pavement, where the detectives stood stolidly surveying her. This was a piece of bravado. She knew what she faced. She studied the men openly, appraising them in her shrewd way. This was her first direct encounter with the sturdy, bearded Mr. Pinkerton, a strong antislavery man. No doubt he studied Rose with equal interest as she stood silently challenging him, her vivacious face clearly exposed in the sunlight.

Having taken their measure she decided on her line of conduct. In her own words, she felt that "the fate of some of the best and bravest belonging to our cause hung upon my own coolness and courage." It was a moment of decision for Rose, and she showed no hesitation. Her crinoline rocked as she approached her house with the long graceful stride characteristic of the spirited belle. As she started up the steps Major Allen and his assistant, one in the

140

fatigue uniform of the Union Army, the other in mufti, were at her heels. Then, as Rose tells it:

"Is this Mrs. Greenhow?" Allen demanded.
"Yes," said Rose. "Who are you, and what do you want?"
"I come to arrest you."
"By what authority?"
The man Allen, or Pinkerton (for he had several aliases) said, "By sufficient authority."
"Let me see your warrant."
He mumbled something about verbal authority from the War and State Departments, and then both stationed themselves upon either side of me, and followed into the house.

Rose skillfully whisked her handkerchief to her face, glanced to see if her agent had caught the signal, and then observed grandly: "I have no power to resist you, but had I been inside of my house, I would have killed one of you before I had submitted to this illegal process."

All mention of threatened gunplay on Rose's part is missing from the Pinkerton narrative of her arrest. Her memoirs have the added flavor of her own reactions to each episode, sometimes spiced with a dash of theatrical effect. On essential points, however, they dovetail with established facts.

Using her intuition she decided that a careless and sarcastic manner might be the most effective, even though "agonizing anxieties filled her soul." She had determined to test the truth of the old saying that "the devil is no match for a clever woman."

"What are you going to do now?" she asked Pinkerton when they reached the front parlor.

"To search," he told her bluntly.

"I will facilitate your labors," said Rose.

She went to the mantelpiece and drew from a vase a torn slip of blue paper dated Manassas, July 23, and bearing the message: "For

141

Mrs. Rose Greenhow with the compliments of Col. Thos. Jordan who is well but hard worked."

The rest of the letter had been torn off before it reached her, ten days earlier. Suspecting a trap, she had cautiously shown it to Henry Wilson, Major Alexander D. Bache, Captain Richard D. Cutts and other friends, she now informed the detectives. Did Rose introduce these names at this juncture for purposes of intimidation? Whatever her motive, she threw the note to Allen with the remark: "You would like to finish this job, I suppose." He took it at once but discarded the city envelope in which she had received it.

"My cool and indifferent manner evidently disconcerted the whole party," Rose's account continues. "They had expected that under the influence of the agitation and excitement of the trying position, I should have been guilty of some womanly indiscretion by which they could profit."

A number of detective police now appeared from different quarters, and the hunt began. As Rose viewed it:

Men rushed with frantic haste into my chamber, into every sanctuary. My beds, drawers, and wardrobes were all upturned; soiled clothes were pounced upon with avidity, and mercilessly exposed; papers that had not seen the light for years were dragged forth. My library was taken possession of, and every scrap of paper, every idle line was seized, even the torn fragments in the grates or other receptacles were carefully gathered together by these latter-day Lincoln insurrectionists.

Rose was particularly outraged by their invasion of Gertrude's room. She had left it untouched since her daughter's death, with all her bijouterie and toilet articles spread on the dressing table. Everything was scooped up. Rose's library had always been her particular sanctum. It was associated strongly with her life with Robert. His books lined the shelves from floor to ceiling. They were in several languages and on many subjects, representing his wide and scholarly interests. It was here, too, that she schooled her children. Now even

142

little Rose's "unlettered scribblings were tortured into dangerous correspondence with the enemy."

Her two parlors were divided by portières of shadowy crimson Indian silk. These were drawn aside when Rose entertained, making one room large enough to hold the gatherings she frequently assembled. A tête-à-tête was drawn up before the grate in the front parlor. A painting of Gertrude, blue-eyed, auburn-haired and faintly smiling, hung on one wall. The rosewood pianoforte with pearl keys and candles in gold sconces stood in the back parlor. Portraits of America's most important statesmen were on view. She had much bric-a-brac and choice pieces of furniture.

When alone Rose passed most of her time in her library, which was upstairs, adjoining her bedroom. Here she attended to her correspondence, which was entertaining and widely circulated. Most of the important names of the period figured in it and when the Pinkerton quest was over, one of the searchers—the only one whom Rose considered an educated man—complimented her on its scope and quality. It did her honor, he said and was "the most extensive private correspondence that has ever fallen under my examination, and the most interesting and important; there is not a distinguished name in America that is not found here. There is nothing that can come under the charge of treason, but enough to make the Government dread and hold you as a most dangerous adversary."

To Calhoun, to Buchanan, to Seward, to Lord Lyons, to Martin Van Buren, to Stanton, to Breckinridge, to Reverdy Johnson, to Bishop Kip and innumerable others, she was always "My dear Madam" or "My dear Mrs. Greenhow." They were always most respectfully hers. The quality of their friendship for her, and their regard for her views, showed up clearly in her correspondence. But notwithstanding his colleague's opinion, her papers quickly persuaded Pinkerton that the "irresistibly seductive" Rose had been trading the sweets of love for the secrets of war. The H letters had come to light.

143

The havoc wrought in her surroundings changed Rose's tantalizing air of indifference and scorn to blazing anger. Her home was only two blocks from the White House and efforts were made to keep her arrest secret. A high wall surrounded three sides of it, so that the guard was not on view from the street. But the little rosebud saw to it that her mother's couriers had ample warning not to approach. In the midst of all the confusion she ran into the garden, climbed a tree, and chanted over and over again: "Mamma has been arrested. Mamma has been arrested."

Detectives dragged her down, protesting and screaming, but she had raised the alarm. Soon all Washington knew that Mrs. Greenhow had been nabbed. Four hours after her arrest Lily Mackall appeared. The detectives marched Rose and Lily upstairs together, after a slight scuffle between Rose and Captain Dennis, the only ruffian who dared to lay hands upon her.

Rose took stock of the situation and saw that they had failed to find the really vital material. It was hidden in a folio on her library shelves. She carefully laid plans to corner it before the night was over. Commenting on the material they had so far found she said: "I had a right to my own political opinions, and to discuss the question at issue, and never shrank from the avowal of my sentiments."

Dennis never knew it but, according to Rose, his life for a few moments was in danger. She had asked to retire to her chamber to change her dress. The day was intensely hot. Actually, Rose had papers in her pocket that she intended to destroy—"even at the expense of life." They included some messages in her cipher. She got rid of them "without such a fearful sacrifice" just as Dennis knocked at her door, peered in, then withdrew when he saw her apparently "legitimately employed."

"Had he advanced one step," Rose commented at this point, "I should have killed him, as I raised my revolver with that intent; and so steady were my nerves that I would have balanced a glass of water on my finger without spilling a drop."

144

A woman detective named Ellen, with a face "like an India rubber doll," next took charge and searched Rose's person. A guard waited outside for the evidence. None was forthcoming. Rose had forestalled them. She prided herself on remaining perfectly self-possessed throughout this humiliating experience. It was no small ordeal for proud Rose, but again her fervor restrained her. She had already resolved to set the house on fire from garret to cellar, if she could not get rid of certain papers during the night, for she did not believe that they would escape a second day's search.

By evening Lily's sister and mother, who had come looking for her, were all in custody upstairs along with Rose. When Pinkerton left for the night she adroitly steered his aids to her best rum and brandy, with resulting chaos. When they became quarrelsome among themselves she whipped up further excitement by encouraging racial disputes—pitting English, German, Irish and Yankee against one another. Finally drowsiness overtook the drunken guards. This was the effect she desired.

With moonlight only to guide her, Rose slipped softly into her library. She mounted to the topmost shelf and from an old folio took "papers of immense value to her at that moment." She hid them in the folds of her dress and got back to the bedroom without being missed by her guards. Remembering that when she was searched, her shoes and stockings were not disturbed, she quietly helped Lily to stuff the papers into her hose and boots, although a slumberous guard was in the room with them. Rose told Lily that if held for searching as she left, she was to express compunction about deserting her friend, and return "to share the honors of the conflagration." Rose had thought of everything.

Between three and four in the morning the Mackalls finally were permitted to go home. Rose thankfully snatched some sleep. Later in the day Lily was back, having disposed of the papers. For several weeks she shared Rose's confinement. She was allowed to come and go at first, seemingly with freedom. Actually she was being used as

145

a decoy to light the trail to other agents. When she had served thi
purpose a guard accompanied her everywhere. Rose clung to Lily's
company as a link with the outside world. Since her pistol had beer
taken from her, for the first time in her life she felt the "dread o
personal violence."

For the next week the search continued. Rose's papers were par
celed off in bundles labeled "highly important," "political," "legal"
and "personal." The day after she emptied the folio, every book ii
the library was pulled down and examined, page by page. Robert's
lawbooks were torn apart. His French and Spanish classics were rif
fled through. His volumes of poetry, of history, of exploration, were
closely studied. Rose suffered through this, but recovered her spirit
enough to jeer as she watched the jigsaw proceedings conducted by
a War Department clerk—half-burned scraps rescued from her grates
torn odds and ends slowly being pieced together on her Duncar
Phyfe tables. She had no further qualms, however, since she main
tained that right under their eyes she had destroyed or sent off al
incriminating papers.

Rose rejoiced that the "basic clue" had escaped them and main
tained that even Jean François Champollion, the decipherer oi
Egyptian hieroglyphics, might have been baffled by what remained
Here she was overestimating her cipher. Jordan later dismissed it as
a crude and amateur effect which he had dashed off in a hurry, know
ing its weakness and vulnerability. He was working on a better one
when Rose was arrested.

But one important item had escaped her. She was thoroughly
aroused when the alert Lily abstracted from a heap of papers a sheet
of blotting paper bearing the impress of her vital dispatch to Manassas
on July 16—"another evidence that Providence watched over me as
an humble instrument in a glorious cause."

This, Rose knew, was specific evidence. She felt that many tricks
were being played to get a solid foundation for a case against her. A
guard named Pat flirted with Lizzy Fitzgerald and treated her at the

146

confectioner's, but Lizzy kept her counsel and "led him a dance." A Scot named Robert offered to carry letters for Rose—a transparent ruse. Various techniques were tried. Subordinates threw themselves in her way, pretending disgust with the task assigned them and with "hearts overflowing with kindness, and hands ready to be bribed, discoursed most fluently upon the outrage committed in my arrest."

Rose was not taken in. She was well aware that each move she made was reported to Provost-Marshal Andrew J. Porter and she had word that some of her messages were sent directly to Seward. But she flattered herself that she had her captors cowed—at least where manners were concerned. They took her orders for meals, and "even my lawless captors were rebuked into more quiet and reserve before me, although they still presumed to seat themselves at table with me, with unwashed hands, and shirt sleeves." Most mortifying of all was their continual presence by her side. Rose was never alone for a moment. A detective sat close to her bed while she slept. She had to change her things with open doors, and men peering in at her.

During these first dismaying days she was perfectly posted on outside events, largely through Lily Mackall. The most vital piece of news reaching her was the story that her seized papers had come under discussion at a Cabinet council, called with Scott and McClellan in attendance, and that "several Republican officials had been summoned, amongst the number Wilson of Mass., as being implicated by my information."

The H letters unquestionably had caused a sensation, so Rose may not have been deluding herself that Wilson was called to account for his undisputed association with her. There is no record of the way in which he met this ordeal, if indeed he was called on to face it squarely. The prevailing feeling in political circles at the time was that he had not betrayed his trust, but had been bedeviled by Rose. However, there was much rude laughter in Washington saloons and messes over the H notes, whatever their authorship. Clearly they had come from Capitol Hill.

147

Rose's papers were a matter of concern to several members of Lincoln's Cabinet. She reported Simon Cameron's defalcations to Jefferson Davis before they were known to the public. She foreshadowed many of McClellan's reorganization plans for the army. She also felt it her duty to report all dissension in the inner councils, as well as to supply military information. Her own view of this is precise:

I had deemed it important that the political intrigues then going on at Washington should be clearly understood by the Confederate Government; and as I might almost be said to have assisted at Lincoln's Cabinet Councils, from the facilities I enjoyed, having verbatim reports of them as well as of the Republican caucus, I was thoroughly competent of the task of giving a faithful synopsis of their deliberations.

There were many allusions to Seward that must have caused him uneasiness. One of her letters to Jefferson Davis described in detail the intrigues to get rid of Winfield Scott by elevating McClellan, and the reasons pro and con for leaving Seward where he was as Secretary of State. Some of this must have been galling news to Lincoln's chief Cabinet member.

She quoted a conversation she had with James Gordon Bennett in which she described Seward as the "only statesman in the Black Republican Party." Bennett replied that Seward did not have "enough blood in him to entertain an honest opinion on any subject but wished to be a great man and would truckle to anything for power."

Rose gloated when she heard that Seward turned scarlet with fury over this. She was well enough used to his squirmings and ambiguous smile to know that he must have been deeply stirred to redden, for he did not show his feelings lightly. He was further embarrassed by another item in this same letter. Rose maintained that Chevalier Henry Wikoff, the ubiquitous adventurer who had been preying on Mrs. Lincoln, had besought her to go with him to General Beauregard

148

and get him safe conduct to Richmond, there to send out a peace letter—an idea which Wikoff insisted was approved by Seward.

"Your reputation is so bad, that no lady would travel in your company," Rose told him. "I should consider President Davis derelict in his duty if he did not cause any man to be hanged who would do what you propose." Peace was out of the question, added Rose, on any basis other than separate independence, since the "South had been driven to draw the sword in self-defense."

She was greatly flattered by the reaction of Lincoln's Cabinet members to the duplicate drawings laid before them of their fortifications and weak spots. They were pronounced "a very able production worthy of the best engineers"—as well they might be, Rose commented, having full knowledge of their source. She preened herself a little at this point:

I had at least the satisfaction of knowing that Lincoln and the assembled wisdom of Abolitionism did justice to the zeal with which a Southern woman executed her patriotic duty. Their fears elevated me to a most dangerous eminence, and they deliberated whether I should not be publicly tried for treason, and made an example of. . . . My social position was such that they did not dare follow out the suggestions of their first excited consultations in disposing of me; for in their own ranks I had many devoted friends, who openly expressed their admiration of the position I took under the circumstances of danger and difficulty which environed me.

Rose, who had always prided herself on her knowledge of law, was now familiarizing herself with the technical aspects of warfare. Jordan pushed her for precise data, and she left no stone unturned to supply him with what he wanted. She rounded up Winfield Scott's *Infantry Tactics*, Dennis Hart Mahan's *A Treatise on Field Fortifications* and James Allen Hardie's newly compiled journal on artillery operations. Rose was a student who had done much research for Robert. What would she not do for the Confederacy?

149

CHAPTER X

Spy Ring Broken

With the arrest of Rose a long skein of espionage operations came unraveled, and a series of arrests followed. She proved to be the binding knot in the system of communication, although Jordan kept his agents working in the dark about one another, and had little trust in any of them, even Rose. He quickly learned that the women spies worked poorly together when their paths chanced to cross. But he kept a tight personal grip on the group at all times, and in the early days of the war his espionage system was remarkably successful.

Jordan took particular pains with Mrs. Greenhow, who was at the very heart of his plans. Her great value lay in the fact that she had easy access to the persons who had military knowledge to divulge, and had the wit and knowledge to extract and apply it. Others could serve as conveyances, but Rose supplied the powder. Her house was soon the acknowledged headquarters for Confederate espionage in Washington.

She had exceptional opportunities through the diplomats for stirring up foreign sentiment on behalf of the South, and they often supplied her unwittingly with military items. She had the inner trail in army and navy affairs. She could summon men of authority to her parlors, then strip them of vital secrets. She was constantly primed on the conflicts that raged around Lincoln, and the confused strategy involving his generals and war maneuvers. She had always had entrée everywhere.

In short, Rose's connections were only slightly less potent than her own masterful personality. But she had one great drawback as a spy, and this must have worried Jordan. She believed so thoroughly in what she was doing that she scorned the need for discretion. The boldness and dash of her operations left her victims breathless.

Sometimes her daring backfired and she was betrayed. But much of her success was attained by open drive. When cornered she met a situation with pride and defiance. Had she been more discreet she might not have been caught so soon. Her arrest was a blow to Davis and Beauregard. She was less than five months in the open field after the outbreak of war although, by her own admission, she had been guilefully employed for years, preparing for the day of disunion.

She lived on a high peak of excitement during these few dedicated months, however. By the time all of her papers were assembled it was clear that she had wasted no time in getting to work after her interview with Jordan in April. On May 4, 1861, she supplied the detailed plan of organization for the increase of the Regular Army, issued by the War Department that same day.

Manassas was followed by a barrage of messages, some highly detailed, others cryptic. One dated July 31, read:

All is activity. McClellan is busy night and day, but the panic is great and the attack hourly expected. They believe that the attack will be simultaneous from Edward's Ferry and Baltimore. Every effort is being made to find out who gave the alarm. A troupe of cavalry will start from here this morning to Harper's Ferry. . . . Don't give time for reorganizing.

On the 5th, the 8th and the 9th of August Rose sent detailed information of a precise military nature, and assured her friends that notwithstanding orders and requests the newspapers "were chronicling the movements of troops correctly." On the 9th she reported that every approach to the capital was being strengthened and soon would offer powerful resistance at and above Chain Bridge.

All arrivals and departures had been noted by "eye witnesses placed at the out- and inlets for such purposes" and there would be an aggregate of ninety thousand men around the capital. Rose said that McClellan was vigilant and there was no boasting this time. She detailed railroad operations and indicated where masked batteries were located. It was quietly reported that many of the guns were rifles, and that great reliance would be placed thereafter on artillery and cavalry.

Two days later Rose came through with a precise account of the defenses and fortifications around Washington, later labeled in the National Archives as "Important Intelligence for the Rebels." It conveyed minute details. It was scientific and itemized the earthworks and their dimensions; the number of guns and their caliber; how they were mounted and where they were stationed. Her report, accompanied by maps, began in general terms:

The principle fortifications for the defense of Washington are in Arlington Heights and are of such a character that military men believe that five thousand men could hold them against ten times that number. . . . A most formidable array of field artillery is being brought into service, and upon its quantity, calibre, quality and efficacy the most sanguine hopes are founded. . . . From the neighborhood of Arlington House to that of Alexandria, there are now between thirty-five and forty Regiments, some of them in a state of demoralization and fears are entertained that they cannot be relied upon in emergency. Sickness and insubordination prevail more or less in all the regiments with perhaps twelve or fourteen exceptions. . . .

Here Rose launched into the technical military details. This happened to be the report that chilled the Cabinet with its exactitude.

Another dispatch supplied the Confederates with a list of McClellan's thirty-two "works" in the vicinity of Washington. The detectives had a difficult time piecing together the torn fragments of an undated dispatch, which conveyed such random items as:

152

There are 45,000 Va side. 15,000 around the city, to wit, up the river above Chain Bridge . . . across Anacostia Branch and commanding every approach to the city. . . . If McClellan can be permitted to prepare, he expects to surprise you, but now is preparing against one. . . . Look out for batteries wherever you go. . . . Their reliance this time is an abundance of artillery—which they have disposed formidably. . . . At proper time an effort will be made here to cut their telegraph wires and if possible to spike their guns wherever they are left unmanned. . . . A line of daily communication is now open through Alexandria. . . . Send couriers and afford other facilities en route.

As McClellan stiffened his resistance and drilled and disciplined his army, Rose followed him every step of the way. Technical reports of the utmost secrecy passed through her hands and reached headquarters at Richmond. The movement of troops and ordnance munitions was duly recorded. Artillery placements were accurately pinned down. The spirit of the men was appraised. The shortage of blankets was cited. Nothing escaped Rose.

A clue to the way in which she received some of her information was a note, unsigned, undated, but on officially stamped paper, written in ink and bearing the following message:

DEAR MRS. G.

I heard from a good source that a large force was to have been sent to Aquia Creek and under the protection of the vessel's guns land a large force and take possession. I send you this information as you may not have heard it. I think I heard Wednesday mentioned. Please make a note on't.

Yrs.

The form of the "secret conveyance" system maintained by Rose, showing how material was passed from hand to hand, is illustrated by a penciled note found in her fireplace:

Regt. Evansport Landing. Send to Col. W. B. Bates, camp near Evansport landing—ask him to send it to Chapmans by Mr. Ray of his Regt. Nat Chapman will deliver it to Dr. Wyvill who will bring it here so that I can get it.

There were other more intimate touches in Rose's papers, such as a letter in French addressed to *Mon Ami* and asking for some French novels to read, the love letters from H and Joe Lane, and also Lane's genealogy. But the documents found by Pinkerton's men, destined to repose in the National Archives in Washington, were scarcely redolent of lavender and old lace. They were tough, grim reminders of a war between brothers.

They included, besides words of love, a torn fragment of the famous cipher, a swatch of figured silk suggesting a pocket to which a message had been glued, old newspaper clippings, both American and English, dealing with the battle of Manassas, torn scraps of transparent paper bearing disconnected words and phrases, and defiant communications in Rose's own handwriting as clear as the day on which they were written. Through all the papers ran the firm impress of her own personality.

Her small maroon diary was eloquent in itself. On the flyleaf was the name of one of her agents, Frank Rennehan, of 408 20th Street. She had long lists of names and addresses—some of them belonging to well-known Washingtonians. She entered business and social friends as well as fellow agents. One was Cornelius Vanderbilt, listed for 5 Bowling Green, his office, and 10 Washington Place, his New York home. Colonel Turner Ashby, well on his way to fame along with Thomas (Stonewall) Jackson, was on her list. There were also a number of Mexican names.

Clearly, Jordan held the master key, and Rose was at the heart of his operations. Although he maintained that he used his early crude cipher for her alone, the same symbols turned up in different parts of the country, linking various agents to Beauregard's hierarchy of espionage. The ring functioned from Boston to New Orleans, with links touching London, Paris and Liverpool.

Before Pinkerton had finished, the involved pattern was unscrambled, and a curious collection of characters emerged—some well known, others obscure—a lawyer, a banker, a dentist, a professor,

154

cotton brokers, a maniac or opium smoker, soldiers, government clerks and a group of women endowed with worldly charm and good looks.

The diplomatic corps figured in her dossier too. Either implicated or named as suspects were William Preston, who had already fled on a warning from Rose; Richard K. Meade, a Virginian who had served as Minister to Brazil; and Charles J. Faulkner, Minister to France, who was taken into custody ahead of Rose. He was accused of getting arms from France for the South, and of having his sons distribute palmetto cockades in Paris.

Arrests came in a wave during August and September. James G. Berret, Mayor of Washington, was surprised to find himself a captive two days after Mrs. Greenhow's arrest. He was sent to Fort Lafayette, but soon was released after taking the oath of allegiance. Three weeks later the instigators of a plan to pass an act of secession in the Maryland Legislature were rounded up and taken to Fort McHenry. One of these was S. T. Wallis of Baltimore, to whom Rose had been expressing her views by letter a few weeks earlier.

But the first two men to fall into the net directly after her arrest were lesser figures who chanced to call at her house that night. They had not heard small Rose's warning cries from the tree top. Little dreaming that the Greenhow home had become a prison they walked right into the trap. Both maintained they were merely making social calls. The first, Frank Rennehan, who was listed in Rose's maroon notebook, managed to evade custody. The second, William J. Walker, a clerk in the Post Office Department, had a stiff time getting out of prison. Floods of letters on his behalf reached Seward before he was freed three months later after taking the oath of allegiance and promising not to live in Washington without permission from the Secretary of State.

Michael Thompson, a South Carolina lawyer, described by Pinkerton as a "man of subtle intellect, finished education, practical energy, polished manners and attractive address," was a bigger catch and his

155

arrest on December 21, 1861, led to several others. He lived on G Street. After he had been shadowed for a long time, so as to establish his connection with other members of the ring, his home was entered and among his papers was found the cipher used by Mrs. Greenhow in her correspondence with the rebels.

Suspicion first fell on Thompson through scraps of a note taken from Rose's fireplace and pasted together. It was from the same George Donellan who had conveyed two of her warnings before the battle of Bull Run. Dated July 20, 1861, it introduced Colonel Thompson as a "true South Carolina gentleman who would be happy to take from your hand any communication and obey your injunctions as to disposition of same with dispatch." Donellan asked for news of the military movements of the next few days, feeling sure there would be something worth sending.

The trail lead from Thompson to Lewis Linn McArthur, his confidential clerk, who was also a law student. McArthur was found to have a rebel flag in his trunk, and a new cipher worked out, which still had symbols recognizable as Rose's special code, with a little hocus-pocus thrown in to create confusion in case of interception.

Further evidence against these two men came to light with the seizure of papers from the schooner *Lucretia* on December 19 by the U.S. brig *Perry*, operating close to Alexandria. More than a dozen letters were from Thompson but were written by McArthur and were addressed to individuals in the rebel states. Some contained checks and all were said to be treasonable and to convey important military information. Eight, wrapped in a cloth envelope, were directed to William A. Maury, cotton broker of New Orleans.

These papers turned the spotlight on various members of Matthew Fontaine Maury's family who were already in trouble for espionage activities. The noted oceanographer, who had resigned his position with the National Observatory to become a commander in the Confederate States Navy, in charge of sea coast, harbor and river defenses, was closely related to the cotton brokers who now drew fire.

156

His cousins, Matthew Fontaine Maury, and Rutson Maury, Jr., were placed under arrest, and Rutson had no hesitation in saying that he had conveyed more than a thousand letters from the South, many of them addressed to Confederate agents abroad. Charles J. Ballard, of the Collector's Office in Cleveland, where Rutson was taken into custody, reported to Salmon Portland Chase that the "whole Maury tribe was as full of Secesh as an egg is of meat."

This caused much excitement because of the prominence of Commander Maury, internationally known for his scientific achievements. Today his birthday is a national holiday in Virginia. He is in the Hall of Fame. His geography books are known to past generations of children. He conducted research on ocean winds and currents, charted the ocean floor, and when the Atlantic cable was laid Cyrus W. Field said of him: "I am a man of few words; Maury furnished the brains, England gave the money, and I did the work."

Rose always remembered that Calhoun considered Maury a "man of great thoughts." He successfully mined the rivers and harbors for the Confederacy, used torpedoes against the enemy, and was largely responsible for the effective naval operations of the South in the early months of the war.

When the Commander's cousin Rutson was arrested as a spy it was instantly recalled that he had figured earlier in the year in the international row over papers addressed to Lord Russell, bearing the official British seal, which were taken from Robert Mure of Charleston as he boarded a ship in New York bound for Europe. Robert was the cousin of William Mure, British Consul in New Orleans, who claimed to have received the papers from Robert Bunch, the British Consul stationed at Charleston.

All this flared up into charges that the British Government was engaged in secret negotiation with the Confederacy. Rose considered the Mure incident a bungling move by the South. It quickly brought Seward, Charles Francis Adams and Lord Russell into a three-way correspondence on the role Robert Bunch had played in spreading

157

the impression that the first steps had been taken by Britain for recognition of the Confederacy. Lord Russell wrote flatly to Adams on September 9, 1861: "Her Majesty's Government have not recognized and are not prepared to recognize the so-called Confederate States as a separate and independent State."

Lord Russell had instructed Lord Lyons in Washington not to approach the Confederate officials even indirectly without advising Seward. And Seward had asked all his representatives abroad to adhere to the Treaty of Paris. But the Bunch correspondence had violated all the rules, and Seward was indignant over papers being sneaked out under the official British seal. He asked that Bunch be removed from office. Mure was arrested but soon was freed and the incident died down, leaving the strong impression, however, that the British consuls in the South were not preserving neutrality.

This feeling grew stronger when Rutson Maury and his brother Matthew, held as spies, turned at once to William Mure to help them. There was no denying that they had conveyed many letters under the official British seal, some dealing with the Maury plan to transfer cotton from the South to England for a nominal price. Their joint system of transmission of letters from one state to another involved a secret partition in a trunk.

Lord Lyons interfered in their behalf. But Seward tartly informed him on December 5, 1861, that much of their correspondence "showed premeditated violation of the blockade; second, the treasonable supply of insurgents with arms and munitions of war." Both men were released after a few months on the understanding that they were not to enter any insurrectionary state.

Meanwhile, Thompson was proving to be a stubborn customer. He refused to name any of his couriers or to take the oath of allegiance. Pinkerton was angered by this attitude and recommended that "as a military necessity M. Thompson be kept in close confinement until the conclusion of the war." The same fate was proposed for his associate, McArthur.

(Spy Ring Broken

The arrest of Thompson, or Colonel Empty, as he was known in the South, brought a major figure into the net, and one close to Rose. While the colonel was being shadowed his trail led to the home of William T. Smithson, a prominent banker living on F Street. Among the letters seized on the *Lucretia* were several signed by Charles R. Cables, the alias used by Smithson in the South.

Like Thompson, he was a cultured man, utterly dedicated to the Southern cause. In one of his notes he wrote:

> Expense falls heavily upon me in my present embarrassed condition. Everything I have after paying my debts is at the command of those you represent. If you should fail to succeed I don't wish to live any longer.

As the picture clarified it became evident that Rose and Smithson worked together on the upper levels of the spy ring. With Thompson they constituted the top stratum of brains. Rose and Smithson knew each other well. The evidence is strong that he was her chief medium of conveyance for messages after her arrest.

Smithson was not taken into custody until early in January, 1862, four months after she was imprisoned. During this period she effected some of her most important espionage operations. It later developed that Smithson was ingenious about getting information through the enemy lines. One of his plans that fizzled out in the autumn of 1861 involved a sister of charity from the Providence Hospital in Washington, who had promised to aid him in getting military information to the Confederate States. He rolled up the documents and stuffed them in a hollowed-out plug of tobacco. But Colonel B. B. Boone, who was to take them from the sister of charity, backed out rather than violate his parole.

In a note addressed to Secretary of War Judah P. Benjamin just before Christmas, 1861, Smithson reported that the Army of the Potomac would march between then and January 5. He commented on Colonel Thompson's arrest, "Letters found on the ducker; poor fellow." But his own turn was to come.

159

Powerful influences worked for Smithson while he was imprisoned in Fort Lafayette "as one of the most prominent and dangerous of rebel sympathizers in Washington." He was released after four months, having taken the oath of allegiance and pledging himself in no way to aid and abet the South. But the War Department had cause later to regret his release. By the spring of 1863 he was in custody again, charged with conducting illicit banking operations for the Confederacy, and with "promoting a treasonable correspondence with a well-known and influential rebel." This was Rose again, after she had been freed and had gone South.

Aaron Van Camp, a well-known Washington dentist, was involved through a letter addressed by Rose to Jordan on October 5. She informed him that she had failed to receive his last three dispatches, because they had been turned over to the Federal War Department by Samuel Applegate, a Union agent who had simulated Confederate sympathies. "The one sent by our other channel was destroyed by Van Camp," said Rose.

This chance mention of his name proved to be the dentist's undoing. He was arrested just before Christmas, charged with being a spy, and with having aided in the escape of Dr. J. C. Herndon, a deserter from the Federal Army who bore important information to the South sewn into his waistcoat. It developed that Van Camp's son was in the Confederate Army. When he was wounded at Bull Run, his father clandestinely passed through the lines and succeeded in having the youth appointed as an orderly to Beauregard.

In the letter implicating Van Camp, Rose wrote:

Our friends here all are ready to cooperate and carry out what I planned. I have signals, take care that the cipher does not fall into their hands. I destroyed it and every paper of consequence, but O my God, with what danger, with twenty detectives following every step.

McClellan is fast making the army efficient; it has been in a deplorable state. They look for an attack, and are greatly puzzled to know what is the plan. They make blunders every day. The appointment of the French

160

princes was one. Foreign ministers all sympathize with us. Spies are employed to every class, and more is spent in the secret service by Mc than ever before. Destroy the cipher; thousands are offered for it, and for weeks the most skillful detectives are at work on it. As yet nothing has been made of it.

Artillery is constant and severe, about sixty thousand troops are surrounding, including McDowell's command. They come in slowly and badly equipped. Meigs asks for private contributions of blankets. You are losing golden moments. Bitter feuds in sections of the party. I am sorry to see that Lincoln is going with the strongest party, that which opposes interfering with slavery. They speak of the mild and beneficent institution etc., etc. Think of me with guards at my chamber door, with bayonet; how long is this to last? Inclosed is a list of the forts, it is a work of the wise.

Did the first line: "Our friends here all are ready to cooperate and carry out what I planned" refer to the scheme by which guns were to be spiked, McClellan was to be taken prisoner, and communications were to be cut from within if the Confederates reached the capital? This was none too farfetched for Mrs. Greenhow.

The most baffling and eccentric of all the members of the spy ring was Parker H. French, alias Carlyle Murray, alias Charles Maxey. Strange voices spoke to Maxey. Apparitions entered his room. He would occasionally write "Specter Ghost" or "Phantom Apparition" in exquisite script on the back of his letters. His quarters were frequently "crowded with the souls of those that lived in other days." He had long and pleasant chats with them, and philosophized: "Great God, on what a slender thread eternal matters hang."

Maxey was variously thought to be a spiritualist, an opium eater or a maniac. The likeliest explanation is that opium was his trouble, since his letters show that he swung from visions to common sense. Everything about his career was veiled in mystery, but at times his correspondence was not only coherent but arresting. He had the backing of Andrew Johnson at one period, as well as a number of important businessmen in Boston, including Amos Laurence, who

161

believed him to be working for the Union. He tried to outfit a privateer at Boston under pretense of arming a vessel for the Union, and he pushed a certain type of propeller.

His letters to his lawyer, H. Ryland Warriner, of Philadelphia, strongly suggest that Maxey was doped, and that he was not talking deliberately in riddles, as some supposed. However, his path crossed Rose's, and he worked for one of her friends, James B. Holcombe, noted Virginian lawyer and educator who had been influential in swinging his state into the Confederacy, and was well known as a champion of states' rights.

Maxey rounded up special maps of the rebel states and other documents for Holcombe. He wrote cryptically of Spanish teachers, presumably meaning couriers, and of Treasury notes which apparently he was sending South. He was interested in the Knights of the Golden Circle, which had 197 "bivouacs" and 1,700 members in 27 states—or so he claimed—by the end of July, 1861.

He was three different men, playing three separate roles. As Maxey he worked for Holcombe. As Parker French he furthered the work of the Knights. As Carlyle Murray he was poet, dreamer and dealer in munitions for the rebels. He was arrested early in November at Branford, Connecticut, and was imprisoned in Fort Warren, but three months later he was freed on parole. No more was heard of the ghostly Maxey.

Pinkerton found his victims slipping away from him through the oath of allegiance almost as fast as he pulled them in. The policy toward them was lenient. When he saw signs of official softening toward Rose, as the authorities debated what to do with her, he moved in with a detailed and confidential report submitted to Provost-Marshal Porter three months after her arrest. It covered the entire field of Rose's operations and emphasized the magnitude of her influence. It gave her the importance she craved and was an effective answer to those who chose to dismiss her as a mere exhibitionist and meddler.

162

Pinkerton charged that she had secret and insidious agents all over Washington and scattered throughout the country. He cited the long list of names arranged alphabetically of persons on whom she could rely. He said she had alphabets, numbers, ciphers and various other ways of holding communication with traitors, known only to themselves.

Above all, said Pinkerton, she had used her "almost irresistible seductive powers" to get her effects. He described her home as a focal center where treason found a resting place and traitors were furnished with information through the "untiring energies of this very remarkable woman." According to Pinkerton:

She has made use of whoever and whatever she could as mediums to carry into effect her unholy purposes. . . . She has not used her powers in vain among the officers of the Army, not a few of whom she has robbed of patriotic hearts and transformed them into sympathizers with the enemies of the country which had made them all they were. . . .

For a great many years Mrs. Greenhow has been the instrument of the very men who now lead in the rebel councils and some of those who command their armies; who have successfully used her as a willing instrument in plotting the overthrow of the United States Government and which she, no less than they, had desired to accomplish; and since the commencement of this rebellion this woman with her uncommon social powers, her very extensive acquaintance among and her active association with the leading politicians of this nation, has possessed an almost superhuman power, all of which she has most wickedly used to destroy the Government. With her as with other traitors she has been most unscrupulous in the use of means. Nothing has been too sacred for her appropriation so as by its use she might hope to accomplish her treasonable ends.

Pinkerton charged that Mrs. Greenhow by common knowledge was openly engaged months before her arrest in giving aid, comfort, sympathy and information to the enemy. He found that she whipped up public defiance by influencing men and women to go around Washington saying they hoped the rebel forces would take possession

163

of the capital and hurl from power by force of arms "the legally chosen and duly constituted authorities of the people of the U.S."

Women agents were sent to the camps of generals, with letters written or collected at Mrs. Greenhow's home. They extended the "right hand of fellowship" to the rebel forces and invited them to come and take the nation's capital, promising them every aid they had power to render.

In Pinkerton's opinion the statistical facts obtained and circulated through Rose could only have been found in the national archives. From this he concluded that they came directly from government employees. He also drew attention to Rose's behavior since her arrest. She had continued to lay plans; to try to bribe members of her guard; to use the sign language at the windows of her house with friends in the street; and to send information to rebels in notes that took much time for the authorities to decipher.

She had been doing much of this under the eye of an officer who had her in charge, and whom she supposed to be her friend. He kept turning over her communications to the Provost-Marshal's office as fast as Rose completed them. Was this the man she considered her good and trusted ally—Lieutenant N. E. Sheldon, who headed the detail of the Sturges Rifles that had supplanted the detective police?

In any event, Pinkerton had gathered up all the loose strings of the espionage ring and woven them into a fixed pattern with Rose in the center of the web.

CHAPTER XI

Espionage Behind Bars

"My castle has become my prison," Rose wrote mournfully as she sat at the desk in her denuded library and surveyed the surrounding chaos. Her parlors had been stripped of their furniture. Soldiers occupied them instead of convivial guests. But she found her military guard preferable to the "detective police—those unkempt, unwashed wretches who had rolled themselves in her fine linen," taken the trinkets off Gertrude's dressing table as spoils, and "blasted every hallowed association of her home"—not to mention what they had done to Rose's prized correspondence.

They had not, however, hauled her off to the common jail. As a gesture to her prestige her home was turned into a temporary prison and other culprits were brought there. At first she was cooped up in the bedroom behind her library on the second floor, along with little Rose and Lizzy Fitzgerald. Her protests brought action on this. The child and her nurse were moved to a front bedroom, leaving the back room and library to Rose. She was not permitted to visit them in their quarters, however, for the windows fronted on the street and Rose seemed to have semaphoric powers of communication.

Her library became living room, schoolroom and sewing room. There Rose sat far into the night, reading, writing verse and laying plans. In the daytime she tutored her child, used her sewing machine, meditated, wrote and read. When messages still got out, even the

165

back windows were barred. Visitors were warned not to walk or drive past Greenhow Prison, as it soon was named.

While her masculine associates were sent to various military prisons, Rose was to meet those of her own sex, first in her home, then in Old Capitol Prison, to which she was eventually moved when her case became too hot to handle with any show of leniency.

The transformation of her home into a jail and the sudden parade of women prisoners seemed an outrage to Rose, although the first to arrive was not unwelcome. In happier days she might well have been an honored guest. Mrs. Philip Phillips was the well-known and clever wife of a Washington lawyer, formerly a Representative from Alabama. She was an open sympathizer with the South and had already aided Rose and Breckinridge in distributing comforts to Confederate prisoners. Her mother was Fanny Yates of Charleston; her father was Jacob Clavius Levy. Her sister Phoebe married Thomas Pember of Boston and later wrote a book about her hospital work in Richmond.

Like Rose, Mrs. Phillips had a bevy of attractive daughters— Fanny, Caroline and Emma. She entertained on a lavish scale and was a well-known figure in Washington society. Like Rose also, she was handsome and magnetic. Her hair curled crisply over her forehead. She had an indented chin, good features, and usually wore hoop earrings. She was known to be both sarcastic and kindhearted, and Mrs. Chesnut sniped playfully at her in her diary as a "mad, bad woman." She linked her with Joseph Holt and Stephen R. Mallory, Secretary of the Confederate Navy, and wrote that it annoyed her to have Mallory tell her so much about his flirtation with Mrs. Phillips, while it greatly amused her "to have him imitate Mr. Holt in love with her—like an old pelican slightly ill from eating too much fish . . . exquisite."

A few days after Rose's arrest the Phillips home was taken over. Mrs. Phillips' papers were ransacked. Then she, her sister and two of her daughters, Caroline and Fanny, were marched to Greenhow

166

Prison. Rose was as indignant for Mrs. Phillips as she was on her own account, although they could do no more than glance at each other in passing. They had no chance for communication.

But powerful influences were invoked at once on behalf of the lady from Alabama. Stanton, not yet Secretary of War, came hurrying in to make arrangements for her transportation south. Colonel Thomas Marshall Key, Judge Advocate and former aide-de-camp to General McClellan, arrived to see what could be done for Eugenia Phillips and her daughters.

They were all sent south with the utmost expedition and settled in New Orleans, where Mrs. Phillips again landed in trouble after the occupation. She was arrested for jeering from her balcony as the funeral cortege of a Federal soldier passed her home. She was also accused of teaching her children to spit at Northern officers. General Benjamin F. Butler, Military Governor of New Orleans, settled the matter by sending her to Ship Island, where she suffered considerably for her defiance. But first he asked her why she had laughed as the funeral passed.

"Because I was in a good humor," said Mrs. Phillips.

"If such women as you and Mrs. Greenhow are let loose, our lives are in jeopardy," General Butler retorted.

"We of the South hire butchers to kill our swine," Eugenia snapped.

Rose described Mrs. Phillips as a sufferer in the cause of righteousness—"the only circumstance against her really being that she was a Southern woman, and a lady, scorning association with the 'mudsills' whom the upheaving revolution had brought to the surface of society."

But Rose made no attempt to deny that Mrs. F. A. Hassler, the next arrival at Greenhow Prison, coming from the Charles Hotel, was one of her own couriers, assigned by Jordan. She was sorry for the fascinating but uneducated Bettie Hassler, who had blundered into a Federal trap through no fault of her own. It was actually from

167

her hands that Rose's dispatches first reached the War Department, but she was as ignorant of their purpose "as the mail boy of the contents of his bag." Applegate, scorned by Rose because he played the Confederate game in order to trap her, was the naïve Mrs. Hassler's betrayer.

The door between their rooms was heavily barred when Bettie was brought to 16th Street, and they were forbidden all communication. But Rose sent the faithful Lily Mackall next door to warn the new arrival that she must disclaim all knowledge of Mrs. Greenhow. She knew her captors were seeking evidence through Mrs. Hassler. But they did not get it. After two months of imprisonment Bettie took the oath of allegiance and was released, through the offices of a woman friend of Simon Cameron's.

Rose was relieved to see this prisoner go free. Her health was impaired by confinement and she "had paid dearly for a momentary impulse, her sympathy or connection with our cause being confined to the transmission of a few letters." Clearly Rose felt some qualms in this particular instance, and carefully differentiated between the casual and the professional agent.

The other women brought into Greenhow Prison outraged Rose, particularly Mrs. Medora A. Onderdonk, a habituée of the streets of Chicago. When she was assigned to Gertrude's room Rose exploded, and Lieutenant Sheldon hastily had Medora assigned to other quarters. She was supposed to have her meals with Rose, but since Rose would have preferred starvation to breaking bread with Mrs. Onderdonk, whom she felt sure was installed merely to spy on her, Sheldon again made concessions.

Rose was beginning to cast her spell over this young man, who had been McClellan's bodyguard during his campaign in Western Virginia. He was a handsome and good-natured officer, and for a time Rose's blandishments threatened to get him into trouble. However, he held his ground and treated her with consideration throughout her imprisonment. But he turned her notes over to the Provost-Marshal more often than she knew.

Rose's comment on Mrs. Onderdonk's proximity was sharp: "It might have been supposed that my former social position, and that which members of my immediate family still held in the Federal City, would have protected me from this attempt to degrade me."

Miss Ellie M. Poole, alias Stewart, was another irritant, since she took delight in checking up on the two Roses and reporting on their actions to the military guard. She had the run of the house and was a troublemaker. Her political errors were never well established. She was thought to have given information to rebel leaders in Kentucky. She was brought in from Wheeling, West Virginia, having escaped from prison there by sliding down a rope made with knotted sheets.

Other prisoners "of the lowest class" were brought in from time to time, but Rose took pleasure in associating with Mrs. Eleanor Lowe, an Englishwoman whose son was in the Confederate service, and with the Richard Posey family of Maryland "who were most estimable people." They were detained for a few days only, upon suspicion of signaling to the Confederate Army across the Potomac. The wave of a hand was thought to have meaning during this period of apprehension.

On October 29, 1861, Jordan wrote a revealing letter to Judah P. Benjamin from Centerville, acknowledging the receipt of a cipher note addressed to Rayford, his alternate name, and sent to him for scrutiny by the Confederate Secretary of War. The letter looked like a plant to him, although he conceded that Rose conceivably might have written it. He said that further correspondence with her, or use of the cipher, would be futile, now that she was imprisoned.

He expressed some contempt for the crudity of his own handiwork, feeling that an expert should have been able to decipher so simple a code. Yet the War Department in Washington had not yet succeeded in breaking it. He made note of the fact that a reward had been offered for the key to the cipher, and he cannily proposed to Benjamin that he supply it through a friend in Washington, who might then collect the money. It could be of no further use to anyone, he argued, adding that he had used it "with but the lady" and with her it "had served our purpose including the one great service of saving General Bonham from a disastrous surprise on the 17th of July."

In this same letter Jordan mentioned young Callan, clerk of the Senate Military Committee, as giving information on "the place of descent by the Annapolis Armada." He also revealed that "Cape Fear River, Smithville, were to be the real points of attack," a tip he had received from one "with capacity and wit to make a most efficient emissary."

"Circumstances have placed her *en rapport* with me lately," wrote Jordan, "and I expect a good deal of timely, acute observation of a useful character from her, but as I cannot be altogether sure of her faith all will be received with caution and nothing communicated to her, as was my course I may also say, with Mrs. Greenhow."

Jordan was referring to Mrs. Augusta Heath Morris, who was to provide a fresh sensation in the espionage revelations, moving in to take the place of imprisoned Rose. But would Rose have cared to know that Jordan had doubted her own good faith? Or that he had told some of his men associates that in his own case she had surrendered her pride to the thesis that all was fair in love and war? It is doubtful that Rose needed the added fillip of love to augment her already burning patriotism. But she had always enjoyed being courted.

After Jordan's letter reached Benjamin, Jefferson Davis directed Rose to give up her cipher. Apparently he did not know that she had already destroyed it, for reasons "vital to her and fraught with hazard to others actually engaged and still unsuspected." From then on she used a pseudonym, and wrote in riddles that baffled her

170

captors, for her operations continued almost uninterrupted from her guarded home.

She was annoyed to learn from the outside world that her friends as well as her foes were hacking away at her reputation. Her foes had the "infamy to circulate a report that, for a large sum, I had engaged to desert my cause and betray my party." She repudiated the idea of turning informer, saying she had cast her lot "as God and nature directed. Their whole bankrupt treasury could not tempt me to betray the meanest agent of our cause," Rose maintained.

Nor was she too pleased to hear that a party of Secessionist matrons, knitting at one of their homes in the South, had taken some pot shots at her and Eugenia Phillips.

"These poor souls are jealously guarded night and day. It is a hideous tale," said the ever-ready Mrs. Chesnut.

Mrs. Robert E. Lee could not resist a jest: "Think of ladies of their age being confined!"

"Some say Mrs. Greenhow had herself confined and persecuted so that we might trust her the more," Mrs. Chesnut added. "The Manassas men swear she was our good angel, but the Washington women say she was up for sale to the highest bidder, always—and they have the money on us."

By this time Rose had given eminence to the woman spy. False hair was removed and searched for papers. Pistols were sought for, with crinolines reversed. Bishops were suspect. The full tale of Rose's own methods has never been disclosed. In jail she made the broad acknowledgment that a "little bird" was her medium. But the "little bird" was known to lurk in hanks of wool, in an embroidered alphabet, in garbled notes, in signs, gestures and in whispered words through barred doors, in place of the intimate têtes-à-têtes, with wine and candlelight, that had gone before.

Ellie Poole brought up the suggestion that small Rose was the "little bird" who sometimes gave and received communications on

171

the sidewalk. There were others who shared this dark suspicion. But Rose always denied the charge with scorn and anger. However, it became a family legend that she sewed messages into the soles of little Rose's shoes.

In the early days of her imprisonment there was talk of sending Rose south, like most of her fellow prisoners, but nothing would induce her to take the oath of allegiance. Moreover, her continued defiance in jail hardened the authorities against her, and the success with which she continued to operate persuaded her captors that she was no "chatty Secessionist dame" but a skilled and authentic spy, requiring constant supervision. Because of her past relations with them she presented a knotty problem for Seward, Wilson, McClellan and other men of influence around Lincoln. None knew what she might do next, for she had the power to embarrass them, and no qualms about using her knowledge to put them in the wrong.

Rose indignantly rebuffed the suggestion that her house and furniture should be hired by her captors for use as an official prison. James Howard, a youth from the Provost-Marshal's office, conveyed this proposal to her. She told him to go back and tell his superior officer that they had already ruined, destroyed and stolen all that she valued, and that they might as well continue to hold it by the same lawless tenure, since she refused to be a party to her own robbery.

Howard, however, was captivated by Rose during this interview and on his return to his base he declared in front of General Ben Butler and Secretary of War Simon Cameron that his mortification over the part he was forced to play before this noble woman made him feel like ripping off his shoulder straps with shame. This, at least, was Rose's conception of what occurred.

General Butler, never laggardly in scoring a point, exclaimed: "If the Government will take my advice, and consign that haughty dame to my care at Fortress Monroe, I warrant to put her through an ordeal which will no longer endanger the loyalty of our officers."

It soon developed that young Howard was not without stain. In

172

the general unraveling of Rose's operations he too was called to account. A number of young officers who tried to help her during her imprisonment found themselves in hot water. It was not for nothing that Pinkerton had reported on Rose's "irresistible powers of seduction." A good many men of substance had felt their potency.

Rose's legal experience soon directed her thoughts to habeas corpus proceedings. Since no hostess in Washington had dined more notable lawyers and judges in her day, it seemed the natural thing to write to her old friend, Jeremiah S. Black, who had been Buchanan's Attorney General and later his Secretary of State, and to R. J. Walker, President Polk's Secretary of the Treasury, asking them to call on her. Both were eminent lawyers whom she had frequently summoned to her dinner table in happier days.

But now the japonicas and Madeira were absent. Her invitations were ignored and Rose reflected in bitterness of spirit: "Those grave legal gentlemen, influenced by prudential considerations, or sympathy with the inquisitorial hierarchy, gave no heed to my request, and I was thus left in the hands of an unscrupulous cunning enemy, with only my own judgment to guide me."

Both Stanton and Colonel Key called to see Rose when they visited Mrs. Phillips to speed her departure south. She knew Stanton well. He had always been close to Buchanan and he had flattered her in the days of her ascendancy. Their paths, too, had crossed through the Limantour proceedings. Rose considered Stanton a sycophant and a weakling, but a brilliant lawyer. He was not yet in the Cabinet, and Rose told him she wished to employ him as her counsel, to obtain a writ of habeas corpus for her. Her bitter comment at this point on Stanton's defection became part of her memoirs:

This he declined, accompanied by expressions of high appreciation and proffer of service in any other way—to which I of course attached no value. . . . This last effort convinced me that no Northern man had the courage or desire to attempt to stem the tide of Northern usurpation, which was destined to sweep like an avalanche over the land, destroying civil liberty,

173

and establishing in its stead an irresponsible military despotism. . . . I felt now that I was alone, and that the wall of separation from my friends was each hour growing more formidable.

Rose was disconcerting to friend as well as foe. When she heard that Senator William M. Gwin was a prisoner, but on parole, she made strenuous efforts to establish communication with him. She wished to give him verbally "some details which would have been useful to our Government, but which I did not dare write, as it would have compromised the safety of a friend whose position was one of prominence under the Yankee Government."

Rose's note to Senator Gwin reached him without interference, but he was far from pleased to receive it. She told him she could safely arrange an interview with him. He reacted with terror, and she laughed off the incident. He begged her "for God's sake not to attempt to communicate with him, for he was surrounded by the detective police." Out of the depths of her own experience Rose commented: "He had not learned that therein was his immunity to do seemingly impossible things."

Rose's disillusionment was now complete. She had known Gwin from the time of Jackson's administration. Like Robert, he was both a lawyer and physician. She had seen a great deal of him during her visits to California, and had always considered him genial, kind and clever. But she realized by this time that her friends were seeking cover. Mrs. Douglas had not come near her. The Cutts family had chilled off her completely. Nearly a century later a granddaughter of Mrs. James Madison Cutts was to recall that her grandmother had described her sister as a colorful woman, but had not approved of her.

Rose was indeed forsaken by kith and kin, for this was civil war.

When Mrs. Catherine Virginia Baxley arrived late in December, chaos developed at Greenhow Prison. She proved to be a screamer, moaner and whiner. Rose despised her, and commented: "She raved from early morn till late at night, in language more vehement than

174

delicate. I was an involuntary listener to her cries and imprecations, and pity and disgust were often strangely commingled. My chief care was to prevent my child from hearing much that was unfit for her ear."

Mrs. Baxley and Miss Poole alternately had fainting fits. The guard would appear, with fixed bayonets, and handsome young Sheldon would bring up the rear "with the judicial gravity of Sancho Panza, conspicuously flourishing a brandy bottle, that being the masculine panacea for all the ills of life."

Mrs. Baxley was caught at Baltimore on her way north from Richmond, with significant papers tucked inside the lining of her bonnet. She had talked too much on the truce boat and had boasted of having obtained from Jeff Davis a surgeon's commission in the Confederate Army for her intimate friend, Dr. Septimus Brown.

Mrs. Baxley insisted that she had a letter for Mrs. Greenhow, and that she had been instructed to communicate with her at her house on 16th Street. In proof of her veracity she flourished a handful of nuts which she said had come from Jefferson Davis' own dinner table. Rose was scornful of all this, and dismissed the allusions to herself as the vaporings of a "disordered imagination." But in this instance it seems likely that Jordan was moving his pawns without close intercommunication, a favorite trick of his. Like Rose, she received a fee for her services from the Confederate Government when finally they were sent south.

Mrs. Baxley was vehement, derisive, and refused to sleep under blankets bearing the U.S. stamp. In one of her many letters to Seward she insisted she had nothing but a few friendly letters in her bonnet, and was certainly not one to be trusted with state papers, because she was "nervous, impulsive and frank." Her trip to Richmond was merely a "quixotic expedition," chiefly to have a look at Jeff Davis. She suffered now for Dr. Brown. Why make him responsible for her folly, she demanded, when she learned of his arrest.

"I cannot to save my neck shriek 'Union,' " she wrote with candor

175

to Seward, "but I will go home and meddle no more with edged tools. You can fight hereafter without my aid or intervention. . . ."

However, Mrs. Baxley remained in custody, for word had come through from General William B. Franklin's headquarters at Alexandria that her operations were not minor. John L. Brown wrote on December 30, 1861: "This woman is the strongest kind of a Secessionist. She made her brags to me some five months ago that she had sent 200 guns to the Southern army."

Obviously Mrs. Baxley was less of a nonentity than Rose supposed. Her letters to Seward and Stanton bubbled with amusement over the "gullibility" of the people of the South as well as the North. General John H. Winder, the blunt, gray-haired soldier who was accused of issuing passports through the lines too freely, had waited on her in person in Richmond, thinking she had important papers, and had led her to Jeff Davis with much ceremony. "Ha!" jeered Mrs. Baxley in effect.

But in another and more realistic note to Seward she wrote: "I was angry and indignant at the treatment I experienced at the hands of the deputy marshal and his satellites and made boasts of what I had done and what I would do. They were but empty, idle boasts."

However, Mrs. Baxley proved to be a tartar, the most obstreperous of the women prisoners. Much as she despised her, Rose was to have her company to the last day of her imprisonment. Miss Poole took the oath of allegiance and went on her way rejoicing, with "fifty dollars in gold from the Yankee Government." Rose kept her distance from her fellow prisoners but wrote with pride: "Right under the eyes of my eighteen guards I received and answered dispatches from friends—amongst them the order from my President to give up my cipher, upon specific contingencies."

How did she do it? No one knew. Some weeks after her arrest the New York *Tribune* commented editorially:

The Female Express South has discontinued its regular trips, and not a few of its most useful employees have been caught in the act. Communication with Virginia is now attended with difficulties.

176

But the difficulties were merely a challenge to Rose. She devised fresh and ingenious ways of conveying information. It was at this stage that she was suddenly "seized with a taste for tapestry." The wool reached her through the Provost-Marshal's office, wound in balls, "with a memorandum by which I could always know the original arrangement of colors." She had devised a vocabulary of colors which, "though not a very prolific language, served her purpose."

After Mrs. Phillips and her daughters were freed from Greenhow Prison they had three days at their home in which to pack for departure. They were surprised when Rose, out walking with her guards, came up to one of their windows and threw in a ball of pink wool, saying: "Here is the yarn you left at my house." Rose went on her way laughing and chatting with her guard.

Four days later, although she was carefully searched at Fortress Monroe, Mrs. Phillips gave Jefferson Davis the ball of pink wool from Rose. Unwound, it contained a message for the Confederacy.

After abandoning her cipher Rose wrote letters that were mere jargon to the uninitiated, but had meaning for those who received them. She gave a great deal of time and thought to working out these elementary notes and was secretly amused when she heard that in the Provost-Marshal's office they could not understand how such a clever woman as Mrs. Greenhow could write such trash.

A favorite example of Rose's double talk ran as follows: "Tell Aunt Sally that I have some old shoes for the children, and I wish her to send some one down town to take them, and to let me know whether she has found any charitable person to help her to take care of them."

Interpreted, Rose was announcing that she had important information to send across the river, and wished for a messenger immediately. She was also asking if the recipient had any means of getting reliable information. She varied the form of these notes and was remarkably successful in communicating in this rather obvious way. The War Department had at last cracked her code, and both

McClellan and Pinkerton now knew how much information she had managed to convey to the Confederate forces.

Meanwhile, Lily Mackall worked with unflagging zeal on Rose's behalf. She talked to every Cabinet member in turn and finally reached President Lincoln. According to Rose: "He told her 'that she had too much of my teaching already—that I had done more to damage and bring his Government into disrepute, than all the rest of the darned rebels together; and by G–d she should never see me again, if he could help it.'"

Rose sent back a sarcastic message, which probably never reached him, saying that while he was busy reviling a woman prisoner she was making a new disguise for him to wear on his departure from Washington—a gibe bearing on the current gossip about his secretive arrival in the capital.

By the end of September Lily was barred from visiting Rose. She then made a final appeal to Provost-Marshal Porter, who dismissed her with the sharp reminder that she too should have been arrested with Mrs. Greenhow. She left him in tears and sent the prisoner by a "medium unsuspected" a full account of the interview. Rose never saw Lily again. The harassed girl fell ill with a severe cold and exhaustion, and within a week was close to death. She begged Rose to visit her and Rose wrote to Seward explaining that her friend was at death's door. He denied her the privilege but she interpreted his note as a tribute to her capacity in the espionage field:

The Provost-Marshal will please inform Mrs. Greenhow that, in consequence of her correspondence with the general commanding armies now besieging Washington, her request to visit the house of Mrs. Mackall cannot be complied with, as it would be an interference with military arrangements.

This time Seward had the last word and Rose was bitter. When Lily died many tears were shed for her in Greenhow Prison. Rose was now cut off from this sustaining outside contact and felt the full pressure of her isolation. She considered her immurement, without air or exercise, an attempt to reduce her rebellious nature to submission.

"The idea of the Yankees at first," she wrote, "was to hold me up conspicuously before the eyes of the public as a terrible example and a warning. In this they signally failed, for I became even amongst their own people an object of interest." She was flattered to read in the *New York Times* that "had Madame Greenhow been sent South immediately after her arrest, as we recommended, we should have heard no more of the heroic deeds of Secesh women which she has made the fashion."

CHAPTER XII

Seward Challenged

Rose addressed a sensational letter to Secretary of State Seward on November 17, 1861, challenging him "to imprison her soul, if he dared." It was smuggled out of Greenhow Prison and soon had wide publicity, to the embarrassment of Lincoln and his Cabinet, for in it she reviewed her arrest and treatment in stinging terms. Such handling of Mrs. Greenhow aroused the chivalrous instincts of a number of men who had known her.

Rose compared herself to Marie Antoinette who had a "paper torn from her bosom by lawless hands and had to change her linen within sight of her brutal captors." The invasion of her privacy, the rough handling, the general indecency, and drunken brawling that she charged were carried on in her home, all passed in review. She discussed every aspect of her case, from the seizure of her private letters to the aims of President Lincoln.

She cannily sent a copy of the letter to Jordan. It soon appeared in the Richmond Whig and was reprinted in the New York Herald. Later she insisted that she had never intended it for publication. But when she learned how angered the antislavery elements were at having the secrets of their prison laid bare, she became "perfectly satisfied of the superior wisdom of my friends in giving it publicity."

The letter proved to be a disastrous move for her well-being, since it turned the spotlight sharply in her direction. While it invoked some public sympathy and much interest it also brought heavier retribution. However, it was some satisfaction to Rose to lash out at the potent statesman whom she had liked, admired, and now despised. He might subject her to harsher, ruder treatment, she wrote, but he could not break her. She quoted Charlotte Corday: *"C'est le crime qui fait la honte, et non pas l'échafaud."*

She challenged Seward to find a line in her papers that she did not have a perfect right to send or receive. She pointed out that freedom of speech and opinion was the birthright of Americans, guaranteed by the constitution. She insisted that she had merely exercised her prerogative and had openly expressed her sentiments. To her the new regime was a military dictatorship. Rose wrote:

Read history, and you will find that the causes which bring about a revolution rarely predominate at its close, and no people have ever returned to the point from which they started. . . . Even should the Southern States be subdued, and forced back into the Union (which I regard as impossible with a full knowledge of their resources), a different form of government will be found needful to meet the new developments of national character. . . .

A blow has been struck by this total disregard of all civil rights against the present system of government far greater in its effects than the severance of the Southern States. The people have been taught to condemn the supremacy of the law, to which all have hitherto bowed, and to look to the military power for protection against its decrees. . . .

The "iron heel" of power may keep down, but it cannot crush out, the spirit of resistance in a people armed for the defence of their rights. . . . It is your boast that thirty-three bristling fortifications surround Washington. The fortifications of Paris did not protect Louis Philippe when his hour had come.

Rose pursued the matter at great length and considered her letter a masterly production. By the time it had gone into wide circulation she had some support for this belief. All Washington discussed it and Seward was furious.

181

The "refined ladies of President Lincoln's Court" were shocked by Rose's realistic writing. It was all right in a Christian age for a lady to suffer these outrages—only she must not proclaim them, Rose commented with sarcasm. The New York *Herald* called it a "pungent epistle" and commented editorially: "It is just such a philippic as one would expect, under the circumstances, from a spirited, dashing, active, and fearless politician of the South Carolina School of Secession malignants."

Her old friend, James Gordon Bennett, did not back her up in any way. Look at what she had been doing, he said in effect, adding: "Grant all the personal rights of freedom of speech and action which Mrs. Greenhow demands, in the midst of this great rebellion, and we may as well abolish our armies, and turn over the country to unrestrained ruffianism; for under this system of liberty we should all be at the mercy of ruffians and robbers."

Rose's Southern friends were indignant, and on December 6 Mrs. Chesnut made one of her crisp diary entries on the subject:

Last night I read the most bravely indelicate letter from Mrs. Greenhow. She wants us to know how her delicacy was shocked and outraged, and that could be done only by most plain-spoken revelations. For eight days she was kept in full sight of men, her rooms wide open, and sleepless sentinels watching by day and night. Soldiers, tramping by, looked in at her by way of amusement. Beautiful as she is, even at her time of life, few women like all the mysteries of their toilette laid bare to the public eye. She says she was worse used than Marie Antoinette when they snatched a letter from the poor Queen's bosom.

Although the publication of Rose's letter to Seward created a deeper chill in Greenhow Prison and led to more curbs being placed on her, it also brought her some visitors. Shortly before Christmas her sister, Mrs. James Madison Cutts, and her beloved niece, Mrs. Stephen A. Douglas, finally came to see her. She had smarted deeply under the disapproval and neglect of friends and relatives who were heavily committed to the Union cause. "No one suffered in this

182

respect more than myself," she commented, "for many members of my immediate family sided with the despot, and held high official position under him."

But this visit did not warm her heart. The interview was limited to fifteen minutes and General Rufus Ingalls, chief quartermaster of the Army of the Potomac, was an auditor. He earnestly recommended "graceful submission" to the government, and offered to mediate on her behalf with Seward. Rose sharply rejected this counsel and proffer of aid "as inconsistent with my own feelings and derogatory to my honor."

Addie sent her a cake for Christmas, and some presents for little Rose that delighted the neglected child. Lieutenant Sheldon, out of the kindness of his heart, permitted her to attend the Christmas parties of some of her young friends, accompanied by a guard. Her mother received other "tokens of respect and affection through less orthodox channels" and the day passed not too unpleasantly. Some items of valuable information came in with the Christmas fare, and a sensational newspaper story exploded to the effect that a cake loaded with Treasury notes, and a plan for escape and conveyance into Virginia, had been smuggled into jail for Mrs. Greenhow. The money presumably was to bribe her guards. The suggestion was made that she be removed to a more inviolable Bastille, away from sympathetic friends.

All this seemed so absurd to its victim that she laughed at the rumors, but her guard was doubled and surveillance tightened. Even a sprig of jessamine reaching her was closely examined, for she had baffled them all by her ingenuity. To add to the current excitement a fire in an adjoining stable was thought to be a "very daring attempt at rescue of the rebel prisoners." The guard appeared with bayonets, but the fire burned itself out.

Soon Rose was plagued by stories from the outside and clippings from Northern newspapers suggesting that she was losing her mind and might be sent to an asylum. Nothing that had happened shook

183

her like this. "My blood freezes even now," she wrote a year later, "when I recall my feelings at the reception of this communication, and I wonder that I had not gone mad."

The Surgeon-General of Pennsylvania Volunteers visited her at this time, with several witnesses, and Rose received them with "fear and hate in her heart," sure that they were there to appraise her sanity. But he told her that he merely wished to see a lady "who had become so celebrated in the eyes of the world." They discussed politics. Rose was not intimidated. She expressed her usual views, "although the frightful idea was ever present that this man had been probably sent for the purpose of dooming me to a madhouse." She jested with him lightly and defiantly. Finally he said to her:

"Do you never find your mind giving way under this close solitary confinement?"

"Do you see any indications of aberration of mind?" she countered.

According to Rose he replied: "Madam, you fill me with admiration and astonishment, not only by your cheerfulness, but from the wonderful knowledge you have of what is going on. I had never believed that any person could rise so superior to surrounding circumstances. For I know that the government has placed such an estimate upon your capacity, as to resort to measures of unusual harshness in your imprisonment."

Rose quipped back: "Well, Doctor, I defy their skill to thwart any purpose of mine; and so far from succumbing, I never felt my mind clearer or more capable of mischief against your government than at this moment."

The visit ended there, and Rose was never to know if the Surgeon-General, whose name she had forgotten by the time she came to write her memoirs, was her savior or not. But she heard no more of the madhouse. However, from then on she read aloud to herself so as not to lose the power of modulating the tones of her voice. And she studied and wrote verse far into the night, stoking the intellectual fires that sustained her in moments of stress.

184

This was followed by a visit from Colonel Thomas Marshall Key, who had already called on her. On this occasion he had a long and conciliatory talk with Rose. In the past she had always resented what she took to be his attempts at intimacy. He was slightly deaf and leaned close to her when he talked. Once when he took her hand "to find out whether she had ever done any work," Rose promptly withdrew it, saying that her head had labored more than her hands. "There was a certain *laissez-aller* about this officer very offensive to me," she commented.

But this time his manner was "respectful and earnest." He seemed anxious to serve her and told her he thought her imprisonment "impolitic." He said he had discussed her fate with members of the government and they were "greatly embarrassed to know what to do with her."

Obviously he, too, had come as an emissary.

"Oh yes," said Rose with spirit. "They dare not hang me; are afraid to release me; and would like to encourage me to escape, in order that they might catch me and spirit me away. . . ."

He sounded her out about terms. Her heart "beat wildly" over this "chance gleam of freedom." But something in his expression made her skeptical. Hope faded. Suspicion gripped her again. She threw back his challenge on terms.

"None, sir," she retorted. "I demand my unconditional release, indemnity for my losses, and restoration of my papers and effects."

Colonel Key then made it plain that strong influences were working against her and he doubted that he could do anything effective about her personal freedom, but he thought she should let him make the best terms he could.

"Freedom is sweet," Rose replied, "and, although I have suffered much, there are many things dearer to me, and I will not compromise a principle even though I am detained as a prisoner for the war—the sentence, I learn, already pronounced against me."

Colonel Key bowed, and mildly reminded her that greater hard-

185

ships might await her. He professed himself deeply interested in her plight and advised her to think things over. She said she would consider his proposals. He then suggested that if she changed her mind she should write to him care of the Provost-Marshal's office, since he could not call on her again lest he, too, "fall under suspicion of Southern sympathies."

Immediately after Christmas the "little bird" arrived with a disquieting message that Rose was to be removed to Fort Warren, a Northern stronghold, but that her friends were watching the house and would rescue her at a given signal. In no way dismayed, she smuggled two important messages out of her prison that same day, one involving the army, the other bearing on the navy.

The first was a warning that twelve hundred cavalry supported by four batteries of artillery would cross the river and get behind Manassas, cutting off railroad and other communication while an attack was made in front. "For God's sake, heed this," wrote Rose urgently. "It is positive. They are obliged to move or give up."

Then, switching to her own plight, she added with considerable confidence:

They find me a hard bargain and I shall be, I think, released in a few days without condition but to go South. A confidential member of McClellan's staff came to see me and tell me that my case should form an exception and I only want to gain time. All my plans are nearly completed.

This message in code was found among the Confederate papers when Richmond was evacuated. Rose's information on navy movements was of vital importance at the time. She had been following fleet maneuvers with the closest attention. She had learned in advance of Samuel F. du Pont's expedition from Fortress Monroe late in October with seventy-seven vessels and land forces commanded by General Thomas W. Sherman. According to Rose, Seward had let slip information on this to one of his diplomatic friends during the after-dinner hour.

Now she was primed with specific information that General Ambrose E. Burnside would lead a naval expedition from Fortress Monroe for Albemarle Sound, North Carolina, early in January. Such were her resources that apparently she was able to cross-check the report, for she wrote: "Being satisfied by other means of the accuracy of the intelligence, I lost no time in preparing one of these peculiar *square despatches* . . . and with a prayer to almighty God for its safe delivery, committed it to my faithful bird, and sent it across the waters to General Beauregard."

Her courier on this occasion met with fantastic adventures, taking refuge for a time "in the dovecot of the enemy." Nevertheless, this important information got through. As a result of it Jordan, mentioning the dispatch from "our friend, Mrs. Greenhow," forwarded a day earlier, was able to write authoritatively to General Beauregard on December 28, 1861:

Today I have it in my power to say that Kelley is to advance on Winchester. Stone and Banks are to cross and go to Leesburg. Burnside's fleet is to engage the batteries on the Potomac and McClellan and Co. will move on Centerville and Manassas. . . .

This information comes from one of McClellan's aides and from Fox of the Navy Department. As I remarked yesterday be prepared for them on every hand and at every moment. . . . Now, my dear General, look out for a large army, and tell your men (God bless them) to cut and slay until the last man is destroyed. Do not allow one to come back to tell the sad tale. No living man ever made such a desperate effort as McClellan will make. Nevertheless I believe he is a coward and is afraid to meet you. If some excuse is not hatched up you may certainly expect an attack next week. My God! General, give them the most awful whipping that any army ever received. McClellan's army will certainly number 180,000 or 185,000 men—perhaps more. Let our next greeting be in Washington. You shall have a warm reception. I write in some haste.

The Stone referred to by Jordan was General Charles Pomeroy Stone, construction engineer who later planned the foundations of

187

the Statue of Liberty. Banks was General Nathaniel P. Banks, and Kelley was Colonel B. F. Kelley. Fox was taken to be Assistant Secretary of the Navy Gustavus V. Fox, the corpulent, bearded and able assistant to Gideon Welles. The McClellan aide was assumed to be Colonel Thomas Marshall Key, who had visited Rose on December 20 with talk of conciliation. The probity of Fox and Key was never questioned. Rose's methods were such that her victims rarely knew they were being pumped.

No sooner had she successfully transmitted these items of information than she wrote again to Seward, who was in deep trouble over Simon Cameron, whom he had backed through heavy scandals involving war contracts. Her second letter, by a "fatality which it would not be safe to explain," did not reach him directly, although he soon was aware of its contents. At this time the detectives were hot on Smithson's trail.

Rose's second letter was even more definitive than the first. She chided her old friend for bad manners in ignoring her earlier communication. She charged that although it was intended as a "grave appeal to his humanity against gross outrages" he had permitted it to become a matter of vulgar comment among his subordinates in their "drunken orgies in bar-rooms and hotels." Rose made it clear that in her opinion Seward was a cad.

Her first letter had received such wide publicity that she decided to make the most of this medium and state her political credo in her second epistle. She had found a good platform, from which she now reviewed the rise of secession, and defined the forces symbolized in the controversy by Exeter Hall in England and Faneuil Hall in Boston. She showed what the clergy had done, drew in Harriet Beecher Stowe by implication, and attacked all the forces that had backed the anti-slavery cause.

Rose reminded Seward of the criticism he had suffered personally over John Brown's raid. With many flourishes she gave her views on the election of Lincoln, the Peace Congress and the attack on

188

Fort Sumter, which "was planned to force upon South Carolina the initiatory step of resistance." Rose wound up with a burst of patriotic fervor:

You cannot conquer us, Sir. . . . If our men fall in the defence of our rights and our firesides our women will take their places, and die with their natural protectors. . . . Although we may yet wade through oceans of blood, we will achieve our independence, or leave our whole Southern land one howling wilderness, and a monument to all future time of the crimes of your party. . . . Oh, Sir, let this terrible lesson suffice. Give us peace . . . and the crimes you have already committed may be forgotten, and I could find it in my heart to forgive the evils you have inflicted upon me.

Rose had shot her bolt this time. Her guards had chilled after the first Seward letter. A blackout followed this one. She was completely isolated. Even Lieutenant Sheldon no longer smiled. Pinkerton men arrived to search for a copy of the second Seward letter, but she had sent it out with the original. She heard them rummaging downstairs and quickly destroyed all papers in her library that she feared might fall under scrutiny. Rose was still a discursive correspondent. It was second nature for her to write letters.

She noticed that Sheldon looked "pale as marble" when he appeared with Pinkerton at his heels. She was taken downstairs while her quarters were searched. The north window of the library was sealed and nailed up. Her journal and every scrap of paper were taken from her desk and table. Some of her clothing was removed, for Rose did clever tricks with secret pockets.

When she begged for pen, ink, paper and newspapers, all of which had been denied her, Colonel Key sent her a single sheet of paper, with pen and ink. She wrote at once saying that she was ready to discuss conciliation with him. He visited her but this time he was embarrassed and ill at ease. The situation had deteriorated since the second Seward letter had been read. Colonel Key told her regretfully that he had lost the power to serve her. Her letters had "aroused great

189

indignation" against her, and he doubted that there was any hope of release.

Rose turned on him with scorn, saying that she had not taken his conciliatory suggestions seriously in the first place. Muttering about the power arrayed against her, the Colonel left to consult "parties whom he would not name." He returned two hours later and told her that because of the "dangerous extent of the knowledge she possessed, it was deemed inexpedient to release her."

Colonel Key refused to tell Rose who had cracked the whip, but she had no doubt that Seward and McClellan were the culprits, "instigated by the detective Allen," who had already recommended with considerable earnestness that she be kept in custody for the duration of the war. All soft measures were now ruled out. The stream of communication to Richmond had not been stemmed. Rose had sustained it for five months in spite of guards and constant supervision. It was now decreed that she should be transferred to the tighter vigilance and greater austerity of Old Capitol Prison.

On January 18, 1862, she was sitting in her library with her child at her feet, "playing with her dolls and prattling and beguiling me almost to forgetfulness of the wickedness and persecutions which beset me," when word reached her that she was to be moved that same day. No inkling had reached her of what lay in store for her, and she barely had time to collect a few belongings when the summons came.

Her guard was drawn up in front of her home to watch her go. Some of the men had been kind, and Rose acknowledged this as she left. "I trust that your next duty will be a more honorable one than that of guarding helpless women and children," she told them proudly.

She looked up at the familiar windows of her home and saw them crowded with men. Having been a celebrity for so long she recognized the newspapermen among them. She turned to Lieutenant Sheldon and thanked him for the kindness and courtesy he had shown her— even at the risk of embarrassment to himself. He helped her up to the

190

end. He rescued "some cherished memorials from the general wreck of her effects." He spared her the humiliation of being driven to prison in a covered wagon, accompanied by a file of soldiers. As befitted a lady, she rode in a carriage. Little Rose threw her arms around Sheldon's neck as she said good-by. Reporters took note, and her mother later deplored this impulsive act.

The press swarmed through the house as they drove off. For the next few days the public had a close-up view of the Greenhow menage, from Gertrude's portrait to the two bottles of fluid that Rose had mischievously left on her sewing machine. It was instantly deduced that they contained sympathetic ink for code messages, but she had deliberately left the bottles to distract attention from her "real means of communication." The bedevilment of her captors was one of the few diversions now left to Rose, and she made the most of it.

CHAPTER XIII

Old Capitol Prison

L IFE reached its lowest ebb for Rose during the dark days she passed in Old Capitol Prison. Here she had once been a rare young beauty, hurrying down the broad staircase to join Cave Johnson for an evening of dancing and romance. Here the chivalrous Robert Greenhow had wooed her. Here she had sat on a hassock at John C. Calhoun's feet, absorbing the political faith that by devious channels had brought her back a prisoner.

Darkness had fallen on Mrs. Hill's old boardinghouse when Rose drove up, but the familiar hulk of the Capitol, dimly pricked with lights, was discernible through the shadows. She had traveled far since her days of hurrying up the hill, an eager girl in a princess gown, intent on hearing Clay or Calhoun orate. Now she was back as a political prisoner, and was face to face with Superintendent Wood, who struck her at once as being "fully sensible of the honor of being the custodian of so *noted a rebel.*" She was indeed the major catch up to that time, and Wood had been warned that Mrs. Greenhow was hard to handle. However, he had little idea how much they were to wrangle. Neither one was ever to surrender ground to the other.

Little Rose walked in out of the cold with a perky air, tipped her crinoline, and announced to the surprised Mr. Wood: "You have got one of the hardest little rebels here that you ever saw." He was soon to know it well. The eight-year-old was becoming shrill and defiant from the unnatural life she was leading.

"If you get along with me as well as with Lieutenant Sheldon, you will have no trouble," he assured her.

Rose gently reproved her daughter as they walked indoors: "You must be careful what you say here," she cautioned the child.

They were ushered into the bare "search room" on the ground floor. Officers crowded at once around Rose and stared. But there was a long wait. She seated herself on a wooden kitchen chair and a strong tide of remembrance flowed over Rose, as she realized that this was the room in which Calhoun had lodged and died. Forgetting all else, she thought of the past. Back came the words he had whispered shortly before his death: "*I have lived in advance of my time, but you in your generation will witness the fulfillment of my prophecy.*"

"And now," wrote Rose, "scarcely a decade has passed and his prophetic warnings have been realized; and Abraham Lincoln has brought about the fulfillment of his prophecy, and written in words of blood upon the tablets of history that the 'Great Model Republic' is a failure."

Rose recalled the measures that Calhoun had advocated. In her own words:

In the room in which I now sat waiting to be conducted to my cell, I had listened to the words of prophetic wisdom from the mouth of the dying patriot. He had said that our present form of Government would prove a failure; that the tendency had always been towards the centralization of power in the hands of the general government; that the conservative element was that of States' rights; that he had ever advocated it, as the only means of preserving the Government according to the Constitution; that it was a gross slander to have limited his advocacy of those principles to the narrow bounds of his own state; that he had battled for the rights of Massachusetts as well as for those of South Carolina; and that, whenever it came to pass, that an irresponsible majority would override this

193

conservative element, that moment would the Union be virtually destroyed. That our system was not susceptible of long duration; that no government could stand the shock of revolution every four years, and that as our population increased the danger became more imminent; that upon this principle he had opposed the war with Mexico and the proposition for the purchase of Cuba, as all acquisition of territory was likely to bring about the agitation of the slavery question, and arouse the fanaticism of the North, which was destined, at no distant day, to set aside the constitutional restraints which now held them but feebly in check, and eventually bring about a revolution.

Rose at last was led up the familiar staircase, and entered a room in the brick extension to the rear. By her own admission, she had already gone through so many trials that her transfer to Old Capitol Prison was merely the "crowning act of villainy that could only elicit a smile of scorn." The room, facing on the prison yard, was ten feet by twelve, and she was sure was chosen so that she could not see or be seen.

She looked with disgust at the furnishings—the straw bed which was to be a couch of thorns for little Rose; unwashed cotton sheets; a small feather pillow, dingy and dirty enough "to have been on the Mayflower"; a few wooden chairs; a wooden table and a looking glass, six by eight inches, in which Rose could barely survey her distinguished features, or see to arrange her sleek black hair.

Thanks to Lieutenant Sheldon, her desk, sewing machine, some books and writing materials were added in course of time. The room was luxurious compared with the shakedown arrangements, triple-tiered bunks, and general mess of stools, tables, food, pots, pans and valises that most of the political prisoners had.

The two Roses were confined at first to their room, and every effort was made to keep Mrs. Greenhow away from the windows. The day after she arrived they were boarded over with wooden slats. Wood protested the bars, but General Porter insisted, saying: "Oh, Wood, she will fool you out of your eyes." Her magic propensities had already been proved. She could talk with her fingers, the wave of a handkerchief, a stray gesture in the air.

By daylight Rose took stock of the disintegration that had taken place in her aunt's once trim boarding house. The walls were decayed. Large rooms were partitioned off into cells. Doors and stairways creaked. A tall wooden fence enclosed the yard. The trees still stood. Nothing else was familiar, except the shape and general position of the rooms, which she readily identified from the past.

Rose busied herself with her pen at once, but her letters all were subjected to a chemical process "to extract the treason." This amused her. But she now deplored the "notoriety which these dastards force upon me." Her doings had been in the newspapers off and on for five months. If she had found it exhilarating at first to be a celebrity, this attention had now become menacing. Rose was tired of newsprint; of people who stared; of being always on parade and at war with her surroundings. She was a nervous and tired woman when she reached Old Capitol Prison. She had the uneasy consciousness that every word she uttered "would appear with exaggeration in the newspapers and even my child of eight years is deemed of importance enough to have her childish speeches recorded."

As the weeks passed she watched little Rose with growing anxiety. Fearful that her spirit would wilt in jail, she exhorted her: "My little darling, you must show yourself superior to these Yankees, and not pine."

"O Mamma, never fear," said the child. "I hate them too much. I intend to dance and sing that 'Jeff Davis is coming,' just to scarce them."

But Rose felt that the manner of her reception, the newspaper stories that followed and the gaping crowds, all conspired to make a spectacle of her and her child. Soon large parties were arriving with sightseeing passes, chiefly to stare through her ever open door. Sometimes she was amused; at other times annoyed. She liked it when an editor from Rochester compared her with Madame de Sévigné and

195

said she was detained on account of her talent as a writer. She was dismayed when a smartly dressed woman made inroads on a cake that had been sent to little Rose. And she was thoroughly aroused when a Bostonian made "quite a furious onslaught" on her, and told her that love of notoriety was her motive in behaving as she did. This visitor became excited and rushed at Rose with violent words.

After this she asked Wood to debar these sight-seers from her room. "The fishwomen of Paris in the French Revolution were before my mind," wrote Rose, "and I feared that the next party might come armed with sticks or knives."

Wood told her that some of the visitors were willing to pay him ten dollars just to pass her open door and obtain a view of the "indomitable rebel." Rose flattered herself that this was being "damned to immortality."

The prisoners were a mixed lot—smugglers, soldiers, blockade runners, rebel mail carriers, felons and prisoners of state. The section where the Greenhows were confined was devoted largely to Negroes. New ones were brought in daily, and Rose found the "tramping and screaming of the children overhead most dreadful." The prison yard was filled with them. The air was rank and pestiferous, said Rose, and the sights which met her eyes were "too revolting to be described."

Negroes were drilled beneath her window. The sexes were huddled together. They danced, jigged, sang, played cards, made love and squabbled. Little Rose, who was allowed to go down in the yard for brief periods, would often come up crying "from the effects of the brutality and indecency to which she was exposed." Technically the child was not a prisoner, but since her mother elected to have her with her in jail, she was subject to all the rules and regulations.

Rose protested against "these infamies" and threatened to ask for a Senate investigation. She sent out a stream of letters complaining about conditions in the jail. She maddened her guards and flouted regulations. She scorned to take exercise in the yard because of the

196

rabble. She filled Wood with despair. She got Brigade-Surgeon W. D. Stewart, the attending physician, into serious trouble. Their warfare reached classic proportions.

Rose considered him a "vulgar, uneducated man bedizened with enough gold lace for three field marshals." He visited her first in Greenhow Prison to make a "daily inspection of her sanitary condition." This was an unimaginable horror to the delicately nurtured Mrs. Greenhow. He further excited her scorn by writing a prescription for Lily Mackall in English, thereby leaving Rose convinced that he knew no Latin. He also misspelled Brigade-Surgeon. Thereafter she called him the Brigand-Sergeant. By this time she had persuaded herself that he was an illiterate, as well as a villain who invaded her room day after day, so that he could boast he had talked to the rebel Greenhow.

But Dr. Stewart was not easily discouraged. He returned, calling himself Materia Medica, after learning that Rose considered him an ignoramus. She told him flatly to discontinue his visits. Next day he was back, and entered her room without knocking. Rose sent for her friend, Lieutenant Sheldon, who used his authority to end the daily sanitary inspections. But she was again thrown into Dr. Stewart's hands at Old Capitol Prison. When little Rose fell ill her mother asked the Provost-Marshal for her family physician. Dr. Stewart appeared again, walking in unannounced before she was out of bed. She would have none of him, "preferring to trust her child's life to the care of the good Providence which had so often befriended her."

But as the weeks passed Rose became seriously alarmed about her child. Day by day she saw her bloom fade. Her "round chubby face radiant with health, had become pale as marble, the pupils of her eyes were unnaturally dilated, then finally a slow nervous fever seized upon her." Rose had camp measles and again Dr. Stewart appeared.

Mrs. Greenhow ordered him out of the room. Then, as she describes it:

197

He arose also, foaming with rage, and stood confronting me—almost a giant in size—and said, "I will not quit your room; I am here by order of Brigadier-General Porter."

"Sir, I command you to go out; if you do not, I will summon the officer of the guard and the Superintendent to put you out."

With that he attempted to lay hands upon my child. I interposed my own person and said, "At your peril but touch my child. You are a coward and no gentleman, thus to insult a woman."

"I will not go out of your room, madam," he said, this time livid and trembling with rage or fear, I don't know which.

At this point Rose swept majestically across the room to summon help. She was slowed up involuntarily, however, while she waited for her knock on the door to be answered. The room was always locked and bolted when anyone came in. Rose summoned the officer of the guard. Finally a young Ohio lieutenant named Carleton appeared, a youth whom Rose had already intimidated. Since Dr. Stewart was his superior officer, he looked helplessly from one to the other, then chose the lesser of two evils and obeyed Rose's imperious order.

The doctor was told to go. Rose's conception of his departure was that he "slunk" out of sight. As he disappeared she burst into uncontrollable laughter, finding the situation farcical—"a display of valour against a sick child and careworn woman prisoner." She followed this up with a sizzling letter to the Provost-Marshal that led to a reproof for Dr. Stewart.

After this she was visited by the physician she wanted—Dr. C. McMillan, brother of Major James McMillan, a member of her guard and "one of the kindest and most chivalrous souls to cross her path during her imprisonment." Rose considered Dr. McMillan a gentleman and a man of science. She had faith in his professional skill. He ordered more nutritious and palatable food for both Roses, as well as fresh air and exercise. But after his first visit he was not permitted to see Mrs. Greenhow again, except in the presence of a

198

witness. Conversation was limited to medical inquiry and prescription. In commenting on this, Rose made the revealing comment: "An idiosyncrasy common to the Abolition dynasty, was that I exercised some spell over all who approached me, whose natures were not brutalized." Rose inevitably proselytized for the South when a man of intelligence came near her.

By this time she felt ill herself and was in need of medical care. Her health had been undermined by poor food, frustration and confinement. Her magnificent eyes stared forth from deeply sunken sockets. Her cheeks and throat showed hollows. She was constantly ill and the victim of lassitude. She could not sleep. She had nothing to read, papers reaching her only intermittently through the caprice of her jailers. Rose was bored beyond description.

To spice the deadly hours she sewed a Confederate flag on her machine and waved it from the window. From time to time she livened things up by pointing her pistol at a guard's head. This weapon had been taken away from her at Greenhow Prison. It was returned to her at the Old Capitol but without ammunition. However, Rose soon amended this.

Her most uproarious coup was achieved in the yard early one spring morning when Superintendent Wood's produce cart was driven in by one of her friends named Charlie. Seeing Rose taking an airing he asked her if she would like a ride.

Rose leaped in beside him with the greatest agility, followed by the other women prisoners in one of the few gestures of co-operation shown by these sisters in suffering.

"I'm off for Dixie!" Rose exclaimed in her rich, carrying voice.

Charlie cracked the whip and off went the cart, round and round the yard to this dangerous refrain.

Panic and confusion followed, greatly relished by Rose. Prisoners rushed to the windows. Many applauded. There were laughs and shouts. Those in the yard jigged around in excitement. Captain Gilbert, one of her most despised guards, yelled: "Stop that vehicle!"

199

But the horse was excited and so was Charlie. Rose's little drama became opéra bouffe.

A guard was quickly posted all around the yard and Rose felt sure they were getting ready to fire at her prancing equipage. Charlie circled the enclosure three times, then drew up in front of the enraged captain, "who verily believed that an escape had been meditated, and that his timely intervention had alone frustrated it."

Such antics as these were balm to Rose's jangled nerves. She was letting off steam. Some weeks later she created further excitement by lighting a candle near her window when she received news of a Southern victory.

"Put out that light," a guard yelled to her from below.

Rose paid no attention, but lighted another. Then came a chorus of voices: "Damn you, we will fire into your room."

Excited now, she collected all the ends of candles she could find and set up a real illumination to celebrate victory. But soon she heard the "rattle of arms, the clatter of feet, and furious rapping at her door." The soldiery had arrived. By this time Rose had received permission to bolt her door, and she declined now to open it.

"You are making signals and must remove your lights from the window," she was told.

"But it suits my convenience to keep them there."

"We will break open your door if you don't open it."

"You will act as you see fit but it will be at your peril."

None knew at the time that Rose's pistol was loaded. The guard was doubled around the prison. Later she explained to the chief officer that she had lit the first candle merely to find something in her trunk, and that the whole proceeding was absurd, having grown out of nothing. But such incidents were characteristic of her reckless mood. Her pistol was again taken away from her.

At this time she sought the return of her papers, which had been seized months earlier. She sent Wood one of her wordy and formal epistles requesting this favor. He told her bluntly that if she would only be kind enough to dispense with the "God and Liberty style of pronunciamento," and give him plain power of attorney he would do what he could for her.

Rose lashed back with swift repudiation. She considered Wood an infidel and so implied in her answer:

To make reference to God, or Liberty either, behind the bars of this prison, to its admirable *administrator*, would be—knowing *your peculiar views*—in as bad taste as writing in a dead language. As to my papers, they may even remain where they are until I shake off the chains of tyranny.

Rose and Wood warred constantly, yet there was a modicum of grudging respect on both sides. She found him "vindictive, cunning, and ambitious, a man who repelled with warmth any claim to being considered a gentleman, and yet, strange to say, was by no means devoid of some generous inspirations." He was a Virginian and his wife came from Maryland. Tom Paine was his mentor, Rose declared, adding with a grand and irrelevant flourish the thought that "William P. Wood, Abraham Lincoln, and the Emperor of Russia were the most irresponsible absolute despots on earth."

She finally forbade him to address himself to her at all, but as her loneliness deepened she regretted cutting herself off from this excitement, for the "chattering of a monkey would even break pleasantly on the monotony of my life."

She was in deep disgrace by this time for having involved herself in a plot for the escape of Harry Stewart, a fellow prisoner. He was shot by the guard he had bribed to help him, and Rose's evidence was taken. When asked if she would aid a prisoner in an attempt to escape, she readily said she would. "I considered it a point of honor to render any aid in money or otherwise," she commented.

Unhappily, Rose's second sister, Mrs. C. Leonard, was drawn into this. She was arrested and detained for several days when Mrs. Augusta Heath Morris disclosed that she had given Rose the money used by Stewart to bribe his guard.

"I saw my sister but once afterwards," commented Rose, "when she left the city as no longer a safe place for her."

After this incident none of her friends was permitted to visit her, and since she would not associate with the other women prisoners, she was in absolute solitude, an unhappy plight for the eloquent and gregarious Rose. She found it difficult to concentrate on anything but the "unutterable weariness of her lot."

"I try to fix my mind upon the heroic deeds of my countrymen," she wrote, now in great agony of spirit and desolation, "for in them indeed is my trust, my only hope."

Many years later little Rose was to recall some of the horror of these days:

I do not remember very much about our imprisonment except that I used to cry myself to sleep from hunger. . . . There was a tiny closet in our room in which mother contrived to loosen a plank that she would lift up, and the prisoners of war underneath would catch hold of my legs and lower me into their room; they were allowed to receive fruit, etc. from the outside, and generously shared with me, also they would give mother news of the outside world.

The prisoner who tattled on Rose when the Harry Stewart incident came to light was another siren of no mean accomplishment. The two women conducted a running feud. Both were adept at handling men, but Rose used her head, and had a proud and direct approach, whereas Augusta Morris had caressing ways, an amiable nature and the capacity to wring tears from strong men with her piteous tales of abuse. Thanks to the softness of her nature, she fared much better than Rose, but was just as stubborn underneath.

When imprisoned by order of McClellan, Mrs. Morris, daughter of an Alexandria baker, was billed as a second Mrs. Greenhow, involved in espionage activities with Jordan, Smithson and other members of the Confederate spy ring. She had been living in style at Brown's Hotel, having moved there from the Ebbitt House under the auspices of a Quaker named Elias M. Green. Her calling list was one of distinction. She had even tried her wiles on General W. L. Marcy, McClellan's father-in-law.

Among those who visited Augusta were Captain Frederick Buck-lock, J. S. Rollins, Edward and Lovejoy Loring, George A. Hanson, E. W. Belt, Mansfield T. Walworth, Lily Mackall and Rayford, who of course was Colonel Jordan. None but Miss Mackall, Walworth and Rayford figured in any way in the espionage operations, but all were names well known in Washington at that time.

Augusta claimed to be the wife of Dr. John Francis Mason, of the Confederate forces, and produced evidence of a marriage in Paris in 1854, when Rose and others became rudely insistent that she was not married at all. Her story was that she had left a heartless husband, had resumed her maiden name and come north as an alien because of her domestic troubles.

She tried to see McClellan, failed in this, but astonished State and War Department officials by offering them the key to the Confederate signals for $100,000. She proved to be quite appealing to General Marcy, and thereby embarrassing to General McClellan. The Union men had reason to be suspicious of Augusta, since they had intercepted a letter in which she had said that she was assigned by General Beauregard, with the consent of Jefferson Davis, "to go to Washington and see if her feeble efforts could be of use to them."

On the way North she stopped off at Fairfax to call on the blunt and hearty General Bradley T. Johnson, of whom she wrote:

I believe he is my friend—at least he pretends to be, or from policy, seeing that my friends were those that held all in their hand. I staid [sic] a day with him at the station. He was very kind to me and the children. He is a dear funny fellow.

Pinkerton's men shadowed her for some time after her arrival in Washington. They watched her while she nursed a sick child and postponed her arrest until after the boy's funeral, which they attended with an eye on their quarry. Then they pounced on her at Brown's Hotel in the middle of the night. They knew her variously as Mrs. Morris, Mrs. Mason or Miss Ada M. Hewitt.

On the day of her arrest young Mansfield T. Walworth, a clerk in the Adjutant-General's office, was taken into custody as an accomplice. He was the son of Reuben H. Walworth, Chancellor of New York State and a good friend of Seward's. Through his wife's family Walworth had connections in the South. He was a writer in his spare time and had been tinkering with the idea of doing intelligence work, but whether for the Union or the Confederacy remains a little obscure.

He was released soon after his arrest, the finding being that his connection with Augusta was social rather than political. But he was required to take a special oath of allegiance, to leave Washington, and to report regularly to his father.

In the meantime Augusta had already managed to send army plans and other information south. "Too late," she blithely wrote to her husband on February 7, 1862. She had charmed McClellan's latest plans out of a member of the Senate Military Committee, and a courier had taken the freshly garnered plums to Jordan.

In this same letter Augusta told Dr. Mason of their child's death, accused him of "appalling cruelty and neglect" and added: "You born a gentleman—where was all manliness gone when you deliberately left me to battle with this cruel, cruel world alone with your two children—reared as one of your own sisters, how did you expect me to live?"

Augusta's social and political operations were closely intertwined. They were at all times markedly obscure, but her opinion of Mrs. Greenhow was not. She thought "the lady enjoyed herself amazingly," and on February 19, 1862, she wrote to Colonel B. F. Johnson, a friend of her husband's in the South:

204

A military necessary compelled McClellan to arrest me two weeks ago. I have excellent society when I get a chance to enjoy it. It's solitary confinement!—but trust to my French sagacity for that. . . . Greenhow enjoys herself amazingly. My friends, or our friends, have supplied me with every comfort. I have no fault to find, but on the whole, rather like it—out of the way of scandal. I can't work so well here as when free. I regret that. . . .

I want you to write me. Give it to Colonel Jordan. That's a good man. I love him very much. . . . You know I cultivate a cheerful spirit as a duty. . . . The sentinels, keeper, prisoners, and officers are all kind. They only keep me here because they hate to part with me. Is it not strange, the only man in the world that ought to love me, does not, when everyone else besides, does. You know my vanity, but really it is so.

Five days later she wrote to Colonel Jordan, complaining of a cabal formed against her in prison by Mrs. Greenhow: "She is drowned by a mean ambition of being known only in the good work, and jealous of everything that surpasses her in loyalty and courage. She makes herself the echo of every evil rumor. . . ."

In this same letter Augusta asked Jordan if he had received the military plans she had sent him. She also wrote that "Mrs. Lincoln gave Wikoff the message you saw when they arrested him to make him tell." Did this link up with Rose's story of Henry Wikoff's attempt to go south and act supposedly as a peace mediator? Were some of the whisperings about Mrs. Lincoln rising from such sources as these?

When Augusta's remaining child, Frank, visited her in jail he raised much uproar by kicking at the door and shouting: "Let me out, you d——n Yankee, you." There is no record that he and little Rose came to know each other in jail. But he had a hobbyhorse there to while away the hours.

If Rose, Augusta and Mrs. Baxley were part of the one pattern in Jordan's calculations, they were singularly aloof from one another in Old Capitol Prison. Augusta had heard from Maryland friends that Mrs. Baxley was there only to check up on Rose, and that actually she was working for the Federal forces. Rose, in turn, scorned Augusta's record of espionage. She thought her merely a scandalous woman.

Mrs. Baxley took some pride in the fact that she and Mrs. Greenhow were the first females brought "to this old Union rattrap and that, strange to say, every lady now under arrest and with but three or four exceptions have been Marylanders."

But both Augusta and Mrs. Baxley viewed Rose with some degree of awe. They did not like her; neither did they dare to flout her openly. Rose took slight notice of their existence. Communication was denied them in any event, unless they met outdoors, or passed one another on the stairs, as they did one day when Mrs. Baxley engaged in a scrimmage with a guard who had barred their path to the front stairs with a bayonet. She and Augusta decided to crash through. Mrs. Baxley grabbed the man's musket. He cursed her. She walloped him in the face, making his nose bleed. He knocked her down and kicked her wholeheartedly. Sobs and lamentations followed, all of which proved to be a "humiliating experience" to Rose, a degradation of her sex, although she considered Mrs. Baxley the aggressor. To Rose association with these women was only a shade less obnoxious than with the "degraded servile class" cluttering up the prison yard.

Augusta was quite successful in jail. She was less of a snob than Rose, although she was also a persistent and ingratiating letter writer. Food, favors and kind deeds were her happy lot. She felt she was very well liked. This gave her a sense of elation, even in depressing surroundings. Above her mantel she scrawled a verse from Byron's "Prisoner of Chillon":

> Eternal spirit of the chainless Mind!
> Brightest in dungeons, Liberty! Thou art,
> For there thy habitation is the heart—
> The heart which love of thee alone can bind.

206

This verse was at once observed by Colonel William E. Doster when he visited Augusta after his appointment in March, 1862, as successor to Provost-Marshal Porter. She drew his attention to the Byronic challenge and asked if the Federals really expected to subdue her. She referred to Stanton, newly appointed Secretary of War, as the "inexorable Danton."

But Colonel Doster found Augusta an "exceedingly fascinating and pretty woman of about thirty, and of a temper so good that even imprisonment did not sour it." In his way he was a diplomat and managed to establish much better relations with Rose than Porter had had. In fact, his exasperated predecessor had said he would rather resign than continue to guard Mrs. Greenhow. But Doster was worldly, intelligent and only twenty-five at the time of his appointment. Rose talked to him without difficulty and she came close to liking him. He was greatly interested in her, and his first act on taking up his duties was to pay her his respects.

On that occasion the Colonel viewed Rose with a sharply appraising eye. She had maintained her grooming standards under the most trying conditions in jail, and was becomingly dressed in black silk with net ruffles when he visited her chamber. Her hair was carefully coiffed and little Rose was neatly dressed in warm material, with lacy pantalettes in view, a fashion introduced for children by Mrs. James Monroe.

Colonel Doster described his distinguished prisoner as being tall and well formed, about forty-five years of age, with black hair that was beginning to turn gray. He noted that she had black eyes, an olive complexion, firm teeth and small hands and feet. Her carriage was graceful and dignified, but he found her enunciation "too distinct to be natural and her manners bordering on the theatrical."

She was reading when he arrived and when the doctor who accompanied him inquired about her health she did not deign to reply. Had Dr. Stewart dared to show his face again—this time with the backing of the new Provost-Marshal? It seems likely, for Colonel

207

Doster noted their antagonism and commented: "As we were going, she inquired what this intrusion meant. Thereupon the doctor told her when a Union man called on a Secessionist it was not an intrusion but a favor. This doctor rasped up her sensibility. To me alone she was always communicative."

Nevertheless, Colonel Doster left written testimony that during her stay at the Old Capitol she "exerted herself to be as troublesome as possible and met her keepers successively with flattery, coquetry, denunciations, and finally with billingsgate, writing continually to everyone she knew about the military authorities."

Colonel Doster characterized the fifty-year-old Mrs. Baxley as the "most defiant and outrageous" of all the female prisoners in his noted jail. Another arrival who caused disquiet was Mrs. J. Barton (alias Mrs. McCarter), an Englishwoman who wore men's attire and who tried to get through to Richmond with the offer of a projectile invented by her husband. Rose deplored her trousers but considered her a woman of cultivation and scientific attainments. She was a keen observer and both wrote and spoke well. Rose approved her politics. The newcomer had supreme contempt for the "Abolitionist government." Rose admired her spirit and independence and wished her well when she was freed. Their rooms adjoined and they communicated through the keyhole. Mrs. Barton's predecessor, a man, had enlarged the opening with a penknife and Rose had pushed through many a note, as she did again with Mrs. Barton.

She also enjoyed briefly the society of Mrs. William Henry Norris, of Baltimore. They met in the prison yard, getting a breath of air, and their Maryland accents fell into happy unison. "She was a most excellent lady," said Rose, and was glad to see her released on parole through the influence of her own old friend, Reverdy Johnson.

During this period Rose did her best to follow the course of the war, but she was more cut off than at any time in her life. However, she caught some echoes of frivolity that interested her and caused her to make the charge that "perhaps at no period of its history had

208

there been such unrestrained indulgence of revelry and mirth in the capital." The "court journals" gave daily accounts of balls, dinners and routs, and exultantly proclaimed the fact that the "Abolition ladies could dress and dance, and give brilliant suppers in spite of the withdrawal of these Secesh dames, and demoiselles—the Greenhows, Slidells and Clays—and the foreign Ministers who were wont to sympathize with these fair traitors."

Rose did not hear of it until later but her sister-in-law, Mrs. Lee, was also in hot water in March. She had been smuggling out large batches of letters through W. Buxton, of the London *Morning Chronicle*. He was caught and it took the combined efforts of Lord Lyons and Seward to extricate him. General Nathaniel P. Banks accused him of consorting with Winchester women and he replied that he had traveled all over Europe and America and they were equal to any he had seen anywhere. Banks finally gave him a pass, and back he came to Mrs. Lee's door. A neighbor warned her to be careful. "I will give all the information I can, whenever I can, and risk the consequences," said the intrepid Mary Lee.

After the seizure of the Buxton letters, however, she kept her valise packed and ready for emergencies. She was flattered to learn that Seward went back to Washington from a near-by battlefield declaring that all the men of Winchester were in the army "and the women were she-devils."

"We will become thoroughly demoralized if the Yankees stay longer," Mrs. Lee agreed. "Mild and ladylike language is not strong enough to express our feelings and I fear we will never be fit for refined society again. Even Laura Lee, the good, the perfect, indulged in some profanity today. Our masters have announced that . . . the country shall be thoroughly devastated—that we shall be starved into submission."

On March 6 General James S. Wadsworth, Military Governor of the District of Columbia, called on Rose and she was drawn at once to this tall soldier, blue-eyed, white-haired, noted for his good humor,

209

courage and common sense. She found him "gentlemanly and kind, one who seemingly recognized the right of a prisoner to be treated with humanity and respect." He ordered that she get the usual exercise allotted to other prisoners, for since Harry Stewart's death Rose had been in solitary confinement. Two weeks later her enemy, Brigade-Surgeon Stewart, or Cyclops, as she now called him, walked into her room with her old friend, General John Adams Dix.

This was preliminary to summoning Rose for an official hearing before the United States Commissioners for the Trial of State Prisoners. She happened to have great respect for General Dix, whom she had known for many years. He was one of the Senators aligned with the antislavery elements, but he was also close to Buchanan and had always been her friend. Rose regarded him as a man of charm and scholarship, lofty purpose and good manners. He spoke French and Spanish fluently, wrote well, and was interested in music and the arts. The one thing Rose had against him was his political outlook.

She noted that his lean, contemplative face had changed little. His hair had grayed, as had hers, and was brushed back in the old crisp manner. She quickly recalled that he was one of the few Northern politicians in "whose integrity she entertained any confidence, or for whom she felt any respect."

He told her that he had come as a United States Commissioner to ascertain her wishes and offer his mediation and services. He offered to serve her as an old friend. Rose thanked him but said that in his capacity of "minister of a tyrant" she could not accept any service other than that he would present her simple demand for justice against his government. Rose told him she believed in the old Mosaic law of an eye for an eye and a tooth for a tooth. She fenced about appearing before his commission. Compliance was voluntary on her part.

But General Dix handled the matter with tact, and Rose eventually agreed to appear. He felt her child's forehead as she lay on her bed

210

of straw, and exclaimed at once: "Why, the child has fever. Here is a physician."

Rose turned her back on Brigade-Surgeon Stewart. "I have sent for one," she announced, "and decline the services of that gentleman."

No sooner had General Dix left the room than Rose and Stewart engaged in a furious argument. Rose summoned the General back before he was out of earshot and claimed his protection. She told him that she had already been forced to have the guard expel the Brigade-Surgeon from her presence. Dr. Stewart held his ground and protested to General Dix. But the General quietly led him away, and Rose went straight to her diary to enter the comment: "I confess I enjoyed his crestfallen discomfited look more than any incident of the day."

Although Governor Dix's visit had cheered her, she had no real belief that freedom was in sight. She had become completely cynical by this time. Her spirit was unbroken, her resistance was as firm as ever, but her health and optimism were failing.

CHAPTER XIV

Mrs. Greenhow on Trial

ON A March day in 1862, with snow driving in heavy flurries against the carriage windows and its wheels sinking deep in slush, Rose set forth from Old Capitol Prison bound for the Provost-Marshal's headquarters. She reflected gloomily on the filth and deterioration of the city. The constant flow of marching men, ammunition wagons and ambulance trains, had made things worse than in the time of Andrew Jackson. Everything she saw was depressing to Rose. Even the sun seemed "obscured as dark as Yankee deeds."

General Dix's visit had been followed by a summons for a hearing before his commission, the closest Rose ever came to trial for espionage. She viewed it as a farce and a minor proceeding. She had already announced that she did not shrink from trial for treason. "Let it come," she wrote. "I will claim the right to defend myself, and there will be rich revelations."

But her challenge was ignored. Feeble though this substitute was for the flamboyance of public trial for treason, Rose entered upon the ordeal as a star might walk across the stage. This time she was Mary Queen of Scots, dressed in ruffled black, with a lace snood holding her graying hair in place. She had the worn and ravaged look occasioned by grief, hardship and the inevitable inroads of age. Rose had suffered much in recent years. She had lost both husband and

212

daughter. Her life had changed abruptly from a milieu of luxury and influence to the sordid horrors of jail. Through it all her unquenchable faith in the Confederate cause had sustained her. All that she had done seemed right to her, with the future of the South at stake. In her own eyes she was armored in righteousness, blessed by the gods of the martyrs, and she feared nothing from her inquisitors.

The hearing was something of an ordeal for kindhearted General Dix. He was much attached to Rose. He had dined often at her home, and had known her intimately for years. As Buchanan's Secretary of the Treasury, he had watched her move as a bright star in the firmament. To see her worn, haggard, vituperative, mendacious and at bay, was a disturbing experience for a man of his sensibility. It was obvious at first that he could scarcely bring himself to probe too hard, but Rose's responses soon chilled him. His fellow commissioner was Judge Edwards Pierrepont. Both had trouble pinning her down.

Rose considered the entire proceeding an outrage. She wasted no time in announcing that it was a mock trial, and took the attitude that she had obeyed the summons merely out of curiosity. Contemporary commentators were of the opinion that Rose was theatrical and loved publicity, and that upon this occasion she sought the limelight. In her memoirs she denies this with many conflicting arguments. Her situation in itself was spectacular, and her slightest act was dramatized. She was now in a tangle that invited public comment.

Ironically enough, she was questioned in the old Gwin house, where she had attended many parties, including the spectacular masquerade held before the war. As she passed through "filthy halls and stairs, and saw the filthy crowd of soldiers and civilians who lined the way" she recalled some of the gatherings in which she had mingled and the "goodly company" that had enjoyed Senator Gwin's hospitality.

Rose mentally contrasted the denuded rooms and battered floors with the shining surfaces of the past, the fine furnishings, the echo of violins playing, the scent of flowers, the flounced beauties and

213

handsome men who had gathered there. Like her own home, it had been a Secessionist center.

But no one welcomed Rose on this occasion. Instead of liveried attendants a guard stationed at the door rattled his musket to remind her that she was a prisoner. She was kept waiting in a fireless room on the third floor until her hands and feet were numb with cold. Officers in assorted uniforms walked in and out, on one pretext or another, but actually to have a look at her, Rose concluded with some justification. Whatever her situation, she never failed to interest the opposite sex.

She was in a lofty and injured mood when finally ushered in before the commissioners. "Gentlemen, resume your seats," she told them haughtily. "I recognize the embarrassment of your position. It was a mistake in your government to have selected gentlemen for this mission. You have, however, shown me but scant courtesy in having kept me waiting your pleasure for nearly an hour in the cold."

They apologized and said they were ignorant of her arrival. After a few courtesies the proceedings got under way. Rose was seated between them at a long table, and she promptly announced that since it was only a mimic court, she assumed she could answer or not as she saw fit.

Judge Pierrepont reminded her that she was charged with aiding the enemy with military information. Rose challenged him to produce his proofs. When she saw notes being taken she jumped up and addressed General Dix: "If it is your object to make a *spectacle* of me, and furnish reports for the newspapers, I shall have the honor to withdraw from this presence."

Both commissioners reassured her and explained that an official record was being made for the War Department. Rose subsided for the moment and Judge Pierrepont reminded her that at the time of her arrest papers containing information on military operations were found in her possession and some had been destroyed.

"That is false," Rose protested. "I had no occasion to destroy any

214

papers. People were constantly at my house, and I don't know what they may have done. I had removed all the papers I desired to have removed before I was arrested."

She pointed out that letters written long before the war, and having nothing to do with military operations, were seized. She had been unable to recover them. But Judge Pierrepont flashed back at her with a question about the Seward letter and its publication in Richmond. Rose quickly hung the blame on Seward for its release, and with some inconsistency, in view of her earlier pride in it, said that it was an "outrage to allow a private letter of mine to find its way into the public prints." Next she would be charged with counseling Jefferson Davis on how to lead his armies, she snapped. But when her great coup, Manassas, was mentioned, she could not wholly deny this scintillant piece of espionage, although not conceding her role in full.

"It is certain that if I had the information, I should have given it," she acknowledged. "I should consider that I was performing a holy duty to my friends."

Judge Pierrepont took another tack and asked her how she would feel about going to the other side of the lines. Would she then consider that she owed allegiance to the government and would she be willing to be bound by the laws of war?

Rose would not. "This is my home," she protested. "I have been taken from my home and carried to a prison, to be insulted, and subjected to treatment of the most outrageous kind. Every association of my home has been broken up and destroyed. If the government design to send me across the lines as an exile, I have no alternative but to go as such."

Rose asked if she would be forcibly exiled or permitted to go of her own free will.

"Would it be exiling you, to send you south among your friends?" Judge Pierrepont inquired.

"It is exiling me, to use any force, to send me south, from my home."

Judge Pierrepont backed down hastily. It was a mere suggestion, of course. He made it amply clear that the proposal had come from the higher realms of government. Rose was a diplomatic problem of no mean order.

"I suppose it is hardly worth while to ask you to take the oath of allegiance, or give your parole of honor?" he pursued.

"You would blush to do that," Rose retorted, "because I belong to a religion and a section of the country, which makes an oath binding. . . . If I took the oath of allegiance—no matter how galling it might be—I should consider myself as being bound by that oath."

"Have you any peculiar religion?" asked the literal-minded Pierrepont.

"None but that which relies on the mercy and goodness of Providence."

Pierrepont turned to his companion. "General, I think you had better talk to Mrs. Greenhow. You are an old friend of hers."

But General Dix had had enough. "I don't know as I have anything to say."

Rose turned to him, briefly sympathetic: "You both see how pleasant it is."

The General stiffened up at this challenge and suggested that Rose be questioned about the cipher. This brought on a lively interchange and gave her a chance to air her opinion of the detectives who had searched her house. But Dix now pressed hard. He brought into view one of the most damaging exhibits—Rose's dispatch on the number and disposition of troops quartered around Washington. She denied all memory of this item, but wavered sufficiently to say: "I think that is false. I won't swear it is. I have been in the habit of entertaining guests in my house. So far as I am myself concerned I pronounce it unequivocally false."

216

"The charge is not that you wrote those letters but that it was through your agency that they were transmitted," General Pierrepont broke in, having found a chink in Rose's armor.

"That I pronounce to be false. . . . I am no one's agent. They might have been there, and they might not have been there. I am not to be made accountable for my guests."

Rose was becoming repetitious and self-contradictory. General Dix grew colder: "You know, Mrs. Greenhow, that in a contest like this, while the very existence of the government is in danger, the communication of such information as this, which tends to subvert the interests of the government, should certainly be considered a very serious offense."

At this point Rose swung her antislavery friends into the forefront. After abusing Lincoln and saying she detested his party in her very soul she went on: "I lost my child a short time before. I have not been in the world during that time; therefore any information I may have got, must have been brought to my house, and brought to me. Brought to me by traitors, as you call them, in that party. . . . If Mr. Lincoln's friends will pour into my ear such important information, am I to be held responsible for all that? Could it be presumed that I would not use that which was given to me by others? If I did not I would be unjust to myself and my friends. It is said that a woman cannot keep a secret. I am a woman; and a woman usually tells all she knows."

"If you got the information as a secret, what then?" asked Judge Pierrepont.

"That doesn't make any difference. I haven't any intention of working against my friends. I have written as much as any man against the party now in power; because I believe it is this party that has brought all the present trouble upon the country. . . . I believe it religiously. . . . The government is gone. You can never re-establish it."

217

Rose said she saw no treason in anything they had brought up.

Judge Pierrepont observed acidly: "I don't think you are bent so much on treason as on mischief."

This launched Rose on a fresh tirade: "Let me tell you, I have studied the Constitution and Laws of this country. I have informed myself about the Constitution as well as I have about my Bible. Your government ought to be ashamed of itself for allowing me to be so scandalously treated; in allowing such scoundrels as it did to get my letters, and read them, and laugh over them. I have been made the victim of every kind of villainy. It has sent its emissaries to betray me, and persons who advised me to write letters but to betray them to the government."

"The question is not as to whether you have only written the letters, but, also whether you have a right, knowingly, to try and subvert the purposes of the government," Judge Pierrepont reminded her.

"I look at it in an entirely different light. I have a right to write what I please. I always did so."

"You are charged, Madam, with holding communication with the enemy in the South."

"If this were an established fact, you could not be surprised at it. I am a Southern woman, and I thank God that no drop of Yankee blood ever polluted my veins; and as all that I have ever honored or respected have been driven by ruthless despotism to seek shelter there, it would seem the most natural thing in life that I should have done so."

"How is it, Madam, that you have managed to communicate, in spite of the vigilance exercised over you?"

"That is my secret, sir; and, if it be any satisfaction to you to know it, I shall, in the next forty-eight hours, make a report to my government at Richmond of this rather farcical trial for treason."

At this point General Dix picked up a letter written on pale pink paper and addressed to her daughter Florence, whom he knew well.

218

He also knew that her son-in-law, Treadwell Moore, was in the Union Army. He asked her if she did not have relatives fighting for the North. Rose admitted reluctantly that she had both a son-in-law and a nephew in the Union Army, adding: "Unfortunately, I have a great many relatives who are benighted on the subject."

Forced to look at the letter, Rose could not well deny the words she had written to Florence. She had aired her views with considerable frankness. She quickly acknowledged that the letter expressed the sentiments she still felt.

The intercepted letter was dated March 15, 1862, and was from Old Capitol Prison. She described conditions in the jail and said that all her letters would reach Florence thereafter through "our underground, as these despicable scoundrels, the detectives, now examine all letters and exercise their discretion about sending them." Rose continued:

My God! you cannot conceive the outrages practiced here. . . . I will have my revenge, and bear these outrages better on that account. I have no feeling but hate towards this detested, demoralized nation, and I thank God that it is in its last throes. McClellan has got his congé, having served the purpose of killing off Scott. Stanton has been brought forward to get rid of McClellan, and he will be put aside in his turn. These men let their vanity blind them as to their real position, and content themselves with the applause manufactured in advance to suit the role they are intended to play, and lose sight of what a light observation should point out to them; the necessity of making a party. Stanton is now fooled to the top of his bent. He writes magnificent orders for Lincoln and lords it in the most approved fashion; he does not see what others see, that his own fall is not distant.

The abolition policy is now fully avowed. Frémont has been again galvanized into prominence; if he was a man of talent and nerve, he would be the first American dictator; as it is, he will be the catspaw to draw the chestnuts out of the fire for somebody else to eat. I am pressed for time, darling. The naval engagement has been a glorious victory to the Confederate States, unprecedented in daring in any age. The retreat from

219

Manassas is also a most masterly success, and I don't wonder at the howl of indignation of the whole North at being so outwitted. I shall try to give you a full account of things here. I do not care to speak of Mrs. Cutts. I shall publish an account of my experiences. When I tell you that I am now seven months a prisoner, that in that time, she and Addie have been three times to see me. That only once during that whole period have they ever sent me the smallest thing, and that was on Christmas, as an ostentatious display. But I am content. I shall send you some colored clothing for yourself and Leila; as for myself I shall never lay aside my mourning.

God bless you, darling. My love to dear Leila and Minnie.

Your devoted mother,
(Signed) ROSE GREENHOW

General Dix looked severe. "This letter is equal to declaring determined hostility to the government."

"I should have been the meekest, lowliest Christian in the world, if, after being smitten on one cheek by the government, I should have turned the other. Well now, have you any other letters of mine?"

General Dix said there were a great many others of the same purport, but Rose did not yield an inch of ground. "The government knows what my feelings have been, and always were. I have not changed them. I have no other feelings than those now."

General Dix gave up. "Judge, I don't know as we wish to ask Mrs. Greenhow any more questions."

Rose added her own characteristic touch: "In these war times, you ought to be in some more important business, than holding an inquisition for the examination of women. I look upon this as nothing more than an inquisition."

This was official transcript, but in her memoirs Rose gave a much more spirited account of the proceedings, and indicated that she had drawn blood a good many times. She also pictured herself as parting courteously with the court and saying, with all her attention focused on General Dix: "On examining this evidence, you can but smile at the absurdity of the charges, and the extreme care not to

220

extract any information from me. I have, however, sir, to return my most sincere thanks to you and your colleagues for the delicacy and kind feeling which have characterized your bearing toward me, and to congratulate you upon the conclusion of a task which can be but little in unison with the feelings of a gentleman."

The upshot of the Dix-Pierrepont proceeding was that Rose was ordered sent south. There were many complications and delays before this was effected, however. Characteristically she had proved to be a handful, and a number of confusing newspaper reports followed her official hearing.

A reporter who had been offered five hundred dollars by New York and Philadelphia papers for a story on her ordeal submitted his copy to Rose. She approved it, doing a diplomatic rightabout face on the question of publicity. She had been persuaded that a distorted version of the hearing might leak out otherwise. However, according to Rose, Seward promptly vetoed the article, and an authorized statement was given out that she had made a full confession. It is a fact that an item to this effect appeared in the Philadelphia *Inquirer* on April 2, 1862, another thorn in Rose's crown of martyrdom.

She denied the charge heatedly, as she did a similar story in the Baltimore *News*, writing to the editors:

I have made no confession of treason, or treasonable correspondence; neither was I subjected to an examination intended to bring to the light my sources of information. I but claim the right which our fathers did in '76—to protest against tyranny and oppression.

No sooner had Rebel Rose bowed out from the commissioners' presence than Augusta Morris moved in, proving to be a more malleable witness. She was persuasive and ingratiating where Rose was proud and thorny. The "gay, sprightly and dashing" grass widow presented herself effectively in the role of helpless femininity and injured womanhood. But it was equally difficult to pin her down.

"You dragged me from my bed, with my little child—a delicate and fragile woman—to a loathsome imprisonment," sobbed Augusta. "I have nothing more to say. I don't think I owe any allegiance to a government that could do such a thing. The Southerners haven't come to seizing women and children yet."

"General," said Judge Pierrepont, "if Mrs. Morris declines to answer any question, of course we don't desire to press her."

"No, oh no! Certainly not," agreed the General.

Augusta, like Rose, showed no great desire to be sent south, "to be chased into the Gulf of Mexico." Her domestic troubles had driven her forth and she begged her judges not to press her about these.

The sympathetic pair said they would let that matter rest. But they pushed on about her contacts with Smithson. She insisted that he was "one of the most innocent men in the world." Judge Pierrepont was skeptical about this.

Augusta admitted three visits to seek his advice on investing money she had brought with her from the South. She also acknowledged a social acquaintance with Walworth. Her arrest was due entirely to the malice of her mother-in-law, she insisted. And Seward, whom she had believed to be her friend, had failed her completely, after giving her a letter of introduction to McClellan, whom she never saw. But she had found a substitute in his father-in-law, Colonel Marcy.

"I gave these people political information of great value," said Augusta. "I did it because I did not want to be suspected. . . . I told General Marcy that the Southerners would never fight them at Manassas; that they never would fight General McClellan on his own invitation. That they would never have a Bull Run battle again."

This had come direct from General Beauregard, according to Augusta, who quoted him as saying: "We'll wait until we get General McClellan in the heart of the South, and then we will give it to him; where there will be no retreat or cutting off."

"Could I have harmed you with your seventy thousand bayonets?"

222

Augusta demanded. "Is such a thing possible? You are gentlemen, deserving of some better employment than this."

"A woman can do harm when she wants to," Judge Pierrepont interjected, but Augusta pushed on: "I tell you truly I am the most intensely selfish woman in the world. I am thinking of nothing but myself and little child. I know neither North nor South—yet I have strong Southern proclivities."

"I thought you considered you were a Union woman when you came here," General Dix reminded her.

"I was just feeling that way. I wanted to make myself comfortably easy. I wasn't particularly in favor of secession; nor was I going to take an active part with either side. In fact, to tell you the truth, Judge, I believe I have been badly treated."

Augusta expatiated on her vulgar treatment in jail. Judge Pierrepont, studying her carefully, and still dubious, commented: "Those little, fragile, delicate women can sometimes be of service in aiding strong men, and strong governments."

Her judges then politely asked her if she would take the oath of allegiance. They had no doubt of the answer in Rose's case; they were not so sure of Augusta. But she, too, proved to be stubborn, though playful: "Gentlemen, I will tell you the truth. I feel spited toward you. You have treated me so badly that the feeling against you is too strong. I am the most revengeful person in the world. . . . Am I to go out free?"

"I do not know," said Judge Pierrepont. "We'll have to talk with the President about that."

"I think the President will let me out," said Augusta confidently. "I'll write to him on the subject, providing the General does not intercept my letter."

"Perhaps Mrs. Lincoln would help you," Judge Pierrepont suggested.

Augusta looked dubious. "I don't know anything about that. . . .

I bid you all good morning, gentlemen. I shall remember you with pleasure."

Augusta had had some dealings with Henry Wikoff and so considered that she had a link with Mrs. Lincoln. But she came out of the proceedings more triumphantly than Rose. Both women wondered what might befall them next as they settled back in their prison quarters. When Rose learned that "banishment" was the verdict she wrote to General Wadsworth on April 4, registering protest and refusing to bind herself not to return.

Moreover, she assured him with sarcasm that while preparing her own and her daughter's clothes for departure she would not blow up the White House, equip a fleet, break open the Treasury or "do any other *small act* which you may suppose comes within my limited powers to perform."

On April 14 Rose reported to General Wadsworth that she was ready for departure. On the same day she sent an indignant letter to her old friend, James Gordon Bennett. The New York *Herald* had published a report that she protested being sent south, and preferred to remain a prisoner in Washington. In Rose's note, which was intercepted, she reversed some of her earlier statements:

So far as regards myself, I should consider it a great trial to be obliged to live in this city under the present regime, for, according to my peculiar political ideas, all the refinement has departed with my brethren of the South; and I shall only too gladly avail myself of the edict which banishes me from my whilom home to go amongst kindred spirits, and to a land made glorious by its heroic resistance of the invader.

A copy of this particular note found its way into some books she sent to Jefferson Davis' home in Richmond after she was freed. Months later he returned it to her with the comment: "Accidentally I have thus been made acquainted with another of the many bitter trials to which your free spirit was subjected while your person was in the power of a vulgar despotism."

224

March and April were full of unrest and excitement for Rose, but with the appointment of Stanton as the new Secretary of War, and Doster as Provost-Marshal, her status changed and some of the pressure was lifted at Old Capitol Prison. Stanton issued an order permitting members of Rose's family to visit her without passes or witnesses.

Rose wrote at once to Mrs. Douglas, conveying this information. She said that little Rose had been very ill as a result of her close confinement, and that they were now allowed a half-hour's exercise in the prison yard but were followed by soldiers with bayonet in hand ready to cry "Halt!" if they veered right or left. She complained of the vermin, which were so thick on the walls that she had to burn them off with old pieces of candle. It had all become a "tragical farce," said Rose, and if she were not writing to "so loyal a supporter of the Imperial Powers, she would say 'May Heaven confound them.'"

This letter was held up and Rose wrote at once to Stanton, complaining. She received a letter from Addie on March 30 and was bitterly hurt to have her beloved niece write: "I do believe you have a stern joy in your martyrdom, else you would embrace the opportunity to escape from it." Rose replied at once in a reproachful vein, saying that someone had imposed on Addie's credulity, since in eight months no one with real authority had come near her until General Wadsworth showed up. She detailed all the efforts she had made to achieve her own freedom. They had indeed been considerable, although most of her letters had been waylaid. Rose then gave Addie her true view of the "exile" that had been decreed for her:

Do not, my dear, believe that I have any "stern joy in martyrdom." I am too keenly alive to the enjoyment of God's blessings to covet any such thing. I know now that hardships and severe trials are before me in the future. I am to be driven forth from my home by this magnanimous Government, in the midst of the bloodshed and carnage with which they are pursuing all who cherish my own political faith. I may witness the

225

horrors of a sacked city, or sleep within sound of the cannon's roar on the battlefield. These probably frightful vicissitudes do not appal me, for a true woman has her mission, even in scenes like this, in the exercise of the gentle charities which are her peculiar attributes. . . .

I would to God I could obliterate the recollections of the outrages of the last eighteen months, for I fear now that my capacity of hate will overshadow every other feeling.

I have been betrayed into writing this long letter, my dear, when I only intended to correct the impression that the Government had ever signified, in any shape or form whatsoever, its desire to release me; else why not have sent me South, with the Phillips family, seven months ago?

Come soon to see me, for you are almost the sole link with this place, which was once my happy home.

Rose was incredulous when New Orleans fell to the enemy late in April. She had many friends in the Lousiana city and she cried: "Oh! better that she had buried her whole population under her smoking ruins, than to have been given over a bloodless victory to the invaders; and from my soul I pray that heavy retribution may fall upon the dastards in the dark tragedy."

By May 11 she was mourning the evacuation of Norfolk and the loss of the *Virginia*. She would rather have lost both of her hands than to learn of these calamities, she wrote in her diary. But her confidence in the ultimate result was still "strong as the faith planted on the Rock of Ages and even in this dark hour the star of hope rises steadily beyond the gloom guiding us on to victory and to empire."

Rose viewed these adverses as stimulants to fresh effort, and more resistance of the "ruthless invaders." She ridiculed stories coming up from the South that President Davis had had a subterranean passage made to ensure his own escape, and that Richmond would be evacuated at the first sign of the approach of the Federal Army.

As time went on and no order came through for her release Rose grew restless and uneasy. She begged Senator James M. Bayard, of Delaware, an old classmate of General Wadsworth, to let her know

226

what fate was in store for her. The doubt and uncertainty hanging over her were more trying "than the darkest reality." He visited her but could hold out little comfort, for General Wadsworth had told him that McClellan was unbending and had countermanded the order to send her south. She received the same information from Congressman Alfred Ely, of Connecticut, who had been taken prisoner by Confederate troops but had received such generous treatment in Richmond that he wished to help Rose. He had been freed in exchange for her old friend, Charles J. Faulkner, Minister to France.

After investigating he reported back to her that McClellan objected to her release and did not wish her sent south at that time. Rose lost hope. Spring seemed to rush across the countryside as she and her daughter pined in jail. Crocuses, tulips and snowdrops bloomed as the snows cleared. Crab apple trees burst into bloom close to the Capitol. Then, on May 18, Henry Wilson walked into Rose's little chamber.

This must have been a strange encounter. Rose noticed that Wood looked uneasy as he ushered in the man who was widely believed to have been her lover. Wilson said he had come as a member of a senatorial committee. He must have battled for Rose behind the scenes, for he told her that he had held out for sending her south, although "Seward, McClellan and the rest" thought differently. Knowing Rose's love of flattery, he acknowledged that she was the most important prisoner they had taken. Soon she would be free in any event, he predicted, since the "rebellion would shortly be crushed out and Richmond would fall."

Rose told him tartly that if Richmond fell it would bury the Abolitionists under its ruins, and rise from its ashes the capital of a mighty empire. Wilson must have noted that his old friend's fire had not dimmed down. Yet he could not have failed to observe the physical changes—the look of strain, the emaciation, the sunken features of the invincible Mrs. Greenhow.

Usually discursive in her diary, Rose summed up with brevity what

227

must have been one of the most curious interviews of her life. She admitted throwing into their conversation all the bitterness and contempt she felt for his kind. Wilson must have talked freely to her, since she had the "satisfaction of seeing the jealousy and division amongst themselves" which she interpreted as the "avant-courier of the bitter retribution—in the shape of civil war in the North."

Rose sank into deep depression and indifference after Wilson's visit. The outside world was gilded with the light of early summer, but in the Old Capitol Prison "the heat was intense, the stench terrible, and hunger gnawed at her vitals." She could no longer force down "fowl which must have been the cock that crowed thrice to wake Peter." She "beguiled the heavy hours" by reading Piero Maroncelli's "*My Prisons, Memoirs of Silvio Pellico*," but the similarity of her own fate to that of "other victims of tyranny" did not lessen her sense of suffering.

Desperate at last, Rose passed final judgment in her diary: " 'He who entereth here leaves hope behind' is written in letters of blood over the portals of Lincoln's prison." But next day, May 28, she was aflame over Stonewall Jackson's victory outside Winchester. The news was brought in by arriving prisoners. And Mrs. Lee added her footnote:

Joy, joy. The battle has been fought; the victory won; we are free; our precious soldiers are here, in Winchester, with us all the time, morning, noon and night. . . . I opened the parlour window and as I did so a Confederate soldier dashed a Yankee knapsack on the steps and asked me to take care of it. Then we all rushed out and the streets resounded with our shouts and cheers as soldiers—our own men—came rushing by. We shook hands with all who would stop long enough.

Rose burned with excitement as she learned of the feats of Jackson and her old friend, black-bearded Turner Ashby, whose lightning forays and white horse by this time had become proverbial. She had heard that he rode eighty miles in twenty-four hours, using two horses. But within a matter of days he was to die in a Valley cavalry

228

skirmish, crying at the end: "Charge, men! For God's sake, charge."

She rejoiced when she heard that Jefferson Davis—"our great and good President"—was well, although the Yankees had reported him in a critical state. "May angels guard him for his country's sake," wrote Rose, who was to join him in Richmond within the week.

Deliverance had come at last.

CHAPTER XV

Return to Richmond

√ R OSE left Old Capitol Prison on a June day in 1862, wrapped in a Confederate flag concealed beneath her light summer shawl. Her bearing was proud; her spirit triumphant. The marks of her long imprisonment lay deep upon her, but her hair was neatly coiffed; her black kid gloves were tightly buttoned over her small wrists; her gophered dress flared in a modest hoop. Little Rose was crisply flounced, but her face was pale and weary.

Mrs. Greenhow was headed for freedom and the South. News of her departure had been kept secret, but her movements soon stirred up the usual furore. Feuds were forgotten. Her military guard softened at the end. She was escorted through the prison to bid farewell to her companions in suffering. Rose carried this off in brave style. She exhorted them all to bear up under their misfortune—"not that they needed it, for all burned to be free, to share in the glorious struggle now going on."

Never had Old Capitol Prison harbored a queen like Mrs. Greenhow, although Belle Boyd would move in soon to take her place. The banners of revolt would be waved again by a younger, more flashy siren.

Rose was gratified to see that the War Department had honored her departure with a worthy escort. The yard was full of "military gentlemen making quite a display, dressed in full uniform, with sword and carbine in hand." Her old feuding partner Wood was going with her, since no one knew what deviltry Rose might start before leaving Northern territory.

The guard drew up under arms. The twelve mounted men curbed their horses. Prisoners waved lovingly from behind barred windows, but this was more for bewitching Augusta than for the haughty Mrs. Greenhow. Everyone was glad to see the last of Mrs. Baxley, the screamer. The press watched the cavalcade from across the way. The three irrepressible ladies from the South were not without notice in the manner of their departure.

But suspicion still plagued Rose. A Northern prison might yet be her destination. She turned to the young lieutenant who headed her escort and said: "Sir, before I advance further, I ask you, not as Lincoln's officer, but as a man of honor and a gentleman, are your orders from Baltimore to conduct me to a Northern prison, or to some point in the Confederacy?"

The lieutenant was chagrined. "On my honor, Madam, to conduct you to Fortress Monroe and thence to the Southern Confederacy," he assured her, showing the order of transportation.

Rose took a careful look, then stepped into the carriage, bowing to her audience, which by this time had grown large. She had a nervous headache and felt quite ill, thanks to Mrs. Baxley, who had rowed with Superintendent Wood the night before and had raved and ranted until morning, keeping Rose awake with her noise. There was no telling how Mrs. Baxley felt, but both she and Augusta were to annoy Rose greatly before the day ended, with their truculence and bad manners.

Rose must have watched the passing streets with some emotion as the cavalcade drove to the depot. The scene fading from view encompassed the span of her life—her youth, her happy marriage, her social and political triumphs, her friends, her loves and idols, as well as her hours of profoundest misery. She knew she was saying farewell to Washington. Much as she loved the South, the capital had been her home for nearly half a century. Rose must have turned her back on it forever with mixed emotions.

Another military escort awaited her at the depot—"to prevent communication with sympathizing friends." But these precautions failed, "for many a word was stealthily whispered, and many a hearty 'God bless you!' spoken." The prisoners rode to Baltimore in their own private car, heavily guarded. All other passengers were allowed to depart before the trio of agents and little Rose set foot on the platform. The two Roses rode to their hotel in one carriage; the two thorns in another.

Baltimore was a danger spot. There was much feeling for Rose in Maryland, her native state. Sentinels were stationed at the hotel doors and although she imprinted her bold signature on the register of the Gilmor House, General Dix, who was on his way to take command at Fortress Monroe, and more or less supervised the prisoners' journey, ordered it removed. There might well have been a demonstration in Baltimore.

General Dix was summoned back to Washington early Sunday, the morning after their arrival. Superintendent Wood relaxed his vigilance and permitted Mrs. Greenhow to receive some friends. Almost at once she "found her soul expanding once more under the genial influence of a kindred race." But a few days later General Dix, through an aide, was busy denying a report printed in the New York papers that she "had held a levee in Baltimore."

There was no question about the ovation given the travelers as they boarded the vessel headed for Fortress Monroe. Friends had gathered around, all cheered by the news of the battles fought and won around Richmond. Skirmishing was still going on at Seven Pines, but Rose as yet was unaware of the terrible toll in Confederate lives that this victory exacted.

Handkerchiefs were waved. Tears were shed. There were cries of good luck, and a guard with bayonets stationed at the boat had to thrust back Rose's crowding admirers. When General Dix arrived on the scene he promptly paid his respects to his emancipated prisoner, and congratulated her in "very kind terms." But Augusta and Mrs. Baxley flouted the General. Rose was outraged and "rebuked them by her manner." Neither quailed. Mrs. Baxley all but spat. They were being emancipated from Mrs. Greenhow as well as from the Federal Government. It seemed to be a real relief to Rose's two companions.

General Dix left them at Fortress Monroe. Here Rose and her companions on June 2 signed a statement pledging their word of honor "that in consideration of our being set at liberty beyond the lines of the U.S. Army we will not return north of the Potomac River during the present hostilities without the permission of the Secretary of War of the U.S."

This was a measure of surrender by Rose. The oath of allegiance was not mentioned.

Captain Van Valkenburgh, who skippered the ship, provided a bumper luncheon. It was some time since Rose had drunk champagne. Without a moment's hesitation she raised her glass, her black eyes swept the shoreline, and she toasted Jefferson Davis and the Confederacy right under the guns of Fortress Monroe. Her guard took fright and tactfully turned his back. But they were now within range of the promised land and Rose's buoyant spirits soared. Wilson Barstow, General Dix's aide-de-camp, formally asked her where she wished to go.

"To the capital of the Confederacy, wherever that might be," she responded grandly.

He told her that it still was Richmond, although it might well be in Northern hands before they arrived.

"I shall take my chance on that," Rose retorted.

In the late afternoon they boarded the ship chartered to take them to City Point. It was broiling hot and they had a troubled night on the James River, which was difficult to navigate, the buoys having been removed by the Confederates. Rose gloried briefly in the sight

233

of the wrecked *Congress* and other vessels destroyed by the *Virginia*, which was the old *Merrimac* reconstructed. She looked with interest but disdain at that "low black ugly thing"—the Federal ironclad *Monitor*.

"I was under intense excitement," Rose later recalled, "for, after nearly ten months of imprisonment, I was in sight of the promised land. In a short time we reached the shore, and my foot pressed the sacred soil."

At this point she was tempted to unfold the battle flag she wore under her shawl and cast it to the breeze "as a parting defiance to the Yankees," but she prudently decided that she might have further use for it. She was welcomed to Virginian soil by Colonel W. S. Ashe and other Confederate officers "whose bold and soldierly bearing contrasted most strikingly with the Vandal race" whom she had seen, she hoped, for the last time.

The New York *Tribune* took a dimmer view of Rose's reception and pictured the "three graces, when last seen, making their way to the arms supposed to be outstretched to receive them via an open mule cart, with their trunks for seats."

Mule cart or not, Rose bore herself with her usual poise and no longer hid her Confederate flag—the token of her allegiance. It was June 4 when she arrived at her destination and she was taken direct to the Ballard House, where General Winder, commandant at Richmond, called upon her, so as to dispense with the usual formality of her reporting to him. Rose was in the service.

There was no demonstration for her in the Southern capital. Her work was secret, and the papers did not emphasize her return. It was noted inconspicuously but soon the story was all over town that Mrs. Greenhow was back. Jefferson Davis called on her the evening after her arrival. He bowed gallantly over her hand and told her: "But for you there would have been no Battle of Bull Run."

This gesture repaid her for all that she had endured, had it been magnified tenfold, Rose commented later in her memoirs. "And I shall

234

ever remember that as the proudest moment of my whole life, to have received the tribute of praise from him who stands as the apostle of our country's liberty in the eyes of the civilized world," she added.

Jeff was shocked by the sight of Mrs. Greenhow—her sunken eyes, the deep lines furrowing her face, the harassed manner and fast graying hair. On June 13 he wrote to Varina, who had left Richmond before the Battle of Seven Pines:

Mrs. Greenhow is here. Madam looks much changed, and has the air of one whose nerves are shaken by mental torture. General Lee's wife has arrived, her servants left her, and she found it uncomfortable to live without them.

The Richmond *Dispatch* welcomed Mrs. Greenhow back to her native South with a modest notice: "If the tyrant has released her, it was because that even he quailed before the might of her power as representative of the feelings of every true Southern lady."

The *Daily Examiner* on June 5 editorialized on the influence of women in the war, pointing out that "what the Yankees most do deprecate in this war—the influence of lovely women—is our greatest boast and pride. . . . Instances are on record already of displays of moral heroism surpassed by the woman of no revolution either in the past or present century."

In inescapable juxtaposition was the announcement that Mrs. Greenhow, Mrs. Morris and Mrs. Baxley had arrived by flag of truce train from City Point to Petersburg, and thence by train to Richmond. Soon items about Rose began to appear all through the Southern press.

On June 16 the *Daily Enquirer* of Richmond showed that spy-minded little Rose was still on the alert. The elf had spotted one of McClellan's officers, disguised in a Confederate uniform, dining at the America Hotel, and "when he discovered her eying him very suspiciously, he cut out and disappeared before information was given in time to capture him." Little Rose had become almost as well known as her mother.

Richmond was no longer the leisurely city Rose had known when she visited it with Robert. Its external beauties were unmarred—the spacious homes and wide streets, the rolling hills and verdant gardens, with the James River flowing placidly through it. She arrived during a lovely week in June when the outer façade ironically was one of "bouquets, summer bonnets, gossamer and pink lawn; front gardens and green trees devoid of dust, and rich and moist as the dew itself; the sky an ethereal blue." But, like Washington, the streets were jammed with unfamiliar figures. The tension was marked, for the capital was still in danger.

Rose could not yet relax in her soft bed, or enjoy her meals, or stroll idly under the heavily foliaged trees, for the blues and grays were desperately engaged around Richmond, ending with the Confederate victory at Malvern on July 1. She was now within close range of the guns. During the last week of June the Seven Days' Battles raged, and she climbed with her friends to the rooftops to watch the drifting plumes of smoke that indicated how the fighting went. The relief was overwhelming when at last the Federal forces were driven back. The capital was saved but thousands were dead; thousands more lay wounded or dying in the hospitals.

Rose's personal affairs shrank into insignificance as she witnessed the intense suffering around her. Tears streamed down the cheeks of old friends, mourning their dead. In the words of Mrs. Roger A. Pryor: "Richmond had no language but a cry." Years later Mrs. Clay recalled this period with equal intensity: "After the terrible Battle of Seven Pines a mere mention of the deadly conflict for years was enough to start the tears in Southern eyes."

As Rose accompanied old family friends to the tobacco warehouses turned into hospitals she realized that although it was victory, it was also slaughter. She helped Miss Emily Mason, sister of James M. Mason, with her hospital work. Rose had been well trained in the

236

feminine arts. She was practical and determined, and knew how to cook, sew and tend the ill. Her nerves steadied in self-forgetfulness as she watched the suffering of the soldiers brought in.

When the dust and smoke of battle had somewhat subsided a storm of talk was whipped up by the ladies of Richmond about the presence of Mrs. Greenhow among them. Remembering her in full bloom, old friends commented on the change in her, and the urgency of her manner. Mrs. Chesnut took note of her presence in the capital with one of her crisp paragraphs:

Mrs. Rose Greenhow is in Richmond. One half of these ungrateful Confederates say Seward sent her. Mr. Chestnut says the Confederacy owes her a debt they never can pay. She warned them at Manassas, and so they got Joe Johnston and his Paladins to appear upon the stage in the very nick of time.

Early in July Mrs. Chesnut noted that Rachel Lyons was in Richmond, hand in glove with Mrs. Greenhow, adding: "Why not? 'So handsome, so clever, so angelically kind,' says Rachel of the Greenhow, 'and she offers to matronize me.'" Miss Lyons was a quick-witted beauty from Columbia, South Carolina, who had come with her father after the battles around Richmond to look for her missing brother, Captain I. L. Lyons. Some of the incriminating letters found in Rose's library were addressed to a Rachel.

In the midst of all his worries Jefferson Davis gave thought to Rose's affairs. On August 1 Judah P. Benjamin, by this time Secretary of State, sent her "on instructions from the President a check for $2,500 appropriated by him (out of the small fund placed at his disposal for secret service) as an acknowledgment of the valuable and patriotic service rendered by you to our cause."

At the same time the sum of five hundred dollars was sent to the obstreperous Mrs. Baxley, but there is no record of money being paid to Augusta Morris, who was in extreme disfavor when she left the South.

237

Rose was an old friend of the ubiquitous and genial Benjamin. She was familiar with his epicurean tastes, his fine Havana cigars, his fondness for a good glass of wine, his ingratiating manners and strong drive for power. Varina Davis likened him to fire and tow. He got on reasonably well with her husband, but Rose had not been back in Richmond long before she saw that Davis was having the same sort of trouble as Lincoln with his Cabinet members, his generals and the press. Unlike Lincoln, Davis was abnormally sensitive to disapprobation, and reacted with acute dyspepsia. He grew nervous under criticism. As a professional soldier he was baffled by congressional attack. Political opposition was whipped up by Robert Barnwell Rhett and his son. They owned the Charleston *Mercury*, and functioned much like the Blairs in Washington.

Until Robert E. Lee took command of the army and catalyzed the military elements, Davis also suffered with his generals as Lincoln did with his. Strategic retreats were not confined to the North and McClellan. But all approved of General Lee, and on July 19 the Richmond *Dispatch* commented:

The rise which this officer has suddenly taken in the public confidence is without precedence. . . . The operations of General Lee in the short campaign which is just over were certainly those of a master.

Rose was disturbed to find that her own particular favorite, Beauregard, was now at odds with Davis. The stiff-necked Mississippian and the vain Creole had never understood each other. Davis felt that Beauregard had been "placed too high for his mental strength." He disliked his braggadocio, his strategic retreats, his dependence on surgeon's certificates. He found it "hard to see incompetence losing opportunity and wasting hard-gotten gains." But he cultivated hope and patience and trusted "to the blunders of our enemy and the gallantry of our troops for ultimate success."

Rose had long been aware of the tension between the small, compact and alert Beauregard with his Gallic manners, and the warm-

238

hearted and vigorous Joseph E. Johnston. Knowing as much as she did about Manassas, she understood this well. In July she went to Charleston to visit General Beauregard, but cannily wrote first to James A. Seddon, Secretary of War, asking him to make her the bearer of dispatches so as to ensure her transportation.

"I am sure you can find time to lecture Beauregard or Bragg either —so as to oblige me," wheedled Rose. Her letter never reached its destination, for it was intercepted, but Rose did, and Beauregard gave her a warm reception and sent her across to Fort Sumter with an escort. Rose observed the piles of cannon balls, the clanking spurs and sabers, the sentinels pacing the ramparts. She took shrewd stock of the fortifications, an old interest of hers.

Mrs. Greenhow was an object of interest as she prowled around this historic citadel. She had genial relations with Beauregard, who had aged and grown gray since her last contact with him. They had much in common. He was the brother-in-law of John Slidell, having married Caroline Deslondes, Mrs. Slidell's handsome sister. The little General with his chivalrous manners, imaginative plans and wide reading on historic campaigns, always interested Rose. He treated her with deference and she continued to write to him and encourage him as he fell deeper into disfavor. In a sense she had helped to bring him into prominence. Nor had she lost touch with Jordan, who was thought to be Beauregard's amanuensis and to be responsible for some of his boastful writings. But on her return to Richmond Rose worked directly with Jefferson Davis.

After the Battle of Seven Pines Varina returned and the President moved into the handsome old Brockenbrough house on the brow of a hill. Cherry, apple and pear trees grew in the terraced gardens. The Carrara marble mantelpieces made a handsome background for Varina's entertainments. Rose frequently called on the Davises if the President happened to be at home. When a moment of freedom came, he would clatter up the hill on horseback with General Lee and their staff officers. The ever gallant Lee would apologize to

239

Varina for the mud splashed over her light carpet. She served him café au lait in Sèvres cups, using a little silver saucepan on the hearth and eking out the scanty herb.

Varina sometimes read verse to Jeff to distract him in these troubled days. He was fond of heroic songs, could speak Indian fluently and was familiar with Indian traditions from his days in the West. He also knew Spanish, Greek and Latin, and he and Rose had many common talking points from their joint pasts. She was not one of those who agreed with the Richmond Examiner that Varina was trying to create an "unrepublican court by being snobbish, by aping royalty, by putting her servants in livery and not returning calls."

In fact, Rose put on a vigorous campaign against the Examiner soon after her arrival in the South. It was controlled by the anti-Davis faction and was backed by such powerful politicians as Robert Toombs, who had been Secretary of State, and Alexander H. Stephens, Vice-President, both of whom had moved from friendliness to antagonism with Davis. The Rhetts and their Charleston paper were powerful factors in this fight.

Rose reported to Davis that the Examiner was having a pernicious effect in the North, "by exaggerating our internal differences and exposing our difficulties." While in prison she had found ample opportunity "to know the important information which they derived through its columns." Davis learned a great deal from Rose of conditions in the North, for her imprisonment had by no means dulled her knowledge of what was going on outside.

Although beset by opposition of all kinds, he would not hear of suppressing the Examiner, and Rose finally conceded that his reply befitted the head of a great nation. It was simply this: "Better suffer from that evil which is temporary, than arrest it by a still greater one. It is a dangerous thing to interfere with the liberty of the press, for what would it avail us if we gain our independence and lose our liberty?"

Rose was never close to General Lee in the way that she was to

240

Davis and Beauregard, but she viewed him with much respect. As the weeks went on the tempo of life in Richmond became hectic. There were bursts and flurries of gaiety as reaction from strain, and even Lee acknowledged: "My boys must be entertained." For the time being the enemy had been driven back, and except for those in mourning—and they were everywhere—the stream of life flowed on at a fast and desperate pace.

The days were given to hard work; the nights to dancing, music and romance. Rose now heard "Lorena," "Bonnie Blue Flag" and "Dixie" over and over again. From sewing circles the young and the gay went on to "danceable teas," for the men had to be cheered and the pulse beat of youth still called the tune. "We were young and in a garrisoned town, where officers and gold lace flourished," wrote one young belle. "Ergo, it became us to look beautiful in their eyes, to put on goodly apparel, and to the extent of our ability, we did."

"Oh! the seduction, the novelty, the fascination of life in Richmond," wrote Malvina Gist. "If patriotism is its master chord, pleasure is no less its dominant note, and while it is indescribable as the sparkle of champagne, it is no less intoxicating."

Mrs. Roger A. Pryor, always ready to coin a phrase, noted that "the soldier danced with the lady of his love at night, and on the morrow danced the dance of death in the deadly trenches of the line." Another belle exclaimed with some abandon: "We exist in a tremor of ecstasy. More men, more lovers, more music and dancing, more picknicking, flirting and singing. Brass buttons, epaulets and sword-belted manhood."

Rose was a sharp observer as she moved in and out of the homes of old Richmond families. She was grave and urgent as she made battle flags with skill and familiarity, handled heavy cloth, tenting and flannel, and knitted with some of the energy of Mrs. Lee, who, with her daughters, supplied General Carnot Posey's Brigade with 196 pairs of socks and gloves.

241

But Rose felt her age. She could no longer detach herself from the more somber realities of the moment. It was something like the early days of the war in Washington all over again—the campfires, gambling, prostitution, parades, tournaments, picnics, military balls, formal receptions, promenades, amateur theatricals, war weddings—and innumerable war funerals.

She watched girls dance at the Spotswood with flowers in their hair, their crinolines spreading like mushrooms from their narrow waists, their eyes alight with excitement, and she thought of Addie, Gertrude and Florence. There were dances at camps, in the open air, by the glow of wood fires. Evergreens garlanded the tents. Candles glowed through the darkness and lanterns flickered. The girls sat around in blankets after supper and rode home in wagons provided by the army.

The Richmond nights were heavy with the scent of magnolia. Fuchsia bushes showered their magenta and scarlet bells over white walls. Jessamine dangled from trellises. The wide streets meandered over the hill-based town to the banks of the James, starred with summer blossoms. Girls in bright dresses sat on porches and lawns in the daytime scraping lint. Their mothers promenaded or drove slowly under tulip and maple trees, worrying over husbands and sons. Fine carriages still moved along Franklin Street, drawn by Kentucky horses. A few liveried footmen remained, but the slaves no longer sang, rolling the tobacco leaf. Children played at war. Some had model camps manned by wooden soldiers, which they drilled with the intensity of their years.

Food was fabulously dear for the average home but famine had not yet set in. Turkeys, cured hams, terrapin, saddle of mutton, stuffed mangoes and oysters were still to be had, at a price. The gold fringe was not entirely frayed or gone. The silk gowns and jewels had not all disappeared from circulation. But darkness was gathering and none knew it better than Rose, as she compared notes with Mary Boykin Chesnut, Mrs. Louis D. Wigfall, Mrs. Joseph E. Johnston, Mrs.

Stephen R. Mallory, Mrs. Clement C. Clay and a number of older men who might jest and make gallant gestures, but grew ever more serious as the months rolled on and optimism declined.

Some of the women Rose had known in Washington returned to their plantations or went to the hills for the summer months. Although the fields were largely unharvested, beef, mutton, pork and fowl, eggs, milk and butter were produced on the plantations, and life went on to somber echoes, away from the constant rumble of fife and drum, and the slow beat of the funeral march continually heard in Richmond.

Rose worked quietly in the midst of alternating revelry and woe. She was no longer the flambuoyant Rose Greenhow, stared at as a curiosity. Her friends soon became used to her presence. She was back in their social circle as Robert Greenhow's widow. Her gaunt, handsome face was recognized wherever she went. But the legend of Manassas persisted. None believed that she was wholly out of service. Some were a little afraid of her. Few knew that she was quietly putting her prison diary into shape for publication. She had recovered some of her basic notes, and was reconstructing the whole while her memories were fresh.

And again she was summoning men to do her bidding. On her return from Charleston she wrote to a Major Alexander on a scrap of lined paper:

I have something to say to you officially. I suppose that is the orthodox mode of expression of the times,—so as soon as convenient you will do me the favor to call. The *right* man has turned up for the duty we spoke of the other day.

Was this Major G. W. Alexander, commander of Castle Thunder, who had stood by while Timothy Webster, one of Allan Pinkerton's most skilled assistants, was hanged for espionage? By a curious turn of the wheel, since her arrival in Richmond, Rose had been asked by two of her old detective foes, Pryce Lewis and John Scully, to inter-

243

vene with the Confederate authorities on their behalf. Pinkerton had sent them south to find Webster when he dropped from sight. Through their operations all three men were arrested. Lewis and Scully talked. Webster kept his counsel. In the end he was hanged, and the other two after a long interval were freed and sent north again.

There is no positive proof that Rose helped them, although a story circulated widely that she, Mrs. Morris and Mrs. Baxley were freed for purposes of exchange, after Pinkerton and Colonel Key appealed personally to Lincoln to take strong measures to save the three detectives. After this conference a message was sent to Richmond threatening retaliation and pointing out that Confederate prisoners had received lenient treatment in the North.

Was an exchange the issue that caused McClellan to jockey for months over Rose's release? Was this the proposal that Key put up to her in prison, that she considered and then rejected, fearing that in the end she would be betrayed? Congressman Ely, who visited her at about the same time, had been freed in exchange for her old friend, Faulkner, the former minister to France.

It seems likely that an exchange of some kind may have been proposed. Everyone knew that Rose had real influence with the Confederate Government. On the other hand, she was an uncompromising hater, and would have scorned to admit having helped two of her persecutors, or having bartered her freedom in this manner.

By winter a sharp decline had set in. Soldiers' rations were tightened up. Food was scarce as well as dear. All kinds of substitutes were in use. The blockade had begun to tell. Rose's operations during the winter of 1862-63 had a slightly hazy note. She had taken up speculation in cotton and tobacco.

This situation came to light in May, 1863, when Joseph Holt, by that time Judge-Advocate-General, reported to Stanton that W. T. Smithson, the Washington banker who had been arrested for the second time in the North, was engaged in illegal negotiations with

Rose. He was buying and selling Southern securities and bank currency on a widespread scale. He had negotiated sight drafts on Richmond as well as 8 per cent Confederate bonds, and had filled orders for Confederate notes in amounts ranging from five hundred to fifty thousand dollars, buying them in some instances from persons straight from Richmond. Couriers sent by Rose perhaps?

She was deeply involved in these negotiations and a certificate for 120 shares of railroad stock belonging to her was found in Smithson's bank after his arrest. She had given him power of attorney to act as her agent and to sell and collect all stocks, securities and dividends which she held in the North.

Beauregard had fallen from favor but Rose still pushed his cause and encouraged him. Some of the bravest of the Southern generals now were dead. Albert Sidney Johnston met his end at Shiloh. In May the South lost its most picturesque warrior—Stonewall Jackson, the bearded soldier with vizor cap and enormous cavalry boots who died in the blossoming Shenandoah Valley after being accidentally shot by his own men at Chancellorsville and then developing pneumonia.

"Let us pass over the river, and rest under the shade of the trees," he said at the end. And Jed Hotchkiss, who had made his maps and been his constant companion, added: "We miss him all the time and a void is made here which time can hardly fill."

Winchester was again being lost and taken by the two armies and Mrs. Lee wrote:

I wonder how we can live through this perpetual excitement and anxiety—still every day life goes on as usual, we read, sew, eat, lie down after dinner, dress for the evening, persons come in to visit. High and low are bound together by the same interests and the same sympathies and we talk to all the passersby. We lead a strange life and are growing callous to danger, and, I fear, callous in many other respects.

Mrs. Pryor, in the Blue Ridge Mountains, viewed the valley carpeted with moss and tender grass, and thickly gemmed with daisies

245

and purple asters. The skies looked "as if made of roses, but oh, the anguish of anxiety, the terror, the dreams at night of battle and murder and sudden death." Soon she would be back in Richmond, selling her laces, her jewels, her fans, her silks, the shaded roses she wore at Lady Napier's final ball.

For the high optimism of the South was fading. Soldiers were deserting. Gold was scarce, and the Confederate currency was looked on with suspicion. Although cotton and tobacco still got out, much of it was lost at the bottom of the ocean. Confederate negotiations with the British and French governments were faring badly.

By midsummer it was settled that Rose should go to Europe, to get her book published in London and stir up whatever sympathy she could for the Confederacy. Shortly before her departure James M. Mason wrote urgently to Benjamin, saying he believed the "true mode of raising money in England would be through cotton sales in the form, if not the actual terms, described by the Cotton Certificates from the Treasury." This market had not yet been tested. Cotton would be offered in exchange for ships or other goods.

Rose was commissioned to do what she could for the South. She was to function as an unofficial ambassador at a moment when France, as well as Britain, was chilling toward the Confederacy. As Douglas Southall Freeman puts it: "One cannot think of a more appealing agent for the support of the chivalrous element in Britain than this beautiful dark-haired widow, who knew every social art and had mastered the none-too-complicated technique of winning masculine sympathy." Or, in the words of Carl Sandburg, a woman with a "gaunt beauty, education, manners and resourceful speech . . . her proud loyalty to the South and her will and courage set her apart as a woman who would welcome death from a firing squad if it would serve her cause."

It was with this spirit that Rose prepared to sail for England in August, 1863, with Jefferson Davis' blessing. The South was staggering from the defeat of Gettysburg. Davis suffered. Lee had offered to resign. Right up to the end Rose worked for the cause. Late in July she made a special plea for the heavy guns and mortars needed by Beauregard for the defense of Charleston.

Jefferson Davis seemed deeply concerned and told her he was quite alive to the importance of this matter. With bewilderment he asked: "But where am I to get them?"

General Samuel Cooper, who was present at the interview, added: "I have sent him every available gun."

"Such I found from careful enquiry to be the case," Rose reported to Beauregard, ever alert to his interests. "All eyes are turned to you now—and although the deepest anxiety prevails—the fullest confidence is felt in your being able to do more with the means at your command and to drive back the invaders than could be effected by anyone else. But alas! Providence just now seems in the line of the heaviest artillery."

Thus Rose whipped up the flagging spirit of Beauregard. She took mournful note of Gettysburg and deplored the causes which led to the failure of the campaign in Pennsylvania, forcing Lee to fall back. They were "too humiliating to think on," she wrote. It was the first time that the Southern men "had faltered or fled ingloriously from any battlefield."

But again Rose sounded an optimistic note. She believed that the army of Pennsylvania by this time was in a more admirable condition and was eager for the expected battle. Then, with the old technique cropping out, she added: "Meade is crossing at various points and pressing us heavily. This information comes from the most reliable source." She finished with reassurance for Beauregard and an intimation that she still had influence with Davis: "The President mentioned incidentally that it had been the intention of General Lee to call you to the army of the Pa but that the report of the enemies' movements of Charleston have prevented it."

Up to the moment of sailing Rose worked for Davis along individualistic lines. On August 4, 1863, her last night in Wilmington, ⅄

North Carolina, she saw General W. H. C. Whiting and he promised her he would raise a cavalry brigade among persons he knew, provided the officers were promised commissions. Men were getting scarce in the Confederate ranks.

Shortly before she embarked Rose wrote to Davis, giving him this piece of news, and also expressing amazement over the number of blockade runners in the city "who ought to be in the army." She also showed a touch of concern on her own account as she faced the blockade. Rose had never been abroad and this was not a healthy moment to cross the Atlantic. She wrote:

The Yankees are reported as being unusually vigilant, a double line of blockaders block the way. Still, I am nothing daunted and hope by the blessing of Providence, to get out in safety. . . .

And now, my dear sir, I must say good-bye. I can never sufficiently thank you for your goodness to me. May He ever guard you, sir, and keep you in health, is my most fervent prayer.

There is no doubt that Rose was still in the best of standing with Jefferson Davis, was sharing in military counsels and was exercising some degree of influence in her old authoritative manner. She sailed next day on the *Phantom*, a fast new ship whose captain preferred to enter her as an ordinary passenger, instead of listing her as an agent of the Confederate Government, or carrying her anonymously. Rose reported this to Davis, and also told him that Dr. Gwin and Lucy were sailing at the same time on the *Ella and Annie*.

Rose carried letters from her President to John Slidell and James M. Mason, the Confederate Commissioners in Europe. She had the completed manuscript of her book. She was up to the minute on cotton and blockade operations. And she was well equipped to plead the Confederate cause to all who might listen. Rose prepared for this new adventure with some of the fervor of Harriet Beecher Stowe, whose *Uncle Tom's Cabin* a decade earlier had been powerful propaganda in Britain for the antislavery forces, and had sold to the tune of a million copies.

248

The *Phantom* put in at Bermuda, and before Rose left the turquoise waters washing the island, she sent back several items of news to Jefferson Davis. She reported favorably on Major Norman Walker, the Confederate agent "who has a difficult and delicate post here." She discussed with him his monetary difficulties in processing funds into gold and silver, when there was no bank in Bermuda. She reported on a decision reached by the crown attorneys there that all vessels on the high seas were lawfully subject to capture, even though owned by British subjects. And she gave Davis the latest news of a blockade runner which had jettisoned 150 bales of cotton to escape the Union gunboats.

As further proof of Rose's official status on this journey she sailed from Bermuda to England in a British man of war by "President Davis's special request." She was accompanied by little Rose, whom she intended to enter in a convent in Paris. Florence was already abroad, awaiting their arrival. This was the way in which mother and daughter had planned to meet again, without the armies of the North and South between them. Moore had become quite affluent through his mining investments. Leila was happily settled in a boarding school in Pennsylvania. Rose was eager to draw the family together after the dark days of her imprisonment. She longed to see her oldest daughter again. Crossing the Atlantic Ocean was the roundabout way in which they bridged the gap.

(CHAPTER XVI

Triumphs in Europe

M RS. GREENHOW was received by the Emperor of France
in a small salon in the Tuileries on a January day
in 1864. It was an official audience and she was there to plead the
cause of the South with him. Beyond doubt she did it both eloquently
and well, and was an impressive figure into the bargain. The Emperor was courteous to Rose, but she had come too late. The open
door between France and the Confederacy was closing decisively at
the time of her arrival, and her eloquence was wasted.

John Slidell reported to Secretary of State Benjamin from Paris
on January 25, 1864: "Mrs. Greenhow has had an interview with
the Emperor, the particulars of which are to be found in the accompanying letter to the President."

Rose was the final card played by the Confederacy with the
Emperor. She was working closely with Commander Matthew Fontaine Maury in his efforts to get ships from France. In September
the British Government had held up the ironclad rams that were
ready to sail from Liverpool to the Confederate States. Lord Russell
had favored their going. When he informed Charles Francis Adams
that the government could not interfere in any way with these
vessels, the American Minister quietly replied: "It would be superfluous in me to point out to your lordship that this is war."

The North won. The rams were held. Gettysburg, too, had made

250

an impression. France chilled off. And immediately after Rose's audience with the Emperor, Commander Maury sailed for Richmond to make a personal report to the Navy Department on the "total failure of our efforts to get out ships, either from France or England." He feared that written dispatches might be lost at sea, since much else was going to the bottom.

At the same time Mason reported to Benjamin from London: "From England we have long since had nothing to expect; from France we had a right to entertain a belief of other results. . . . I confess that I see neither excuse nor palliation in the defeat of our expectations in that quarter."

Commander Maury had been in Europe since the autumn of 1862, using his international prestige to win support. He had been making headway with the French Emperor by working hard on the synthesis of international relations involving Mexico, France and the United States. He was a friend of the Archduke Maximilian of Austria who, like most European rulers, was familiar with the work of the distinguished geographer. Maury had hopes that Maximilian might be a factor in swinging French support to the Confederacy. He even envisioned a plan to separate California from the Union and restore it to Mexico, should the South win. This was strong bait for Maximilian, but the French Emperor backed down on these intrigues when England declined to join him in recognition of the Confederacy.

When Rose saw the Emperor she was well aware that his plans for Mexico were a complicating factor. None who visited him had closer knowledge of recent Mexican political history than she, or could talk more glibly on the subject. But by that time the Emperor's plans were changing, partly because of the uproar created a few months earlier in the British House of Commons by John Arthur Roebuck, champion of the South who, with William S. Lindsay, aide to Lord Palmerston, was received at Fontainebleau in June, and discussed with the Emperor the British and French attitude to the Confederacy.

Roebuck promptly created international complications by announcing in the House of Commons that the Emperor told them he was prepared to recognize the Confederacy if Britain would move in the same direction. He was forced to back down abruptly and withdraw his motion for recognition of the South when the Emperor repudiated this stand. The storm that blew up at this point hampered the Confederacy interests from then on. The attack was expertly led by John Bright. The vehement Roebuck was an ardent champion of the slaveholder and boasted that Lord Palmerston had confessed to him that he was on the same side.

The situation was still ambiguous at the time of Rose's arrival. There seemed to be a remaining thread of hope, and everyone concerned prayed that she could soften the Emperor, on the question of ships at least. She did all that she could on Maury's behalf, knowing him to be a prized agent of the Confederacy, and a man respected in all the countries of Europe. Beyond that, she was working for her sacred cause.

Aside from her private audience with the Emperor, she was formally presented at court. The Empress, of mixed Spanish, Scottish and American blood, was known to lean strongly to the South. Eugénie must have observed Mrs. Greenhow with interest—an espionage agent who had long been a favorite of the French Legation in Washington, and was the special pet of the Comte de Sartiges and his wife. Rose had done France some favors, and had sought some in return, during the long years of her ascendancy. At a magnificent ball given by the Emperor, she alone was singled out for press comment, aside from royalty.

Worried though she was, Rose gravely took note of the enchantments of Paris. Fresh from the anguish of a country torn by civil war, she found brief relaxation in a city that could still afford to be gay.

252

She had never been abroad before, and she viewed Paris with appreciation—its shops filled with luxury goods, its salons brisk with the bright interchange of thought on which she thrived, its streets rich with historic meaning to one so politically minded.

Soon after their arrival from America Florence had brought little Rose over from London and had entered her in the Convent of the Sacred Heart. Her mother was glad to find her happy and thriving when she crossed the Channel on her political mission. Mrs. Slidell, with all her Creole grace and her old friendship for the Greenhows, paved the way for them in Paris. The American rush of presentations at court had tapered off, since the diplomatic complications were acute, and the planters and financiers who had swarmed into Paris each year with their families were now in uniform. But a number of American girls were there in school. They attended literary and scientific lectures and, as one observer of the American colony of that period said of them: "Utterly self-reliant, they walk as daughters of a conquering race, who have made themselves a place under the sun."

While in Paris Rose followed the American war news through the papers in the reading room of the Grand Hotel. It got no better. She talked persuasively to French bankers and diplomats, discussing cotton and cotton bonds. She looked up friends she had known in the French Legation in Washington. She was welcomed in various salons and drew the interest of some of the literary figures of the day.

Rose was glad to have Florence with her again and in the afternoons they drove together in the Bois. She recovered some of her old zest for fashion as she viewed the open carriages with footmen in powdered wigs and satin breeches, and women sporting the gorgeous trappings of the Eugénie era. Until Robert's death Rose had always been one of the most elegantly turned-out women in Washington, getting many of her clothes from Paris, but her months in jail and her saddening days in the South had reduced her wardrobe and

253

dimmed her interest in dress. Now, with the financial help of Florence, she bought new clothes for herself and for little Rose.

Her youngest daughter was especially dear to her. They had suffered much together. She had worked hard over all her children, and the better part of their education had come from Rose herself. She had carefully supervised their work in their younger years and had personally coached them in French, composition and history. She and Robert had always planned a thorough education for their daughters. Now there was an added reason for placing Rose in a school in Paris. She wanted to get her as far away as possible from the horrors of war.

Rose feared greatly for her youngest child's future. Deceit, terror and brutality had already impinged on her consciousness. She had been witness to revolting sights in Old Capitol Prison, and the hysteria that prevailed had taken its toll. She must also have been confused by the role her mother had played, and the curious events of recent months.

Actually, little Rose's life was to take many strange turns. Could her mother have foreseen her fate, as she kissed her good-by in Paris for the last time, she would have learned that Rose developed into a handsome girl at the convent, and came out of it at seventeen, seemingly sweet, unspoiled and quite tamed after her lurid experiences in jail.

American friends took her home to the Moores. By that time Treadwell was a general, and commandant at Newport, Rhode Island. There Rose fell in love with a young West Pointer, Lieutenant William Penn Duvall, who was to have a brilliant military career, fight in the Spanish-American War, in the Philippines and the First World War, winding up as a general with many decorations and honors.

They were married before Rose had turned her eighteenth birthday, but Duvall, a severe disciplinarian both in and out of the army, eventually divorced her after much marital discord. For a time she appeared on the stage. Then she returned to France, became deeply

254

religious and retired from public view. She had one daughter, Lee, who became Mrs. Louis Marié and lived in California for many years.

But knowing nothing of the future the elder Rose hoped for the best as she established her daughter in the convent and returned to England, where her book, *My Imprisonment and the First Year of Abolition Rule at Washington*, was selling well and being widely discussed. Richard Bentley, Publisher in Ordinary to Her Majesty, had brought it out in November, immediately after Rose's arrival from America. She dedicated it "to the brave soldiers who have fought and bled in this our glorious struggle for freedom."

It was promptly used to whip up sentiment for the South, and was thought to be backed by Confederate funds. On a lesser scale it stirred up talk in the way that *Uncle Tom's Cabin* had done. But the point of view was vastly different. Moreover, it purported to be fact, not thinly veiled fiction. Rose used names with pungency and irreverence. Lincoln, Seward, Wilson, Stanton—all the "lords of abolition," as she called them—passed in acid review.

The diary was accepted with some respect and much interest in Britain. It made Rose a celebrity at once. Echoes of the stir it was causing reached Washington, and Colonel Doster imported a copy and paid sixteen dollars in gold for it. He was anxious to see what Rose had to say about Old Capitol Prison, and with good reason, for her book dealt largely with her days in jail. It covered only one year of her life, with an occasional flashback to prove a point.

Yet it remains an illuminating testament to the life, aims and personality of Mrs. Greenhow. Her pride and prejudices come into view on every page. Her shrewdness, guile and romantic drive are quite apparent, and her personality is defined through her knack for dramatizing the volcanic events of her life. Rose's undeniable knowledge of men and affairs, the sweep of her experience, her genuine passion for the South and her warm familial feelings are clearly magnified through the spectrum of one year's intensified living.

In her introduction she concedes that some of her comments are more "bitterly vituperative and sarcastic" than become the personal narrative of a woman. But she asks her readers to consider her position. Then, detailing some of the horrors of Old Capitol Prison, she adds: "No wonder if my nature grew harsh and vindictive, and if the scorn and wrath that was in my heart sometimes found vent by tongue or pen."

She explains why she used the names of some of her informants and concealed others. She had no hesitation about naming statesmen who had broken bread at her table; whom she had once considered friends, but now were mortal enemies. Seward and Wilson were in this category. But she felt that the Federal officers whom she "had induced without scruple to help her" had earned her protection.

The text that follows her introduction, in which she amply illustrates her self-accusation of using men without scruple, proved to be a sensational personal confession story that made her a center of discussion in 1863. The literary set took her up. Rose swiftly established herself with Thomas Carlyle and became a regular visitor on Cheyne Walk. Carlyle gibed at Lincoln, while Robert Browning championed him. Rose urged Carlyle to write an article on the Southern Revolution. He agreed, but no more was heard of it.

She was swept into the literary and artistic set because of her book and her immediate aura as a political prisoner of Abraham Lincoln's, but she did not neglect the more formal Victorian drawing rooms. Rose was always the grande dame, never the authentic bohemian. She had no wish to call on Abigail Adams, and indeed the American Minister and his wife were still suffering from a social frost in Britain that they would shortly melt, staying to establish themselves as two of the most honored figures ever to fill the British Legation in London.

But many of Buchanan's old friends rallied around Mrs. Greenhow and she soon was in excellent social standing. She was presented at

256

court. Queen Victoria, like the Empress Eugénie, must have noticed her with interest, for she was well known to Lord Palmerston, Lord Clarendon, Lord Russell, Lord Napier, Lord Lyons and all the Englishmen who had wrestled at close range with the complications of civil war in America. Moreover, she was a lady who had served a term in jail for her political convictions, a novel situation.

Rose saw much of Florence Nightingale and of Lady Franklin, widow of Sir John Franklin, the explorer who lost his life in an attempt to discover the Northwest Passage. Both Robert and she had met the Franklins in the past. There were few explorers of world-wide reputation not known to the Greenhows. But Rose was seen most frequently with Lady Georgiana Fullerton, another association from the past, whose brother, the second Earl of Granville, became her particular friend.

Lady Fullerton's father, the first Earl of Granville, was British minister to France, and she had lived at the British Legation in Paris at a time when Robert was most active in the State Department. She was now a serene-faced philanthropist, a Catholic convert, and a friend of Cardinal Newman. She was instrumental in bringing the Sisters of St. Vincent de Paul to England, and was the author of thirty books of a semireligious order.

As the months went on Rose mellowed under the soothing influence of stately Victorian drawing rooms, jeweled women and worldly, traveled men. She was no longer an outraged virago, arguing with jailers. The gaunt look of her prison days was gone. Crystal chandeliers and candlelight cast a softening glow over her aging features. A portrait taken of her in London shows her composed and at ease; her hollows rounded out, and with only a dash of skepticism in her expression evoking the rebel Rose of Washington. She whirled around ballrooms as in the days of her youth. Statesmen paid court to her, and soon she was again, and for the last time, in love—a basic and urgent need of her nature. She was reported engaged to Lord Granville, who had recently become a widower. By this time she

257

had abandoned the mourning to which she had committed herself for life. Red roses appeared in her hair. Jewels sparkled at her throat.

After Rose's death Lady Fullerton devoted a thirty-eight-verse poem to her impressions of the visiting American. She recalled her last view of her:

> I saw her last, one summer eve
> In London in a room
> Where brilliant lights and converse gay
> Banished all thoughts of gloom.
>
> Her head was decked with roses red,
> Bright jewels on her breast.
> Her dark and most expressive eyes,
> The keenest hopes expressed.
>
> She poured in English statesmen's ears
> Her pleadings for the South;
> It was a joy to her to feel
> They heard them from her mouth.

But Rose was so intense in her denunciation of the North that she sometimes alarmed the temperate Lady Fullerton. She felt that her "frantic sense of bitter wrong" rose almost to the pitch of madness when she dwelt on the treatment of the South. She noted the flash of her eyes, the "curl of her proud lip" as Rose vowed to live and die for the Southern cause.

> Fierce was her glance, and fierce her words,
> She loathed the northern foe;
> With that intensity of hate,
> Impassioned women know.
>
> Grand, but appalling was the burst
> Of passion shook her frame,
> When from her breast the rushing tide
> Of Vengeful anger came.

Lady Fullerton, who was working hard to bring Rose back into the Catholic Church, was pleased to see some softening at last. She noted that there were tears in her eyes when someone did her a kindness. But there still was no forgiveness in her, and thoughts of vengeance burned her up. Lady Fullerton worried about her eternal soul and tried to revive her zeal as she watched a conflict rage in Rose "between her natural grace and the tide of passion springing from the might of human love and pride."

But during her last months in London Rose seemed to Lady Fullerton to have mastered some of her bitterness and to have recovered her religious faith:

> It ceased at last, grace won the day;
> She knelt, and though her fears
> And eager hopes for her own land,
> Were strong as in past years.
>
> The frantic curse died on her lips,
> Her own wrongs she forgave.
> The heart that had been fierce became
> Thenceforward only brave.
>
> Her strength, her life, to the same cause
> Were still as wildly giv'n;
> But a dark cloud no longer stood
> Betwixt her soul and Heaven.

Rose's days and evenings at all times were devoted in one way or another to the Confederacy. She talked. She wrote. She lectured. She advocated her cause with flaming passion to the leading statesmen of the day. She presented herself against "rows of lurid lights," running the blockade. She pictured the horrors of a Northern prison. She gave England a heated view of the statesmen of the North.

A century later Rose would have been recognized as an effective propagandist. As it was she was a flexible link in the ring of commissioners and agents working with great assiduity for the South. Able

259

both with her pen and her tongue, she swung easily from one operation to another. Mason's status had become uncertain, since he had lost official standing as a commissioner, and was continually being warned to stay out of London. Charles Francis Adams, in London, and John Bigelow, Consul-General in Paris, worked determinedly against Mason and Slidell, particularly in their efforts to get ships for the Confederacy.

Rose was an old friend of Mason's. She considered him a true patrician, unlike Mrs. Chesnut, who had deplored his appointment and noted in her diary that he said "chaw" for chew, called himself "Jeems," wore a dress coat to breakfast and chewed tobacco. Rose was a regular visitor at his home in Upper Seymour Street, where she used her own form of diplomacy with his many guests to counteract the growing Adams prestige.

The political elements surrounding Rose in England were complex. The press and the cotton trade were firmly aligned against the Union. The greater part of the British working class favored the North, but the peerage was almost solidly in sympathy with the South. Adams, impassively watching the shifting currents of public opinion, had John Bright, Richard Cobden, the Duke of Argyll, Richard Moncton Milnes and other articulate forces on his side. Lord Russell and Lord Palmerston, after some wavering, at last stood firm for neutrality. Adams was critical of Russell for having received Mason and Slidell, but in time these two men swung so close together that Russell eventually was accused of being under the influence of the able New Englander, just as Lord Palmerston was thought to have leaned strongly to the Confederacy.

Unlike Buchanan who, because of his past experience in the diplomatic field, preferred to run his own foreign affairs, Lincoln left the field strictly to Seward. Adams was Seward's appointee. In fact he had backed the Senator from New York for the Presidency and sailed for England in the spring of 1861 still persuaded that although Lincoln was "honest and tolerably capable" he lacked experience. Adams was immediately faced with the fact that Britain had just issued its Proclamation of Neutrality. There was fast work to be done for the North, since the Confederate agents wasted no time in lining up support.

Although prominent on the social front, a hush surrounded the work Rose did with Commander Maury in England. They made a powerful combination as they proselytized for the South in the drawing rooms of Victorian England, but behind the scenes they were involved in a network of quiet activity. Rose had much in common with the Virginian oceanographer who had contributed so much to the early success of the Confederate Navy. He reminded her of Robert in the nature of his interests, and his quiet, patient methods of exploration.

Maury was a barrel-chested figure, lame, small and square-set. He had clear blue eyes, curling brown hair and a massive neck. He was of Huguenot, Dutch and English stock, his family having settled in Virginia. On the day of Lincoln's inauguration he wrote: "The line of duty, therefore, is to me clear—each one to follow his own State, if his own State goes to war; if not, he may remain to help on the work of reunion."

Like Rose, he had profound belief in his principles and no effort was too great for him to make on behalf of the Confederacy. Such was his prestige in Europe that he was thought to be the perfect agent, but he was a practical man of scientific bent, and the frustration he experienced was crushing for him.

He had brought over money with which to buy gunboats, but the immediate drive by all the agents was to offer cotton for ships and other supplies. In the months that followed he sparked a commission of Confederate naval officers in London who worked hard to get ships on any terms. He bought the *Georgia* and *Victor* and tried to persuade shipbuilders with vessels already under construction to sell to him. There was an urgent need for ships of all kinds for blockade running. In the first year of the war the Confederacy claimed that 792 vessels entered or cleared its ports.

But the blockade kept tightening up. More and more of the cotton reached the bottom of the ocean. Maury meanwhile arranged for the rams that were eventually held up. He also pursued his researches on electric mines, torpedoes and other new devices, with the better facilities afforded him at the time in Britain. Meanwhile, he kept a watchful eye on the English agents for treachery.

He made his headquarters outside Manchester and directed the operations of a group of English writers and cotton experts. One was James Spence, a writer and businessman well known in the North. He was the author of *American Union*, which stated the case for the South. It went through four editions and was widely read in Britain. He ran an agency in Liverpool for the sale of Confederate bonds, and worked as "an auxiliary to the purposes of the Navy Department"—in other words, as an aide in the secret work being done by Maury and Commander James D. Bulloch on ships, mines, blockade operations and cotton.

Both Spence and Henry Hotze, another writer, combined commercial and literary operations for the Confederacy. They started *The Index*, a weekly review promoting the Southern cause. They gave out information to free-lance writers who sold to the contemporary magazines pieces favorable to the South. Hotze reported to Secretary of State Benjamin that all this was leading to the foundation of a "school of writers whose services in the moral battles we still have to fight will, from their positions, be more valuable than those of the ablest pens of our own country."

George McHenry, another of the "commerical agents" who doubled in brass as writer and trader, informed Mason immediately after the publication of Rose's book that he was taking it with him when he went north to Manchester "to buttonhole a few of the leading manufacturers and talk cotton with them."

With her dramatic story, her book and her eloquence on a public platform, Rose fitted into these operations with great ease. *The Index* quoted her freely, and her writings were pushed hard in the Northern cotton and shipping centers where Spence and Hotze were most active. Three Southern clubs were organized—in Liverpool, Manchester and Birmingham—and clothing and money were collected for the Confederacy. Public meetings were held in towns and villages, and Rose was in demand for these, as she was for bazaars and gatherings promoted by the peerage on behalf of the South. Since much wealth and prestige lay behind these operations, for a time she floated on a golden cloud.

Both Rose and Maury were active in the Society for Obtaining the Cessation of Hostilities in America, which met at 215 Regent Street and had more than five thousand members by the summer of 1864. This organization was formed "to promote the cause of Southern independence." It was backed by men of both political parties and was organized by Lord Wharncliffe. Its members included the Marquis of Lothian, Lord Robert Cecil, Lord Eustace Cecil, Justice W. S. Halliburton, the Marquis of Bath, A. J. B. Beresford Hope, C. W. Fitzwilliams, G. Peacocke, Robert Bourke, W. S. Lindsay, F. W. Tremlett and other prominent Parliamentarians.

But Maury grew dispirited after the defection of the Emperor of France and the ban on the outgoing rams. He felt that all his work had gone for nothing. He wrote to a Richmond friend on March 23, 1864: "We have nothing to look for from England that money won't buy." It was at this point that he said good-by to Mason, Rose and other Confederate friends in London and returned to Richmond to make a secret report to Jefferson Davis on the shipping situation, and on the various moves involving the French Emperor and Maximilian. He could no longer trust these matters to dispatches that might be lost.

Rose pursued her work without a break. Her stately figure, now gowned in the most modish clothes, supplied by Florence, was frequently seen swirling into 17 Leadenhall Street and the small dark office of Alexander Collie, a shipping merchant who owned the largest fleet of blockade runners operating between British and Confederate ports. He boasted in a letter to Mason, dated December 11, 1863, that in three months he had run out cotton valued at 200,000 pounds sterling for the government.

Now, nearly a year later, he was imploring Rose to help him with the Confederate Government. On August 9, 1864, he gave her power of attorney "to settle certain controversies that had arisen between him and the Confederate States government," showing that her functions were official and that she was still in firm standing. His agent, Theodore Andrea, had been ousted at Wilmington "for bringing the state of North Carolina into violent collision with the general government."

Collie wished the ban raised so that Andrea could return. He considered him the most able and intelligent agent he had ever had and he had found reports of his lack of integrity to be false in every instance. He believed he had been "too successful in his operations and had aroused jealousy."

At this point Collie guilefully mentioned the fact that he had arranged with Andrea to contribute ten thousand dollars a month for six months to Southern charities through Mr. Seddon, and had set aside one branch of his business solely for this purpose. Goods would be sent into the Confederate States for distribution.

"My efforts in this way will now be necessarily limited for want of the intelligence to carry them out," Collie concluded. "If you can aid me in the matter privately at Richmond you will oblige me and I know that thereby you will benefit many of your countrymen."

Rose found a wealth of sympathy for the Confederacy wherever she went in England. She fed the blaze with considerable skill and energy, but every week that passed now brought woeful news from the South. Ulysses Grant had gone into action in the East against Lee and the struggle was grim. The battles of the Wilderness, Spotsylvania and Cold Harbor followed one another in quick succession with frightful slaughter. Rose heard how Lee twice rode at the head of his men to inspire them at Cold Harbor.

264

There was now a desperate shortage of food and wearing apparel, and Rose determined to take clothing back for the women of the South, for she was planning a return trip to make a personal report to Davis, as Maury had done, on the shipping and cotton bond situation. Dispatches were being lost with increasing frequency, and the time had come for Rose to make a personal report on many matters in which she had been involved, including the Mexican maneuvers and her interview with the Emperor.

Rose wrote to Mrs. Lee—the last letter she was ever to send to her sister-in-law and, curiously enough, the only one of many she sent that was not lost at sea—telling her of the people she was meeting and the success she was having in arousing sympathy for the Southern cause. Florence shared her mother's social rounds in London, but she planned on her departure to return to the Continent, to visit little Rose in Paris, then to tour the spas for her health, returning later for Rose's projected marriage. Leila was doing well in a good school in Pennsylvania and was destined eventually to marry a man named Alexander Cravens.

Exactly a year after her arrival in England Rose packed for her return trip to the Confederacy. Again she was going on a mission, but this time she planned a speedy return, for she had definitely decided to marry Lord Granville. But in the meantime she was the bearer of important information. She was laden down with gold, the proceeds from her book. She was bringing clothes for the women of the Confederacy. There was much she planned to reveal to Jefferson Davis, but the hour was later than she knew. The Confederacy was heading for defeat, although Davis still spread optimism. There was little more that Rose could do. But her own last drama was in the making—a climax befitting all that had gone before.

CHAPTER XVII

Death for the Confederacy

Revived in spirit, years younger in looks, Rose sailed for the Confederacy from Greenock on August 10, 1864. She wrote farewell notes to Lady Fullerton and other London friends as she waited in lowering mists for the hour of sailing. Blockade running became more dangerous by the day and no woman crossed the Atlantic at this time without good cause. But Rose had been through it once and had talked much in England of the excitement of running the blockade.

She sailed in the *Condor*, a new three-funneled steamer built in Glasgow and now bound on its first trip to the Confederate States. It was of rakish build, long and narrow in the beam, with three low funnels and two short masts. It drew only seven feet of water and was "swift as a sea swallow," according to the *Evening Mail* of London. Its hull was painted a light lead color. It was three hundred tons and schooner-rigged, with a crew of forty-five.

Unlike Maury who, in spite of his lifelong association with the ocean, got deathly seasick every time he boarded a ship, Rose enjoyed the sea. She found exhilaration in the dash of spray across the bow, and the wild plunging of the *Condor* as they sailed through heavy seas. She was on friendly terms with the six-foot commander, calling himself Samuel S. Ridge on this voyage. Actually, he was Augustus Charles Hobart-Hampden, younger son of the sixth Earl of Bucking-

266

hamshire, a winner of the Victoria Cross in the Crimean War, a favorite of Queen Victoria, skipper of her yacht and one of the highest ranking officers in the British Navy. Tuned to adventure, it was he who led British troops aboard the Russian battleships in the war of 1854 in response to Admiral Sir Charles Napier's challenge: "Lads, sharpen your cutlasses."

As a blockade runner he used the aliases Hewett, Roberts, Gulick and, on this occasion, Ridge. He was legendary along the coast and had already figured in one international incident which had nearly precipitated war when he picked up Slidell and Mason at Provincetown and took them to England in the man of war *Rinaldo*, after their forcible removal from the British steamer *Trent*.

He was then known as Admiral Hewett and he bore a letter from Lord Lyons, who had dined often with the Slidells in Washington, asking him to treat them as gentlemen of distinction. The entire incident was one of intense embarrassment to Seward and had momentarily shaken British and American relations. After escorting the Confederate commissioners to Europe the Admiral must have maintained friendly relations with Mason in London, for he promptly engaged in running ships for the Confederacy—a game that appealed to his adventurous spirit. He took Rose aboard with full knowledge of her role. At the last moment he received dispatch bags from Mason with instructions to give them to Mrs. Greenhow upon landing, since she was headed straight for Richmond.

Fellow passengers noticed that handsome Mrs. Greenhow, who walked the deck in the stormiest seas, wore a large heavy leather reticule suspended by a long chain around her neck. She was never seen without it, either in the saloon, dining room or on deck. They did not suspect that she was heavily weighted with two thousand dollars in English gold, or more than three hundred sovereigns at the prevailing rate of exchange. Some were sewn in her clothing.

When the *Condor* reached Halifax on September 7 with a "very large and valuable cargo" Rose was glad to welcome an old friend

267

and fellow agent aboard—James B. Holcombe. He had been serving for several months as Confederate commissioner to the North American Colonies of Great Britain, and was stationed at Halifax. At the moment he was fresh from the embarrassment of the confused and abortive peace negotiations that he, Jacob Thompson and Clement C. Clay tried to engineer through Horace Greeley at Niagara Falls.

The administration at Richmond had cut the ground from under Holcombe's feet by repudiating the peace feelers. Rose was well primed on this situation, since Benjamin had written to Mason in London saying that although Clay and Holcombe enjoyed the confidence and esteem of Jefferson Davis, they had acted wholly without authority. Rose must have listened with considerable interest to Holcombe's first-hand account of this inexplicable episode as she walked the deck with him and dined at his table. She knew him of old as an eloquent orator and a champion of states' rights.

They were delayed at Halifax, waiting for the moon to wane. Darkness favored blockade runners. It was September 24 before they set sail again. M. M. Jackson, the U.S. Consul at Halifax, notified Seward that along with her cargo the Condor carried clothing and necessities for the Confederate Army. There was no mention of Mrs. Greenhow or the scholarly Holcombe being on board. But Gideon Welles, Secretary of the Navy, automatically notified Acting Rear Admiral S. P. Lee, Commander of the North Atlantic Blockading Squadron at Beaufort, North Carolina, that the Condor was about to depart for Wilmington. Thus the warning was out to catch her.

The Niphon sighted her at New Inlet just off Cape Fear at four in the morning on October 1, and gave chase. The Condor moved up the river, its pilot unconscious of pursuit. When a hulk loomed out of the darkness he mistook for a Federal gunboat the wreck of the Night Hawk, a blockade runner newly gone to its doom. Shifting course, he grounded with a shivering crash on the New Inlet Bar, not more than two hundred yards from the Confederate guns of Fort Fisher.

Rose was tossed from her bunk. She dressed with frantic haste as the settling *Condor* strained and rocked in a raging northeaster. By this time the Admiral had sighted the *Niphon* moving up behind them. Rockets flared. The Confederate batteries opened fire. Commander Edmund Kemble, of the *Niphon*, pulled away to safety as "shot and shell fell in proximity to his boat."

He was a man of caution who reported to his superior officers: "Daylight coming in rapidly, I deemed it prudent to stand offshore. I much regret not being able to destroy the steamer, but the safety of this vessel demanded that I should forego the pleasure of doing so until the coming night when, under the cover of darkness, I shall try to do so."

As things developed, Rose need not have died that night but for her own impetuous nature. They were now lying within range of the protective guns of Fort Fisher, which guarded the last functioning port of the Confederacy. General Lee had declared that Wilmington must be kept open at all costs. It was the gateway for supplies for his starving army.

But the sea was mountainous. The *Condor* rocked and the wind roared, creating a sense of confusion on board. No one knew just what was happening as surf dashed across the deck in great white billows. Rose appeared wrapped in a shawl, dark eyes blazing, her reticule swinging from her neck. She knew that capture meant imprisonment again. She was frantic as she looked for Holcombe and young Lieutenant Wilson, who had come aboard with him at Halifax. Together they sought the Admiral and urged him to send them ashore in a boat.

The craggy hero of many battles assured them they were safe. Holcombe and Wilson were persuaded. But Rose pleaded on. The Admiral told her she would be in greater danger if she tried to go ashore in so rough a sea than if she stayed with the *Condor*. He pointed out that they were under the protection of Confederate guns. But Rose felt that too much was at stake. She had to have her way.

When persuasion failed she raged at the towering Admiral.

269

Shawled, angry, soaked to the skin, gripping her reticule with tense fingers, she engaged in her last battle of wits with a formidable adversary. She had to shout to make herself heard. The blue-coated seaman who was to die as admiral-in-chief of the Turkish Navy, bearing the name of Hobart Pasha, shouted back with equal gusto. The debate took place by the wavering light of lanterns, with much confusion around them as the *Condor* lurched and swung, and no one knew what might happen next.

Rose refused to budge. At last the Admiral gave in, but against his better judgment. He ordered the pilot who had run them aground to take the agents ashore. It took time to launch the boat. Rose waited in a fever of impatience, clutching her reticule. She demanded the dispatch bags, which were put in the boat with her, but were never seen again.

The Admiral must have watched with real concern as the Confederate agents took their places in the boat with the pilot and a crew of two. Dawn was breaking. The waves still roared around them like thunder. They were tossed about and the oarsmen floundered at their task. They had not gone far when a monster wave smashed broadside against the boat, turning it upside down.

The waves broke over Rose's shawled head. She was lost in the spray and the rushing sea. She sank at once, with the added weight of her golden sovereigns. Did a moment of knowledge flash over her before she went under?

Rose had often said she would gladly die for the Confederacy. The moment had come.

The men clutched at the overturned boat and all were saved. Holcombe, battered and bruised, was rescued in a state of total exhaustion. Lieutenant Wilson almost reached the shore before being hauled to safety. Both men lay in collapse on the beach and Rose for the moment was forgotten.

When the wind died down and a gray day followed the storm, the Admiral and some of his men came ashore and the search for Rose

270

was conducted systematically. The *Condor* no longer rocked on the shoals. Peace had settled on the ocean although the day was dark and lowering. None of them knew at the time that Rose's body had already been found by a Confederate soldier from Brunswick County, North Carolina. He had come upon her as she lay in the disorder of death by drowning, with her reticule lying on the sand beside her. The long chain, still encircling her neck, linked it loosely to her body.

The soldier opened the bag and saw the glitter of gold. He tipped it up and her sovereigns spilled in a golden shower around Rose. He scooped up the coins, and stuffed them into his pockets and shirt, then dragged her body to the ocean's edge and pushed her back into the sea. After that he left the scene.

But Rose's body was washed ashore a second time, and her identity was established.* This time Thomas E. Taylor, part owner of the wrecked *Night Hawk*, who was later to write a book on blockade runners, found her as he led a searching party along the débris-strewn beach. Knowing who she was, he carried her gently to the home of Colonel William Lamb, Commander of Fort Fisher. Mrs. Lamb, a bride from New England now wholly committed to the Confederate cause, dried Rose's traveling clothes in her wartime cabin before an open fire of pine knots. Fellow passengers from the *Condor* came and went, and the Admiral stood by her bedside, surveying the dauntless Mrs. Greenhow.

Plagued by agonies of remorse when he learned who she was, the man who robbed her later brought the money back to Colonel Lamb, and confessed to his callous act. He acknowledged that he could neither sleep nor rest, knowing that the drowned woman was the famous Confederate patriot, Mrs. Greenhow. He felt he would go insane if he did not salve his conscience by confession.

Meanwhile, Rose's body was taken into Wilmington where she lay in state in the Seamen's Bethel, with an honor guard in attend-

---

* In her plundered reticule was a small notebook with addresses and the evocative note "Evening Party at Lord Granville's, 16 Bruton St."

ance. On October 2 the Reverend Dr. James A. Corcoran read the funeral service for her at St. Thomas's Church. She was buried with full military honors, the cortege proceeding to Oakdale Cemetery with her coffin wrapped in the Confederate flag. Shops were closed for the day. Crowds joined the funeral procession. A guard of honor accompanied Rose on her last journey. Admiral Hobart-Hampden was among the mourners.

A plain marble cross marks Rose's grave. It bears the inscription:

Mrs. Rose O'N. Greenhow, a bearer of dispatches to the Confederate Government. Erected by the Ladies Memorial Association.

The Daughters of the Confederacy hang a wreath of laurel on Rose's grave on Memorial Day, as for all the Southern war dead. A small Confederate flag is placed beside it and a salute is fired in her memory. Many note the grave in passing. In spring dogwood flowers around it. In summer magnolias and her favorite red roses bloom close to her resting place.

The dispatches that Rose carried were lost with her. Stephen R. Mallory, Secretary of the Confederate Navy, wrote to Commander James D. Bulloch at Liverpool on November 17, 1864:

I am anxiously looking for dispatches from you, having received nothing later than the 6th of August. The Condor's dispatches which are understood to have been in the hands of Mrs. Greenhow were lost, as was also a subsequent important mail in the Hope.

Two months later Mason wrote to Benjamin acknowledging that the dispatches were lost. He said he had asked the Admiral to give them to Rose, since she was going direct to Richmond. Undoubtedly the dispatches that Rose guarded dealt with diplomatic affairs. In any event, she died in the service of the Confederacy, and is so honored in the South.

Florence was in Brussels and planning a trip to the Riviera when word reached her of her mother's death. Leila heard of it in Pennsylvania and Rose in the convent in Paris. Mrs. Lee, still defying

272

the invaders at Winchester, had suffered beyond the point of tears, but she made the following entry in her diary on October 13:

This has been a sad day for me. . . . I was almost stunned by the announcement that my sister, Mrs. Greenhow, had been drowned in running the blockade at Wilmington. . . . It is a horrible event; it fills me more with terror than grief. The manner of her death and the fear that she was unprepared for it are such distressing ideas that I try to shake off the awful feeling but in vain. . . . I have a most affectionate remembrance of her affection for me in our young days, and indeed since the war we have been more drawn together by our common interest in our glorious cause. She labored nobly for the South and was doubtless approaching its shores with a heart filled with pride and satisfaction at the honors she had been accorded by many of England's noblest representatives.

Mrs. Lee deadened her grief with more hospital work, determined not to sadden the soldiers with her personal woes. She no longer "moved from her stance when a cannon ball came near." She had become so accustomed to incurring risk that unless there was excitement she found things dull. "How changed I am—what a life I lead!" she wrote.

No one had stood still in these years of desperation—least of all, after the soldiers, the women in besieged towns. Rose's role was dramatic; Mary Lee's was one of quiet suffering. The Richmond papers, reduced to a double sheet by the end of 1864, had space only for a few lines recording Mrs. Greenhow's death. *The Times* of London gave her a column, which Lady Fullerton saw with a sense of shock and at once composed her thirty-eight-verse poem in memory of Rose. She recalled how her friend had talked of death, but she had not felt foreboding, since Rose was given to extravagant talk. Now she wrote her epitaph:

> She had been faithful to the last,
> To a fond hopeless dream
> She did not live to see it fade,
> Like a delusive dream.

273

In the week that Rose died the Empress Eugénie was at Baden Baden, Queen Victoria was at Balmoral, Mrs. Jefferson Davis was about to flee from Richmond, James Buchanan was living quietly at Wheatland, Henry Wilson was campaigning for Lincoln in Pennsylvania. General Lee's campaign was nearly over. General Philip H. Sheridan was making headway in the Shenandoah Valley. *The Times* of London was thundering:

The Americans are making war as no people ever made war before. Their campaigns combine the costliness of modern expeditions with the carnage of barbarian invasions. Grant squanders life like Attila, and money like Louis XIV. Each party is out for total extermination.

Rose did not live for the melancholy day in the South on which Lee surrendered to Grant. She may even have traveled toward home with some degree of hope in her heart, for although she knew how depleted the Confederate resources were, Jefferson Davis still spread the impression that all would be well. Rose never ceased to have faith in the ultimate success of the South.

News of her death must inevitably have stirred up memories in the minds of a number of famous and harassed men who had known her, some in the South, more in the North. Rose had fulfilled her destiny in many different ways—as a beauty, a wit, a patriot, a spy, an affectionate wife and mother, a siren, a scholar, a writer, but first and to the end, a woman who had "used every capacity with which God had endowed her" in support of the Confederacy. Her death had the epic touch in which she herself would have gloried.

Bibliography

ADAMS, JAMES TRUSLOW, *The Adams Family*. Boston: Little, Brown and Company, 1930.

ANDREWS, MATTHEW PAGE, compiled by, *The Women of the South in War Times*. Baltimore: The Norman, Remington Company, 1920.

AUCHAMPAUGH, PHILIP GERALD, *James Buchanan's Administration and His Cabinet on the Eve of Secession*. Privately printed, Lancaster, Pa., 1926.

BANCROFT, HUBERT HOWE, *History of California*, Vol. VI. San Francisco: The History Company, 1888.

BARBEE, DAVID RANKIN, "Robert Greenhow," *William and Mary College Quarterly*, Williamsburg, Va., July, 1933.

BEAUREGARD, GENERAL P. G. T., *A Commentary on the Campaign and Battle of Manassas of July, 1861*. New York: G. P. Putnam's Sons, 1891.

BEYMER, WILLIAM GILMORE, "Mrs. Greenhow," *Harper's Monthly Magazine*, March, 1912.

——, *On Hazardous Service, Scouts and Spies of the North and South*. New York: Harper and Brothers, 1912.

BOUCHER, FRANÇOIS, *American Footprints in Paris*. New York: George H. Doran Company, 1921.

BOYD, T. H. S., compiled by, *The History of Montgomery County, from its earliest settlement in 1650 to 1879*. Clarksburg, Md., 1880.

BRADFORD, GAMALIEL, *Confederate Portraits*. Boston: Houghton Mifflin Company, 1914.

CALDÉRON DE LA BARCA, FRANCES ERSKINE, *Life in Mexico During a Residence of Two Years in That Country*. Mexico: The Aztec, 1910.

CHESNUT, MARY BOYKIN, edited by Ben Ames Williams, *A Diary from Dixie*. Boston: Houghton Mifflin Company, 1949.

COCHRAN, JOSEPH WILSON, *Friendly Adventurers*. Paris: Brentano's, 1931.

COIT, MARGARET L., *John C. Calhoun, American Portrait*. Boston: Houghton Mifflin Company, 1950.

277

Conway, John Joseph, *Footprints of Famous Americans in Paris*. New York: John Lane Company, 1912.

Curtis, George Ticknor, *Life of James Buchanan*. New York: Harper and Brothers, 1883.

Cuthbert, Norma B., edited by, *Lincoln and the Baltimore Plot from Pinkerton Records and Related Papers*. San Marino, Calif.: The Huntington Library, 1949.

Davis, Varina Howell, *Jefferson Davis. A Memoir by his wife*. New York: Belford Company, 1890.

DeLeon, Thomas C., *Belles, Beaux and Brains of the Sixties*. New York: G. W. Dillingham Company, 1909.

Doster, William E., *Lincoln and Episodes of the Civil War*. New York: G. P. Putnam's Sons, 1915.

Dulaney, Carrol, "Mrs. Greenhow, Confederate Spy," *Confederate Veteran*. Nashville, Tenn., May, 1932.

Eyre, Alice, *The Famous Frémonts and Their America*. Santa Ana, Calif.: The Fine Arts Press, 1948.

Farquhar, Roger Brooke, *Historic Montgomery County, Maryland, Old Homes and History*. Silver Spring, Md., 1952.

Freeman, Douglas Southall, *The South to Posterity*. New York: Charles Scribner's Sons, 1939.

Frémont, Jessie Benton, *Souvenirs of My Time*. Boston: D. Lothrop and Company, 1887.

Fullerton, Lady Georgiana, "Mrs. Greenhow," *Temple Bar. A London Magazine for Town and Country Readers*. London: Richard Bentley, November, 1870.

Furman, Bess, *White House Profile*. Indianapolis: Bobbs-Merrill Company, 1951.

Gouverneur, Marian, *As I Remember*. New York: D. Appleton Company, 1911.

Grant, C. L., "The Public Career of Cave Johnson," *Tennessee Historical Quarterly*, Vol. X, September, 1951.

Greenhow, Robert, *History of Oregon and California*. Boston: Charles C. Little and James Brown, 1844.

———, *Memoir, Historical and Political on the Northwest Coast of North America and the Adjacent Territories*. New York: Wiley and Putnam, 1840.

Greenhow, Rose O'Neal, *My Imprisonment and the First Year of Abolition Rule at Washington*. London: Richard Bentley, 1863.

278

HITTELL, THEODORE H., *History of California*, Vol. III. San Francisco: N. J. Stone and Company, 1897.

HORAN, JAMES D., *Desperate Women*. New York: G. P. Putnam's Sons, 1952.

HUNT, ROCKWELL D., edited by, *California and Californians*, Vol. II. Chicago: The Lewis Publishing Company, 1926.

JOHNSON, GERALD W., *America's Silver Age*. New York: Harper and Brothers, 1939.

JORDAN, THOMAS, "Jefferson Davis," *Harper's New Monthly Magazine*, September, 1865.

KELLY, M. MARGARET JEAN, *The Career of Joseph Lane, Frontier Politician*. Washington: The Catholic University of America Press, 1942.

KEYES, E. D., *Fifty Years' Observation of Men and Events*. New York: Charles Scribner's Sons, 1885.

KIP, RIGHT REV. WILLIAM INGRAHAM, *The Early Days of My Episcopate*. New York: Thomas Whittaker, 1892.

LATROBE, CHARLES JOSEPH, *The Rambler in Mexico*. London: R. B. Seeley and W. Burnside, 1836.

LEECH, MARGARET, *Reveille In Washington*. New York: Harper and Brothers, 1941.

LEWIS, OSCAR, *California Heritage*. New York: Thomas Y. Crowell Co., 1949.

LOCKWOOD, MARY SMITH, *Yesterdays in Washington*. Rosslyn, Va.: The Commonwealth Company, 1915.

MAURY, RICHARD L., *A Brief Sketch of the Work of Matthew Fontaine Maury by His Son*. Richmond: Whittet and Shepperson, 1915.

MAURY, SARAH MYTTON, *An Englishwoman in America*. London: Thomas Richardson and Son, 1848.

MEIGS, WILLIAM M., *Life of John Caldwell Calhoun*. New York: The Neale Publishing Company, 1917.

MOORE, FRANK, edited by, *The Rebellion Record: A Diary of American Events*. Vol. IV. New York: G. P. Putnam's Sons, 1862.

MOORE, J. B., edited by, *The Works of James Buchanan*. Philadelphia: J. B. Lippincott Company, 1908.

MORTON, FREDERIC, *The Story of Winchester in Virginia*. Strasburg, Va.: Shenandoah Publishing House, 1925.

NASON, REV. ELIAS, *Life and Public Services of Henry Wilson*. Boston: B. B. Russell, 1876.

279

NEVILLE, AMELIA RANSOME, *The Fantastic City*. Boston: Houghton Mifflin Company, 1932.

NEWMAN, HARRY WRIGHT, *Seignoiry in Early Maryland*. Published by Descendants of Lords of the Maryland Manors, 1942.

NORFLEET, FILLMORE, *Saint-Memin in Virginia: Portraits and Biographies*. Richmond: The Dietz Press, 1942.

PARTON, JAMES, *Famous Americans of Recent Times*. Boston: Houghton Mifflin and Company, 1884.

PEMBER, PHOEBE YATES, *A Southern Woman's Story*. New York: G. W. Carleton and Company, 1879.

PINKERTON, ALLAN, *The Spy of the Rebellion*. New York: G. W. Carleton and Company, 1883.

POORE, BEN PERLEY, *Reminiscences of Sixty Years in the National Metropolis*. Philadelphia: Hubbard Brothers, 1886.

PRYOR, MRS. ROGER A., *Reminiscences of Peace and War*. New York: The Macmillan Company, 1905.

RANDALL, JAMES G., *The Civil War and Reconstruction*. Chicago: D. C. Heath and Company, 1937.

ROMAN, ALFRED, *The Military Operations of General Beauregard*. New York: Harper and Brothers, 1883.

ROWLAND, DUNBAR, edited by, *Jefferson Davis, Constitutionalist. His Letters, Papers and Speeches*. Printed for the Mississippi Department of Archives and History, Jackson, Miss., 1923.

SCHARF, J. THOMAS, *History of Maryland*. Baltimore: John B. Piet, 1879.

———, *History of Western Maryland*. Philadelphia: Louis H. Everts, 1882.

SCHERER, JAMES A. B., *Thirty-First Star*. New York: G. P. Putnam's Sons, 1942.

SIGAUD, LOUIS A., "Mrs. Greenhow and the Rebel Spy Ring," *Maryland Historical Magazine*, September, 1946.

SIMKINS, FRANCIS BUTLER and JAMES WELCH PATTON, *The Women of the Confederacy*. Richmond: Garrett and Massie, Inc., 1936.

SMITH, GUSTAVUS W., *Generals J. E. Johnston and P. G. T. Beauregard at the Battle of Manassas*. New York: C. G. Crawford, 1892.

SMITH, LAMAR WILLIAM, *The Spy of the Confederacy*. A Thesis. University of Alabama, Tuscaloosa, Ala., 1948.

SOULÉ, FRANK, *The Annals of San Francisco*. New York: D. Appleton and Company, 1855.

STERLING, ADA, edited by, *A Belle of the Fifties, Memoirs of Mrs. Clay of Alabama*. New York: Doubleday, Page and Company, 1904.

280

([Bibliography

TAYLOR, THOMAS E., *Running the Blockade*. New York: Charles Scribner's Sons, 1896.

WAYLAND, JOHN W., *The Pathfinder of the Seas*. Richmond: Garrett and Massie, Inc., 1930.

WILLIAMSON, JAMES J., *Prison Life in the Old Capitol*. Printed West Orange, N. J., 1911.

WINDLE, MARY J., *Life in Washington, and Life Here and There*. Philadelphia: J. B. Lippincott Company, 1859.

WRIGHT, RICHARDSON, *Forgotten Ladies*. Philadelphia: J. B. Lippincott Company, 1928.

Newspapers

Baltimore *American*
Baltimore *News*
Baltimore *Sun*
Charlotte *Observer*, Charlotte, N. C.
Daily Richmond Enquirer
Daily Richmond Examiner
Greensboro *Daily News*, Greensboro, N. C.
London *Mail*
London *Times*
London *Morning Chronicle*
New York *Daily News*
New York *Herald*
New York Times
New York *Tribune*
Philadelphia *Press*
Raleigh *News and Observer*, Raleigh N. C.
Richmond *Daily Dispatch*
San Francisco *Daily Alta California*
San Francisco *Evening Bulletin*
Washington *Daily Globe*
Washington *Daily Morning Chronicle*
Washington *Daily National Intelligencer*
Washington *Evening Star*
Wilmington *Star-News*, Wilmington, N. C.

Index

285

288

Set in Linotype Electra
Format by Marguerite Swanton
Manufactured by The Haddon Craftsmen, Inc.
Published by HARPER & BROTHERS, New York